OGAM

WEAVING WORD WISDOM

ADVANCE PRAISE FOR
OGAM: WEAVING WORD WISDOM

As thoughtful as it is practical, *Ogam: Weaving Word Wisdom* is a breakthrough book, fusing historical scholarship and poetic vision into a toolkit that will be of value to Celtic Reconstructionists and the wider Pagan community alike.

--John Michael Greer
Archdruid and author of *The Druidry Handbook*

It is a delight to welcome Erynn Laurie's clear and well-written exposition of the Celtic Ogam system to the small but growing collection of works on European magical alphabets. The Irish tradition is relatively untouched, and what there is has often been limited to the tree-ogam. Laurie draws on lore and experience to explicate the deeper meanings. Whether you have worked with ogam before or are just beginning, this is a worthwhile addition to your bookshelf.

--Diana L. Paxson
Author of *Taking Up the Runes*

Students of Celtic lore have long been frustrated in their attempts to reconstruct a system of Ogam divination that would both be viable and have the ring of authenticity. Now Erynn Laurie has taken a completely fresh approach, putting Ogam squarely back into the Irish bardic tradition (where it in fact originated). Instead of relying on a set of rigid correspondences, her divinatory practice calls for a poet's imagination and sensitivity. Her book will, without a doubt, become required preliminary reading for any further investigations into the art of Ogam divination.

--Alexei Kondratiev
Author of *The Apple Branch: A Path to Celtic Ritual*

Erynn Laurie, one of the first people to define and promote the Celtic Reconstructionist movement, is here to show us how the Ogham is much more than a simple tree-alphabet. Her presentation has a solid backing in the literary heritage and folk traditions of the Celtic people, far stronger than that of others involved in the movement. Indeed she insists on the necessity for just such a backing: it provides the integrity and coherence which makes Celtic Reconstructionism distinct. Yet at the same time her work displays a sincerity of heart and soul which I find most inspiring. This is a book for the practitioner, as well as for the scholar: indeed this is a book for those who see little reason to separate the scholarly from the practical. I urge the reader to pay special attention to the discussions of Ethics, Deity and the Call to Service, and Poetry, Madness, and Death. Gone are the superficial gratifications of more well known writers. In their place stands a much more honest description of the sacrifices and rewards entailed by living a spiritual life. The Ogham, the magical alphabet of the ancient Celts, forms the foundation of symbols, names, natural correspondences, and ideas which underlies the whole discussion. It is presented to us not like a fossil in a museum, but as a living animal in its natural environment. She wants readers to try things out, and so discover for themselves what she discovered. This is a beautiful book, and I am delighted to recommend it to all those who hear the calling of the Celts.

--Brendan Cathbad Myers
Lecturer, University of Guelph (Canada), author of *The Mysteries of Druidry*

OGAM

WEAVING WORD WISDOM

Erynn Rowan Laurie

Stafford, England

Megalithica books **L**

Cover Photo: Erynn Rowan Laurie
Cover Design: Andy Bigwood
Internal Illustrations: Bob Daverin, Phillip Bernhardt-House and J. Buterman
Editor: Taylor Ellwood
Layout: Lupa
Set in Georgia, Poor Richard and Windlass

Megalithica Books edition 2007

A Megalithica Books Edition
http://www.immanion-press.com
info@immanion-press.com

8 Rowley Grove
Stafford ST17 9BJ
UK

ISBN 978-1-905713-02-8

DEDICATION

To Ogma Grianainech, eloquent creator of ogam,
may your works be known throughout the world;
To Brighid bé n-éces, sacred poet,
may the fire of your imbas touch all who seek it;
And to my mother, Bette, who has always believed in me.
I love you, mom.

TABLE OF CONTENTS

ACKNOWLEDGMENTS

This book is the product of nearly two decades of work, study, conversation, meditation, ritual, and general perversity. It would not exist without the help and encouragement of more people than I can possibly name, but I would like to single out a few who are particularly deserving of recognition. Gordon Cooper first encouraged me to get my material off the computer and into print when I began my ogam studies many years ago (Okay, actually he said, "If you don't try to turn this into a book, I will," and I screamed and tore the keyboard from his hands, thus starting a self-publishing endeavour that eventually led me here.).

Sam Wagar pointed me to the work of Seán Ó Tuathail, whose ramblings inspired me and sent me in search of books and articles I'd never heard of before. Tagh offered dialogue and focus, reminding me that I was doing the right thing when I felt overwhelmed. Bjoern Hartsfvang's superlative divinatory and magical work with the Norse runes inspired me to look at ogam divination with new eyes and to work with three sets of *feda* to represent different aspects of each *fid*. It is with his kind permission that I went on to develop the three currents system presented here in the chapter on advanced divination techniques. Lorrie Wood gave me snuggles and did layout for a short booklet based on some of the core material presented here so that I could have it available for my classes at PantheaCon in 2006 and 2007. Smooches, sweetie!

Alexei Kondratiev argued linguistics, Celtic history, and religion with me on the Nemeton email list for years, helping to sharpen my debate skills and look to the traditions and the importance of language in the development of Celtic Reconstructionist religions. Raven nic Rhóisín went over the first mostly-complete draft of the manuscript in between trips overseas and to clients in the US, making suggestions that have helped immensely. The work she and Kathryn Price NicDhàna have done on the tree ogam has been inspiring.

Phillip Bernhardt-House (conveniently endowed with a Ph.D. in Celtic Civilization) also looked at early drafts, correcting significant errors and stomping out fires left and right. Phillip additionally did photos for the book that I could not do on my own for reasons that will be obvious, and produced the pronunciation guide in the glossary, as well as helping with the tedious task of indexing. He is also to be thanked for the many hours of conversation that were germane to the development and shape of this volume, and for his assistance with the translation of the title into Old Irish so that the ogam title would read properly. It says *Ogam: Fige Briathar nEcnai* ("Ogam: Weaving of Words of Wisdom") for those who are curious. Bob and Brenda Daverin generously allowed me to use bits of ritual that they have developed, and Bob has also provided several of the illustrations for the book as well.[1] Brenda looked over several chapters of the book in progress as they were being drafted. C.L. Vermeers accompanied me on my three-night vigil at the coast, described in the ogam and ritual chapter; you're a fine *fennid*, Chris!

I must mention Paul Remley, an associate professor at the University of Washington, who offered a free class in Old Irish back in the early 1990s that was my introduction to that language. Though I doubt he remembers me, I have a fond place in my heart for him, and for Dennis King and Charles MacQuarrie, who were in an Old Irish reading group with me at that same time. Their influence was critical for my budding understanding of Irish.

My thanks also to Seumas Gagne and Richard Hill, founders of Slighe nan Gàidheal, Seattle's Scottish Gaelic cultural society, for their inspiration, dedication, and tireless work in bringing authentic Gaelic music, language, cultural traditions, and teachers to the area from the *Gàidhealtachd* in both Canada and Scotland. My years singing with Seirm, Slighe's choir, are something I will always cherish.

Over the years there have been more distant friends and literary spies providing me with photocopies of difficult to find and out of print materials than I can possibly thank individually. May the Gods bless you all for your generosity and your encouragement in this project and my research as the years have rolled by. Friends and clients whose names have been changed to protect the indecent kindly offered their permission to use readings I've done for them as samples in this book. May the Gods smile upon them and ease their paths. Thank you to the multitudinous members of the Nemeton and Imbas-Public lists, and to the regulars on the LiveJournal CR_R community for

[1] Bob does ogam bindrunes and artwork on commission. Please check out his website at http://woo.wraptsure.com/

your comments and suggestions as I was working on individual projects necessary to this book and for your private comments and responses to the material.

Thanks are also due to Taylor Ellwood and Lupa at Megalithica, who have been cheering me on as well as doing editing duties. Their support and encouragement, and their laid back approach to my deadlines made this whole thing possible. Without them, this book would not exist in this form. Leon and Allen at Travelers and Shiuwen, Rob and David at Floating Leaves in Seattle gave me chai and tea and great places to hang out and write to get away from the internet when I was too tempted to hang with online friends instead of working on the book. I got great whacking chunks of writing done in those wonderful teahouses.

Last -- and you know we always save the best for last -- my thanks to my momster, who loves me even though I'm more than a little bit crazy.

Adrae buaid ocus bennachtain!
May victory and blessing rise to meet you!

Erynn Rowan Laurie
Everett, Washington
April 2007

Erynn Rowan Laurie

FOREWORD
Walking the Path to Ogam

My journey to the ogam began in 1986, before I'd really discovered my fascination with early Irish and Scottish history and spirituality. I read the usual Pagan sources available in the mid to late 1980s and found myself unsatisfied with what I found there. Being independent-minded and rather stubborn, I set off on my own quest for meaning and found myself enmeshed in poetry, Celtic scholarship, and mysticism.

I am not a scholar. I don't have a degree or any formal higher education to speak of, yet I respect learning and the work of scholars. I hold myself to certain standards of accuracy in my research as well as valuing the importance of *imbas* or poetic inspiration. Within the movement currently known as Celtic Reconstructionist Paganism or CR, both scholarship and inspiration are valued. We who follow this path pursue both *aisling* -- vision -- and archaeology. We seek evidence for the authentic old ways of the early Celtic peoples and attempt to develop what we find into useful and valid ways of living, thinking, and celebrating a vibrant and vital spirituality based in the present that looks to the future as well.

My avocation and my vocation are poetry and the pursuit of a spiritual life. I consider myself a follower of the path of *Filidecht*, the art of sacred poetcraft and mysticism in an Irish and Scottish tradition. I refer to myself as a Druid as well as a *Fili* because while I am a ritual poet and a mystic, I also serve my community in a ritual capacity that goes beyond the more visionary aspects of *Filidecht* to the performance of handfastings, baby blessings, seasonal celebrations, and many other rites and rituals. I am in love with words and the music of them, with history and what it inspires, with the images and symbols of an earlier time and a different place. I live in Everett, in western Washington state, across the street from a lake and close on to the shores of Puget Sound. I am only partly of Celtic extraction and don't believe that one's ethnic heritage has any true bearing on how we hear the call of the spirit. Those forces that call us to their service know who we are and the artificial borders of nation and state, of race and social class are erased in the greater scheme of things. We are all human, and the spirits and deities call upon whom they will. It is for us to answer that call or not by our own choice.

CR is unlike most of the popular forms of modern Paganism. It has its own cosmology, its own technical vocabulary, and its own systems of ethics and social interaction. It treats magic and divination differently than many of the more easily found varieties of Paganism in the US today. And this book is more specific yet, describing a personal and somewhat idiosyncratic form of CR Paganism approached through the agency of the ogam alphabet. My take on ogam has little to do with the more commonly known vehicle of the so-called tree alphabet. It is based instead on language and the possible original meanings of the letter names.

Because words are magic and they can change reality, the ogam has great potential for use in magic. In *Filidecht*, poetry is the root of magic, and words are the root of poetry. Sound is vital, and magic and poetry should ideally be spoken in the practice of *Filidecht*. Ogam is a key to memory within the system, aiding in the interpretation of dream and vision, offering images for omen seeking, and helping give context for the *Fili*'s personal spiritual and ritual practices.

The images found within the ogam alphabet remind us of the early Irish tales, evoke the stories of queens and heroes, poets and seers. They situate us within a world both mythic and natural. The *feda* or letters of the ogam are keys to the universe next door.

Open the gate and walk through.

PREFACE

Seeing the Ogam NOT for the Trees
by Rev. Phillip A. Bernhardt-House, Ph.D.

Contrary to the common assertion found in many popular books on ogam (or, in its Modern Irish form, ogham), this cipher was never truly "mysterious" nor was its knowledge "lost," except insofar as the mysteries of particle physics are now mysterious and lost to the layperson on the street—i.e. they are plainly available in many books which can be found in libraries, or on various internet websites, but the layperson may not know where these are located or how to find them. In ogam, as in so many other things, being an "expert" or "qualified" or "learned" in the pursuit of this knowledge doesn't mean that one knows everything about it. Rather one knows where to look for good and reliable information on it, or knows who to ask to find further resources.

It's therefore a great pleasure to be introducing a work on ogam which takes as its assumption that the cipher, its meanings, uses, and the myths associated with it are not lost or mysterious, and starts from the viewpoint of using what is known and traditional about the system before moving into new and innovative employments of it. Far too many books on this subject play the "Celtic misty-mystic" bluff too heavily, and then spiral off into conjectures and fabrications that, though they may be useful as individual interpretations of the material, are neither traditional, nor based in the definite knowledge of the system which has come down to us from early and medieval Irish literate tradition. Irish poetic culture and the art of *Filidecht* (all things related to the learned craft and artistry of poets) placed an extremely large emphasis on the importance and validity of tradition. Ogam was one of many possible tools in the *Fili*'s repertoire, and it would be highly dubious to engage in study of the practices of ogam interpretation while ignoring the weight and wisdom of that tradition and instead stray off into the vagaries of "Celtic misty-mysticism."

Esteemed and qualified practicing *Fili* that she is, Erynn Rowan Laurie has studied the original medieval texts on ogam, both in the original Irish and in translation, and has also familiarized herself to an admirable (and indeed professional) level of knowledge with the landmarks of scholarship on the subject within the field of Celtic Studies. In far too many books for the popular and the spiritual audience on ogam, there is too great a familiarity with John Matthews, Edred Thorsson, and Robert Graves, and far too little recognition of George Calder, Howard Meroney, and Damian McManus. The bibliographies of some popular writers on ogam have progressively included more and more citations of the latter scholars (compare the early 1990s version of Matthew's book on Taliesin and shamanism to the more recently re-issued version), and yet the reliance on Graves' creative and poetic interpretation of ogam is still pervasive.

Graves' interpretation of the system, in combination with the Welsh poem *Cad Goddeu*—which, though it concerns many of the same trees and has a number of crossovers with the lore of the Irish system, is neither synonymous nor directly related to ogam outside of his interpretation—isn't to be dismissed as irrelevant or meaningless, and indeed remains an extremely influential and in its own way ingenious creation, without which a great deal of modern Neopaganism would be less vital and colorful. But to ignore the very real differences in context between a learned poetic treatise and its mnemonics in Irish, and a mythological poem by the Welsh pseudo-Taliesin, and to lump all of the languages, cultures, and mythologies which can be described as "Celtic" into the same mould is dangerous, uninformed, irresponsible, and even disrespectful practice. The idea of the ogam as a "tree alphabet" owes much to Graves' work, and plays into the widespread idea that "the Celts" were an ecologically conscious race.

Context and the important distinctions in placing individual texts and ideas into their appropriate historical time and place is a cornerstone to a thorough and useful understanding of anything, be it the Platonic dialogues of ancient Greece or the Gettysburg Address. But it seems to be an undervalued concept in popular treatments of Celtic topics.

Unfortunately, the context and the reality of the situation are different than this idealized ecological picture. Many of the Irish poems that are cited as evidence of proto-ecological consciousness aren't the products of a Celtic pagan practice that revered "the Goddess" and recognized the spirit in all things, but instead were the products of learned Christians in monasteries. A cursory examination of the mythological literature of Ireland shows that sense of place and the connection of people and their rulers to the lands upon which they lived were seen as essential to the productive running of society. Despite this, both humans and gods took pride in and placed great importance on exerting their energies to clear away forests in Ireland, and to reclaim lands when they were depopulated by floods and plagues.

Wild and untamed nature was a force to be respected and admired, but the power of the civilizing forces of the arts and crafts—and poetry being the summit of such endeavours—to order and tame these wild forces were also held in deep respect. They were perceived to have their origins in the realm of the gods and the divine. The Irish did see the forest for the trees, but also for the possible fruitful things within it and beneath it, and even without it. Likewise, the tree alphabet associated with the ogam is one possible interpretation of it, but there are many others, and the ogam tract itself assumes that it's the prerogative of the fully-qualified *Fili* to generate further interpretations and mnemonics for it. It is the power of words and what can be created with them, which is emphasized in Erynn Rowan Laurie's work. "Wood-wisdom" is useful, but "word-wisdom" is the very essence of magic and power, which can shape the land, defeat entire armies, and give order and meaning to the world.

It is no surprise, then, that the eponymous inventor of the ogam alphabet, Ogma, was not only a god associated with the "honey-tongued" arts of eloquence and poetry,[2] but also primarily known as a warrior and champion of the Tuatha Dé Danann. Likewise, the Gaulish god Ogmios (who, though his name seems to be related to Ogma's, is not a direct linguistic cognate) was described with Heraclean attributes of strength, but was also noteworthy for the train of henchmen that trailed him by chains from his tongue—indeed, the sweetness implied in being "honey-tongued" might also as easily mean "sticky-tongued," since it is with words and their skillful use that people can sometimes be trapped or deceived and led astray. Ogma's invention of the ogam alphabet is detailed in the "Ogam Tract" included in George Calder's edition and translation of the *Auraicept na n-Éces*, "The Scholar's Primer." However, a much more flashy, exciting and cosmic (as well as syncretistic and pan-

---

[2] The epithets *Milbél*, "honey-mouthed," and *Miltenga*, "honey-tongued," are taken to denote eloquence and sweet speech, and *Milbél* is applied to Cermait son of the Dagda. Ogma is sometimes equated or confused with this figure. These epithets therefore could apply to Ogma because of the skill in poetry and eloquence attributed to him in the sources, but it is to be noted that these epithets are nowhere in any extant text applied directly to him.

21

Celtic) origin-tale for the ogam alphabet is given in John Matthew's *The Song of Taliesin: Stories and Poems from the Books of Broceliande*,[3] making it much more akin to the origin of the runic alphabet. Again, while this is interesting creative storytelling and interpretation (and is totally synthetic, like everything else in that particular volume by Matthews), the more simple origin tale that the Irish themselves used tells us infinitely more about the logic and the beauty of the system, not to mention having the backing of centuries of legitimate and learned tradition behind it. It isn't sacrificing oneself on the wheel at the center of the universe which leads to the word-wisdom of ogam. Rather it's the realization that words, speech, and writing are mighty enough to warn friends, protect oneself from harm, conquer lands, inscribe essential truths, and give shape to the universe.

The Modern Irish pronunciation of ogham is almost monosyllabic, and my own advisor at University College Cork used to say that the word sounds much like *OM* (or *AUM*), the Sanskrit "sound of the universe," or *ohm*, the scientific "unit of resistance." The medieval literate Irish loved this type of punning, which they inherited from the Christian theologian St. Isidore of Seville. It inspired entire texts and genres for them, including many glossaries like *Sanas Cormaic*, the text on personal names called *Cóir Anmann*, and the *Dindshenchas* tales in prose and poetry on the lore of important places. These two definitions of ogham by punning--"the sound of the universe" and "unit of resistance"--are in many respects quite apt in understanding the system. For all words, sounds, letters, and alphabets are fragments of the "sound of the universe," which when assembled correctly can intimate, imitate, and even replicate that same sound. Likewise, all words, letters, and sounds, as well as poetic forms and meters, and other artistic and spiritual laws, are "units of resistance," with their own limitations and properties which must be properly understood, practiced with, and respected in order to produce works which appear truly inspired. The path of *Filidecht* is not the passive path of least resistance, and yet it is a cornerstone of the Irish tradition that poetry and the poet is nothing more or less than a "seer" of reality as it truly is—the "units of resistance" thus reveal the "sounds of the universe."

---

[3] London: The Aquarian Press, 1991

The present work by Erynn Rowan Laurie, like the *Auraicept na n-Éces*, is but a "primer" or "first-instruction" in these arts. Much remains to be said about ogam and its usage, as well as *Filidecht* generally, in future works (which we look forward to with great interest). But one shouldn't assume because of this that the present material is either simple or easy, or that because this is an initial work in this discipline that the arts detailed in it aren't advanced or complex. The great amount of informed and respectful research into these matters, as well as creative usage and practical experience with them, which Erynn has built up over decades of work is a delight to read and should be illuminating for those who pursue this art with diligence. This is a book which Ogma mac Elathan, Morann mac Main, and the Mac Óc, and Cú Chulainn, Finn mac Cumhaill, and Cennfáelad mac Ailella would all be proud of, and to which they would no doubt give their blessings.

Bennacht Dé ocus An-Dé fort! The blessings of the Gods and the Un-Gods upon you!—upon Erynn, for doing this work; upon you who are reading this work; and upon the work itself!

Rev. Dr. Phillip A. Bernhardt-House
Anacortes, WA,
March 2007

Erynn Rowan Laurie

CHAPTER I
Introduction to the Ogam and Celtic
Reconstructionist Paganism

What is Ogam?

At its most basic, the ogam[4] is a Primitive Irish alphabet consisting of twenty *feda* or letters. These letters are arranged in four groups or *aicme* of five *feda* each. The letters consist of lines extending from or across a central line in groups of one to five strokes. There is a fifth group of letters called the *forfeda*, meaning "extra letters", which were added one at a time at a much later date to deal with sounds not native to the Gaelic languages. These letters are more complex in form and do not follow the pattern of the previous letters. They are never found in inscriptions outside of manuscripts. Current scholarly opinion is that the form of the ogam letter system derived from tally marks for counting to define positions in a series of sounds that are quite sophisticated in their ordering.[5]

Each letter of the ogam, called a *fid*, has a name that is usually a word with a distinct meaning. Some of these names include "oak", "a bar of metal", "wound/healing charm", "flame/herb" and "sulfur". A few of the letters have names that are nonsense words, but they still have meanings attached to them within other parts of the ogam tradition, most notably associated with the *briatharogam* or "word ogams" which can be considered a form of poetic kennings. While most people regard the ogam as a tree alphabet, it should be noted that the ogam tracts in the *Auraicept na n-Éces* list nearly 100 varieties of ogam, all considered legitimate; the tree ogam is one of many that are all equally authentic, and the true root of the system is found in the meaning of the letter names themselves.

---

[4] Ogam (og-um) is the Old Irish spelling of the word, though it is occasionally seen as ogum. Modern Irish usually uses the spelling ogham (ohm or oh-am). I've been using the Old Irish spelling for some time now, but you can use which ever you prefer. The glossary beginning on page 291 can be referred to for unfamiliar terms.
[5] McManus, 1997, 11

The earliest known ogam writings are engraved on stone. Amber and bone have also been found with ogam inscribed upon them. Most of the extant ogam stones are funerary or boundary markers, but the inscriptions on bone and amber[6] may have served a magical purpose.[7] Stones bearing ogam inscriptions are found in Ireland, Scotland, Wales and the Isle of Man, though most are found in the south of Ireland.

Current linguistic and archaeological evidence dates the earliest ogam stones to about the 5th or possibly the 4th century CE.[8] Despite the claims of many of the popular books on ogam, it is extremely unlikely that the alphabet originated with the pre-Christian Druids, though the system itself had to be in place by the 4th century CE for it to be in use at that time. To call the ogam *feda* "Irish runes" is also misleading, as they aren't actually related to the Norse runes except by the coincidental feature of having meaningful names. However, this can be said of many early alphabets, including Hebrew. It's more likely that the origin of the ogam letters and their order has some connection to Latin's rules of sound and grammar.[9]

The Irish literary tradition has tales describing druids and others using the ogam for divination and magical purposes[10]. One origin tale of ogam concerns the God Ogma mac Elathan, who created the ogam to warn Lug mac Ethlenn of a danger to his wife.[11] These tales, however, are from well into the Christian period and the Irish manuscripts date no earlier than about the 7th century CE, long after the initial appearance of the first ogam stones in the countryside.

Some people have made claims of finding ogam inscriptions in North America, but these claims have all been

---

[6] McManus, 1997, 132

[7] MacAlister, 1945, 57-58 The O'Connor family of Ennis, Ireland used an egg-shaped amber bead, marked with ogam letters tentatively read as ATUCMLU, as an amulet to cure sore eyes and to aid in childbirth. The method of use was unspecified but obviously magical. The last hereditary holder of the amulet presented it to his employer at the Board of Public Works, from whence it made its way to the British Museum.

[8] McManus, 1997, 40

[9] McManus, 1997, 29-31

[10] The hero Cú Chulainn stalls the march on Ulster in the *Tain Bó Cuailgne* by placing a spancel-hoop engraved with ogam on a standing stone in their path. The army could not move forward until the message was deciphered and the challenges it posed were met. Kinsella, 1985, 68-72. In *Tochmarc Étaíne*, the druid Dallán makes four rods of yew inscribed with ogams to determine where the kidnapped Étaín has been taken. McManus, 1997, 157.

[11] McManus, 1997, 150

specious and are generally associated with the followers of Barry Fell, a marine biologist with no knowledge of either Irish language or archaeology. The protocols that Fell used to arrange and "translate" his alleged ogam inscriptions could result in any number of readings to suit his whims, none of which were actually in the Irish language of any period.[12]

Regardless of ogam's exact historical origins, there's no reason that today's ogam practitioners can't legitimately use the ogam alphabet for divination, magic, ritual, and healing in a modern non-Christian spiritual context. The evidence of the lore shows that the people of medieval Ireland believed ogam had magical meaning and power, and the amber bead from Ennis is physical evidence that ogam-inscribed objects were put to magical use.

Fire and Water: Study and Mysticism

In early Irish mythology, the images of fire and water are deeply linked with those of poetry and inspiration. Fire arises from water at the Well of Wisdom, and poetry is compared both to a fire in the head and to the waters of that well.

When fire and water meet, mist is generated, and this mist is seen in tales as one of the gates into the Otherworld, a place of mystery and transformation. Deep meaning is found within its amorphous embrace. Those who pass through the mist return, if they do, changed and perhaps a little wiser.

Metaphorically, we can say that within CR, the generative forces are the fires of knowledge represented by study and scholarship and the waters of vision presented in dream and trancework. Both are a part of the reconstruction of ancient religions from rare and sometimes difficult sources, cross-cultural comparisons, and the inspiration of the prepared mind. This book is about preparing the mind for that process through the use of ogam as a tool for cultural inquiry and spiritual work.

---

[12] Oppenheimer and Wirtz's *A Linguistic Analysis of Some West Virginia Petroglyphs* at http://cwva.org/ogam_rebutal/wirtz.html offers a lengthy rebuttal to the allegations of Fell and the Epigraphic Society, along with a discussion of Fell's methods.

Why We Do What We Do

Why would anyone want to reconstruct a lost religion anyway? It's a complex question, and the answers vary from person to person.

For some, work on reconstructing pre-Christian Celtic religion speaks to a need for a more visceral connection to the earth and the spirit powers around us. Modern western civilization views nature and culture as separate entities, the activities of humans being prized above all else. Where people interact with nature, that nature is commodified and turned into something to be consumed. Animals in parks are expected to display themselves for the pleasure of vacationers. Forests are treated as resources where leisure activities can be had and trees are valued for their usefulness to humans. Plants and animals are divided into categories of useful things and "pests" or "weeds" to be contained or destroyed.

In looking back to indigenous Celtic spiritualities, we see evidence of a more animist approach, where creatures, plants and places have numinous value in and of themselves. There is danger in dealing with these sacred beings, as well as knowledge that can be shared or discovered. Such places and beings have their own purposes and agendas not defined and delimited by humans. Animals and other beings may, in their own ways, be related to human families as clan-originators through acts of intermarriage or adoption.

There was a time when some families in Ireland and Scotland traced their ancestry to the seals. Songs are still sung of selkies or seal-people, and folktales are still told of encounters with them. They are powerful entities with their own societies and cultures, living beneath the sea. Seeing seals and other creatures as progenitors of your family would naturally lead to an entirely different way of viewing both the seals and the sea, even -- or perhaps particularly -- for those who hunted seals for subsistence. This doesn't mean that cruelty didn't still occur, but it did mean the relationship was potentially very different from that of a commercial fur hunter.

These manifestations of animism profoundly affect the way people interact with the world around them. If we believe that plants and animals, mountains and rivers are alive it shifts the ways we view our responsibilities to the earth and each other. It doesn't mean we never use them to our own ends, but it does mean that such use is more often approached with deep respect and examined for its necessity. They are seen as the personification of forces that act within our world and the Otherworlds.

Some seek to reconstruct early Celtic spiritual paths as a way to reach into the past and connect with their family heritage. For many people, there is value in discovering the ways their ancestors did things, and in practicing traditional crafts. Ethnic musical and cultural festivals are one outgrowth of this urge. Learning the language one's great-grandparents spoke can be a profound influence on a feeling of connection to personal ancestors. Rediscovering crafts like weaving and waulking cloth, participating in traditional dances, and finding value in cultivating and using traditional herbal medicines can be interesting and satisfying on many levels. Participating in modern Celtic cultures can bring connections and richness to life as well as helping to preserve those cultures and languages for future generations.

Others are called by Celtic deities in a direct spiritual sense; urged by them to learn old languages and old ways and to rediscover and reinstate old rituals. Numinous figures appear in dreams and visions, urging us to exploration and discovery. They give us hints and images to lead us along unfamiliar paths.

All of these paths to Celtic spirituality, and others, are legitimate; all these calls to find and reconstruct the spiritual life and views of the pre-Christian Celts are valid and can lead to a satisfying way of life that speaks to our needs in vital and enriching ways.

What does any of this have to do with ogam, you may ask?

In order to understand ogam and how it is used, we first need to understand how it fits into a worldview and a cosmology. Divination and magic occur in specific contexts, with subtle layers of meaning derived from the interrelationships of people with spirits and the natural world around us. The wood we choose to make our ogam *feda* (staves or lots, the singular being *fid*) may have magical or spiritual significance. The sounds of words are resonant and connect with spirits differently in different languages. We draw our divinatory, spiritual, and magical correspondences based on the way we understand the world and our interrelationships within it.

Because ogam and *Filidecht* are so closely intertwined, it is impossible for me to speak of one without speaking of the other. Word and poetry define one another. With poetry, the world is made. While it is certainly possible to use the ogam outside the

29

context of *Filidecht*, its field of expression is narrower and more restricted without the rich web of meaning that the culture and practice of *Filidecht* provides. The response of spirit to symbol is more complex in its native habitat, vibrant with possibility. Ogam and *Filidecht* speak the same language; they are filled with the same symbols and images. Each is easier to understand in the company of the other. *Filidecht* provides a pattern for using the ogam that allows for understanding each letter in the context of ceremony, symbol, healing, and magic. Without the backdrop of Celtic spiritual practice, the ogam loses much of its meaning and resonance. It's like hearing a song in an unknown language. The song may be beautiful, but it tells us little.

The Roots of Celtic Reconstructionist Paganism

Any religion or spiritual path may have a vast spectrum of ways in which it is traditionally expressed or practiced. My personal approach to *Filidecht* is bound up in the techniques of Celtic Reconstructionist Paganism or CR. History and verifiable information about the past is of great importance, but it's also balanced with personal intuition and a lot of thought about how aspects of an older path can be brought forward with respect and relevance for our time.

Scholarship and learning were both important to the *Filid* and *Draoi* of the pre-Christian Irish and Scots, and I follow in their footsteps with my own love of ancient histories, poetry, and the grammar of magic. There is a wealth of gleanable information in the traditional stories, but one must also tread carefully, understanding that everything we have that's written down about Irish and Scottish Paganisms comes from a time after Christianity, and so is thoroughly infused with that influence. It can be difficult work sifting through the pieces, trying to assemble the puzzle, but the rewards are gratifying.

An approach that links scholarship and mysticism can allow for multiple ways of digging down through different layers of the past. By conversation with others following the path, we can compare notes and gain insights that we might not otherwise achieve. We can challenge each other and point each other to resources as well as create shared rituals and contexts for our personal practice.

Within CR, we examine early texts, archaeological records, folklore, and a variety of other sources to discern as best we can how the early Celtic peoples practiced their spiritual ways.

Culture, laws, tales, medicine, and other areas of study all reveal different clues. Language is extremely important within CR as well, for without at least a basic understanding of a Celtic language, it's difficult to understand the worldview that language expresses. And it is the Gaelic language that lies at the root of the understanding of ogam. Personal inspiration has its place, and that place is very important, but it's checked against what can be verified in the historical sources. This, ideally, keeps us from straying too far into fantasy and serves as a series of guideposts along the path.

It is language that reveals the probable original meanings of the ogam letters and gives us information about their potential uses in divination, magic, healing, and spiritual work. While the more easily available material equates each ogam letter with a tree, most of the letter names aren't, in fact, the names of trees at all. Conceptually, they are far more akin to the Norse runes. Lus may be associated with the rowan tree, but the word itself derives from a root that refers to either a healing herb or to the brightness of flame, and it is from these definitions that a depth of meaning can be developed and appreciated.

Reconstructionist Paganisms have been around since at least the early 1970s, particularly through the Egyptian reconstructionist group the Church of the Eternal Source and through the pan-Indo-European group Ar nDraíocht Fein or ADF, but it wasn't until the late 1980s and early 1990s that a specifically Celtic reconstructionist path was developed. Before then, most groups that defined themselves as "Celtic" tended to be based in Wicca or in antiquarian revival Druidism, neither of which have much discernable connection to historical Celtic beliefs or practices beyond the borrowing of a few deity and holiday names. Cosmology was based on that of medieval Ceremonial Magic, with its cast circles and four elements, rather than the Celtic cosmological model of three realms and the tree, fire and well complex.

Most of the ogam knowledge available in these groups was derived from Robert Graves' *The White Goddess* and involved a thirteen-month lunar tree calendar that he created, with its new year at the winter solstice. While this book was a powerful work of poetry, it was never intended as historical scholarship, and in fact his thoughts on ogam were dismissed by the Celtic scholars of his time, including his own grandfather, Charles Graves, who was also a Celtic scholar and an expert on ogam. As early as 1876, Charles Graves was disputing the claim that ogam was solely a "tree alphabet."[13] Robert Graves' theories about the triad of a single Goddess as Maiden, Mother and Crone were also very influential, but not historically accurate regarding early Celtic religion. Johann Jacob Bachofen also influenced this development in his *Myth, Religion and Mother-Right*.[14] While many Celtic Goddesses were in fact triadic, they didn't follow the Maiden-Mother-Crone pattern that these authors proposed.

It wasn't until the advent of the internet that CR really began to gather information, develop a methodology, and gain adherents. Isolated individuals and small groups were doing work with Celtic languages, archaeology, folklore, and mythologies to discover and reconstruct a more authentically Celtic form of Paganism, but the internet allowed these people to come together and compare notes, share sources, and share their successes and failures with ritual, meditation, and techniques. As of this writing in 2007, there are very few books written from a CR perspective, and no good books of ritual or CR spiritual philosophy. There are no books on ogam and divination that step beyond the tree ogam paradigm.

Personal Styles

The web is currently slightly more promising in its resources on CR Paganism, but it's necessary to understand that each website offers a personal, individual style of CR that has been largely created by the person or group that built the site and wrote the material on it.[15] At the moment, there is little agreement on ritual style or on a base Celtic culture from which to work. Where agreement is found, it's in the methods these individuals use to approach the historical information and their personal inspirations and practices. Different CR websites offer information on diverse Celtic cultures, from Gaulish to Scottish to Irish to Welsh and beyond. Some sites are dedicated to individual deities, while others offer rituals used by the individuals and groups who maintain them.

---

[13] Details of the magnitude of Graves' error and a deconstruction of his ogam work in Peter Berresford Ellis' *The Fabrication of 'Celtic' Astrology* can be found at http://cura.free.fr/xv/13ellis2.html

[14] Bachofen, 1967, originally published in German in 1926 as *Mutterrecht und Urreligion*.

[15] The major exception to this individualist approach is the collaborative effort that went into the CR FAQ project, at http://www.paganachd.com/faq/

It is this deeply personal aspect of CR that often makes it so difficult for new seekers to find their way through the thickets. Which culture should I be interested in? Whose site presents accurate information? Whose site is based on shoddy research and sources? What kind of ritual patterns should I use?

Along with different cultural foci in CR, different individuals also worship different deities and follow different paths within those cultural matrices. Some pursue the path of the Warrior, studying martial arts, horsemanship, and offensive and defensive styles of magic. Others who love rural life may follow the path of a homesteader or householder, raising much of their own food and livestock on their land and linking their rituals to the cycles of planting, harvesting, birthing and sacrifice with the slaughter of livestock for food. Some become musicians, following a path of musicianship and learning the harp or other traditional instruments, or learning to sing in Gaelic or Welsh. Others pursue the path of *Filidecht* through the study of poetry, mysticism, and vision. Yet others are drawn to traditional methods of healing with herbs, massage, and charms.

There are also those who focus on individual deities, forming Brigid orders to tend her eternal flame, or revering warrior Goddesses like the Morrígan or Scáthach. Some might follow particular deities who are deeply involved with their personal focus, for instance Dian Cécht, Airmid, or Miach as guides and guardians for healers, Ogma and Brigid as patrons of writers, or Goibhniu as a mentor for someone interested in metal-smithing.

Different people may also interact more or less intensely with the spirits of the local land, or with the spirits of their ancestors. For those whose path includes mysticism, there might be an intense cycle of visiting or camping out in places that are felt to be sacred so as to commune more easily with the spirits there and to develop links with the land itself through their meditations and rituals. For others, there may be a large component of work with animal, plant, and bird spirits. Some work intensively with spirits of trees. Others work on techniques of divination as described in old Irish texts dealing with the observation of the activities of ravens or wrens, or they may become interested in weatherworking through the application of *néldoracht*, or divination by clouds. Some say that *néldoracht* refers to the practice of astrology, and look for the buried lore of stars and planets in the early materials.

Individual CR paths may also emphasize the celebration of certain holidays. Those who work with Manannán mac Lir, for instance, might celebrate the Manx custom of paying him rent near the summer solstice, while others may ignore that day entirely. Those who honor Brigid might focus more on her holy day of Imbolc than on the other days of the year. Most CR traditions recognize four main holidays at the beginning of May, August, November, and February, in contrast to the larger Pagan community that celebrates eight holy days.

My own work with ogam falls within this area of personal style. I also do a lot of work with the local land and waters, the spirits of animals, and my ancestors. It is through a combination of these things that my style becomes manifest, while still pursuing the study of the old ways and trying to apply those concepts and methods to my ogam work in divination, healing, magic, and ritual. Ogma is one of the patrons of ogam work and is said to be the mythic progenitor of the system, carving the first letter of the alphabet seven times upon a birch twig to warn Lug that his wife would be carried off into the Sídhe mounds seven times unless she was guarded by birch.

Much of what I know and present here can be footnoted. It is easy enough to cite books describing what the medieval Irish poets and Christian clerics thought about ogam. There are many available books about tree-lore as well, though only some of that is relevant to the task at hand. The early Irish tales mention ogam here and there, implying it was used for divination and for magic. What I present here, though, is a personal system of interpretation and work based on the sources and on my own intuitions and years of working with ogam in magic and divination for many purposes. It shouldn't be seen as a claim of rediscovering some hidden, ancient truth about how the early *Draoí* used the ogam. That said, the methods I present are effective and useful and it's my hope that you will find them useful as well.

When we look at the ogam with the eyes of a poet, we see beneath the surface. We see into the mists that separate our world from the Otherworld. Come and join me in the universe next door.

The Personal and the Particular

When we rely upon the spirits and our internal voice to guide us on a spiritual path, having reality checks is very important. In early Irish, personal inspiration and vision were referred to as *imbas* and *aisling*. *Imbas* refers specifically to ecstatic poetic inspiration, while *aisling* is a more general term dealing with states of dream and vision.

The development of these qualities was highly sought after and the training of a *Fili* or sacred poet could take up to twenty years to complete. During this time the aspiring *Fili* was taught history, poetics, legal principles, the traditional stories, grammar, mathematics, star lore and genealogies; all manner of things to provide fodder for the creation of poetry. Among the things taught, though, were also techniques of ritual and mysticism, of meditation and the focus of energies that could lead to personal insight, communication with spirits, and ways to open gates to the Otherworlds.

The original *Filid* had teachers to consult and contend with in their education, testing themselves and their knowledge and technique. They had individuals to turn to along the way for advice, to keep them grounded when vision became fantasy, and to sort the useful fruit of inspiration from the dross of delusion. They had a community raised and steeped in the public aspects of the lore and culture to fall back on, with set standards for what a *Draoí* or a *Fili* should know and what they did for that community. For us, without those supports and resources, this is a more difficult proposition, but there are still ways to approach our personal insights and discern their level of usefulness and validity in the context of Filidecht.

One way that CRs talk about this process of validating our personal *imbas* and *aisling* is by reference to personal gnosis. The stages of inspiration, investigation and validation are generally seen as unsubstantiated personal gnosis (UPG)[16], shared gnosis (SG) and confirmed gnosis. In our work, each of us will find pieces of UPG that work for us. Other times such visions will be impractical in the waking world, and while such insights may be noted, they are usually quickly discarded as irrelevant to one's spiritual path.

Now and then, individuals separated by quite some distance may receive the same or similar inspirations or visions. This is most often revealed when people are comparing notes when they talk, online in chats or email, or in person at festivals

---

[16] The convention of referring to "UPG" or Unsubstantiated or Unverified Personal Gnosis originated within the Asatru or Norse Reconstructionist Pagan movement to distinguish between what was in the lore and the things that people discovered in ritual or through other means that worked for them.

or gatherings. Sometimes these insights are the result of small groups working together doing trance work toward a particular goal. When these visions and inspirations are similar enough and there is no evidence that there was any deliberate influence to lead the disparate individuals to the same conclusions, the situation becomes one of shared gnosis.

In both cases, further work is necessary. Going to sources such as the early tales, books discussing archaeological finds, or journal articles in Celtic studies can help focus the information. In some cases, the vision or inspiration may be directly contradicted by what is known about early Celtic societies, though frequently there is no evidence either way. When our personal insights are directly contradicted, this may not mean the insight is invalid, but it does mean that it is not an authentic part of CR and is not likely to be well received in the community. Examples of this sort of inspiration abound in the popular books on "Celtic Paganism" -- for instance, assertions that the Celtic peoples were matriarchal and peaceful, or that potatoes and pumpkin blossoms were an important part of Druidic worship. In both cases, there is direct evidence to the contrary, and while it may make for meaningful personal worship, it isn't in line with CR ritual, cosmology, or practice, and it certainly isn't Celtic in any recognizable sense of the word.

We need to note that personal insight and inspiration, even when it's not an authentically Celtic expression, can still be personally and spiritually valid. This is particularly important when dealing with local spirits and personal ancestors. If you live in South Dakota, what the spirits of the land there want will be different than they would if you lived in Dublin. Local traditional ways of approaching spirits, while not necessarily Celtic, can legitimately be seen as a part of a personal, localized CR practice even though it doesn't related to CR as a whole. That said, these things must be done with the utmost respect for the local people and traditions, and not stolen, twisted, and used without instruction or permission.

Sometimes our personal insights or the images in dream and vision are confirmed while searching the stories and the sources. A reference might be found to a specific ritual act, or an artifact might be discovered that contains an image seen in a dream. At that point, personal gnosis is often shared with the CR community. Frequently, such insights and images are adopted into the practices of other individuals and groups, and in this way the corpus of knowledge within CR and its body of ritual and practice grows and evolves. The body of modern lore surrounding the ogam can be added to in this way. It is through these insights that poetry, ritual, and music are given to the community as well.

Circumambulations

We stand at the center of the world, and each place is the center. Around us, the bright line of the horizon defines the boundary between land and sky. The seasons spin round us in their circle from darkness to light and back into the winter's dark. Day and night are defined by the circles of sun and moon.

The cycle of the year is divided into light and dark halves, and the circle of the seasons determines what work is to be done, when stories may be told, and what rituals are appropriate in a given place. Divination is paid particular attention at different times of year. Samhain at the year's end and the year's beginning is a significant time when divination is done to see who will survive the coming winter, along with other more mundane concerns. Divination helps mark the cycles of time and tide, giving assurance as we seek passage through the darkness and the unknown.

Divination is one of the primary uses for ogam in modern CR practice. Different practitioners have different approaches to it, the majority of them coming to the work from a focus on tree ogam. This works very well for many people, but when a practitioner lives in an environment where the traditional trees are rare or nonexistent, it makes sense to either modify the tree list in some way to conform to local species, or to take a different approach to the material. This is, in part, why I've chosen to work primarily with the name-meanings and the phrases or kennings associated with each ogam *fid*, rather than the trees themselves. Concepts and kennings travel with me wherever I go and are not linked to the species found in one geographical area.

Using the name-meanings allows for a great amount of flexibility. It should be noted that the Celtic tribes needed flexibility as they traveled, as each place they lived had different plants, different trees, and different land features that needed to be acknowledged, learned, and connected with on many levels. This motion is important to remember as we work with ogam. Both the ogam and ourselves are moving and evolving. As we study the ogam we begin to develop our own associations with each *fid*, growing organically from the traditional meanings and associations as well as from our own experiences. This path of learning is also a journey and a circumambulation, leading us back to our starting point, allowing us to gaze into ourselves with greater depth and to understand ourselves at deeper levels of meaning.

Ogam is a mirror held up to our soul. Within it, we can find ourselves reflected, our needs and flaws and dignities revealed.

Land, Sea, and Sky

At the root of Celtic cosmology is the concept of the three realms of land, sea and sky. Oaths were sworn by the three realms and all things are encompassed by them. Land, sea, and sky are ever-present around us, found throughout Irish thought.[17] At a meeting of Alexander the Great with a group of Celts related by Strabo, these warriors said that the only thing they feared was that the sky would fall down upon them.[18]

When we work with ogam, we are placing ourselves ritually in the center of this cosmology, standing firmly upon the land, surrounded by sea, covered by sky. The knowledge of ogam, like *imbas* that sparks poetry, comes from this center, rising through three cauldrons of energy within the body.[19] When we speak of the realms we aren't speaking of an idealized extrapolation, but of the actual physical presence of the sky above us, the water we drink, and the land upon which we walk. These are not abstractions in the way that most modern Paganism postulates earth, air, fire, and water. We cannot invoke or dismiss them because they are always present, and if they aren't then we will surely and inevitably die. "Invoking" the realms makes no sense,

---

[17] A lengthy discussion of the three realms in early Irish thought can be found at http://www.celt.dias.ie/publications/celtica/c23/c23-174.pdf in Liam Mac Mathúna's *Irish Perceptions of the Cosmos*, Celtica 23, 1999, 174-187

[18] Strabo quotes Ptolemy I as saying "Alexander received them warmly and while they were sharing a drink asked them what they feared most, thinking they would say him. They answered that they feared nothing except that the sky might fall down upon them, but that they honored the friendship of a man like him more than anything." Koch and Carey, 2003, 7.

[19] The three cauldrons are originally discussed in an Old Irish poem referred to as *The Cauldron of Poesy*, available in two scholarly translations. My article on the subject at http://www.Seánet.com/~inisglas/cauldronpoesy.html contains my translation and commentary on the poem. The scholarly translations available are Henry, P.L., "The Cauldron of Poesy," *Studia Celtica* #14/15, 1979/1980, pp. 114-128 and Breatnach, Liam, "The Cauldron of Poesy," *Ériu* #32, 1981, pp. 45-93. More information about the cauldrons in a CR context is found in chapter 5 of this book.

as they are already with us. An attempt to "banish" or "dismiss" the realms leaves us in a conceptual vacuum, floating in the depths of space, and this is not a place conducive to healthy human life.

As there are three internal cauldrons and three external realms, there are also three liminal currents of power that I perceive for interpreting the ogam *feda*. Each of these has a rough correspondence to a realm and a cauldron. That said, it's important to remember that each of these currents can manifest within any realm or cauldron and cannot be viewed as strictly a function of or vehicle for a particular realm or cauldron's energies. Celtic philosophy is one of transformative and boundary-transgressing awareness; shape and species change with the blink of an eye and the Otherworlds are everywhere around us. One has only to step into the mist for everything to change completely.

These currents can be viewed as ways that interpretation and energies flow within each *fid* and can be used with more advanced methods of divination for helping to determine which web of meanings is more relevant to a given situation in a reading. The currents are expressions of the depths of each realm, or of ways of accessing meaning within each of the cauldrons. They are different avenues of approach to each *fid*; different categories of experience within the potentials of each *fid*'s meaning.

I've named these currents the chthonic, the oceanic and the celestial. From their names, it's obvious that they have certain resonances with the realms -- the chthonic partakes of the energy of the land; the oceanic is a sea or mist energy; and the celestial is the energy of the realm of the sky. They have general associations and attributes, though none of them are strictly to be interpreted within a dualistic good/bad, dark/light or masculine/feminine paradigm. Good and bad, dark and light, masculine and feminine all arise within each of these currents, and so do the myriad things found outside the boundaries of these polarities.

No current can be solely interpreted as safe territory, nor is any of them inherently more dangerous than any other. Safety and danger lies, at least in part, within the *Fili* herself and the way she responds to what the world brings forth. It is the *Fili*'s ability to bend perception and reality that determines the ultimate meaning of all that happens and whether the manifestation of a given *fid* becomes a danger.

In dealing with the *feda* themselves, chthonic interpretations are body oriented, manifest, and potentially initiatory. Oceanic interpretations are emotionally oriented, transformative, chaotic, and liminal. Interpretations in the celestial category are spiritually oriented, illuminating, and ecstatic. There are specific journey types and states associated with each of the currents and the realms. *Echtrae* are journeys on or within the land; *immrama* are sea voyages into the Otherworld realms beyond or under the waters; *aislingthe* are dream and visionary journeys into the realms of sky and the stars.

Each *fid*'s web of meaning will encompass items within all three currents. They serve as a quick and helpful way to organize categories of interpretation within a reading. They also identify which of a range of meanings is meant when the *fid* appears. These currents are valuable tools for deciding how to interpret the appearance of *feda* that have a wide variety of associations or that may be based on two or more linguistic roots.

The easiest way to work with these currents in refining divination is to create three sets of *feda*. My suggestion is to color code these sets with green for the chthonic current, grey for the oceanic, and blue for the celestial. All three of these colors fall within the semantic field of the color-word *glas* -- which means green/grey/blue[20]. *Glas* is a color that is associated with the Otherworlds and with boundary-transcending states, so the use of these colors in tools to access Otherworldly wisdom is symbolically appropriate.

To make further visual distinctions in low light, the *feda* themselves can be painted in contrasting colors on the *glas* backgrounds -- white for celestial, green for oceanic, and red for chthonic. These three colors come from the Irish Christian traditions surrounding the three types of martyrdom[21], but can

---

[20] Alfred K. Siewers, "The Bluest Greyest Greenest Eye: Colours of Martyrdom and Colours of the Winds as Iconographic Landscape," Cambrian Medieval Celtic Studies 50, 2005, pp 31-66. The Old Irish word *glas* can be defined as blue, green, or grey, within a much larger semantic field dealing with things like "shining" or "the color of sky in water." It is a transcendent color frequently associated with Otherworldly places and things, and with the sometimes-invisible boundary between sea and sky that is a sacred juncture where the *immrama* voyages take place. It is also associated with the natural ecological world of vegetation, natural uncolored wool, ice, the sea, and fog.

[21] In early Irish Christianity, three colors of martyrdom were seen as symbolic of spiritual, emotional, and bodily sacrifice. Red martyrdom was bodily death; white martyrdom was exile or pilgrimage for the sake of God, and *glas* martyrdom --

be interpreted within a CR context as varying forms of personal dedication and sacrifice in the pursuit of wisdom -- bodily, emotional, and spiritual. These colors and currents will be discussed in detail in chapter 8 on advanced divination techniques.

With three visually distinct sets of *feda* the issue of choosing a segment of the meaning web is simpler, relying on cues of color association. It also allows for multiple layers of meaning within a single *fid* to appear in the same reading. While this method relies as much on intuition for interpretation as the single set method, it allows for finer distinctions and more clarity on the part of the reader. It also helps refine focus for magical and ritual work, enabling the *Fili* to concentrate on one particular shade of meaning, excluding energies that might interfere with the desired goals.

Glannad

The curl of rising smoke is an evocative image. Smoke shows the shape of the wind, giving form to its direction. It carries the scent and the essence of the burned offering. These scents connect with memory, setting, and evoking moods. The sense of smell is ancient and visceral, reaching into what is most primal within us.

In many cultures, smoke is used as offering or as a vehicle of purification. In the Highlands of Scotland, according to F. Marian McNeill, the smoke of juniper was used to purify the house at Hogmanay, the new year's celebration. Branches were burned in the fireplace until the whole house was filled with its smoke to drive out any ill luck or bad influence brought in during the year just passed.[22] It was burned in the spring in the Orkneys as well, to purify the cattle as they were driven up to the shielings in the hills for the summer's grazing.

In my own practice, I use smoke as purification and for offerings to the spirits and deities. One of the plants I use for this process is juniper, inspired by Highland practices, but because I live in the Northwest I also use cedar, which is a very important local ritual plant. Sage and other plants sometimes make an appearance, depending on my needs and the desires of the spirits and deities I'm working with. The sage in question isn't the

---

sometimes read as "blue" but usually as "green" -- was the separation from physical desire in fasting or other ascetic practices. Siewers, 2005, 33.
[22] McNeill, 1989, 80

garden culinary sage that you find in your kitchen, but any of the many varieties of white sage or desert sage, which are a different family of plants entirely.

The use of smoke for purification, the act of *glannad* or cleansing, is as much about intent as action. Like any act of magical or spiritual significance, intent and the state of mind used to approach that act are important. No spiritual act is casual, though it may sometimes appear so to an observer. In learning and practicing *Filidecht* and working with the ogam we learn to approach the world around us as sacred, and to uncover or create meaning within our lives and in each of our actions.

The small curl of smoke rising from bowl, shell, or cauldron can induce profound changes in the *Fili*'s consciousness, moving us from the realm of the everyday into a sacred moment. To take this smoke into our personal space in a ritual manner prepares us for our work, whether that is prayer, ritual, magic, healing, or divination. With the smoke of sacred herbs, we clear ourselves of interfering energies and cue our minds to center ourselves for our work.

All one needs for *glannad* is the herb to burn, something fireproof to burn it in, and a way to light the herb so it can smolder. Glass containers are not recommended. Even if you think you will only be burning something in it for a few moments, the heat of repeated use can shatter the glass, and sudden temperature changes are hazardous. Earthenware and ceramic are far better, and natural shell, for instance abalone or a large clamshell, are both beautiful and functional. Smoke can be spread equally well with hands, feathers, fans, or any other object that feels appropriate for your ritual. If you work with particular spirits or deities, you might wish to have something associated with that spirit, God, or Goddess as a part of the process.

You can use a single herb or several, though whole herbs are generally better than ground or powdered for this purpose. Incense sticks or cones can be used, but I tend to find them a very poor substitute compared to the cedar and juniper branches I've gathered with appropriate rituals and offerings made to the trees in question. Sticks and cones also usually have chemicals added to make them burn better, and which can add unwanted energies or even toxins and allergens to the base of plant material.

When performing *glannad*, the intent is that of clearing away anything unsavory that surrounds or has attached itself to you emotionally or spiritually, within or without. The act should be approached with reverence and seriousness, taking time to calm oneself through focus of mind and breathing. While the outer aspect of this cleansing is to brush smoke around oneself, the inner aspect is one of purification and energy working. All things have their own vibration or energy; with intent some of those energies can be brought into and blended with our own to rid ourselves of what we neither want nor need around us. The spirits of the plants used in this process are also asked for their help.

In an animist sense, we give these spirits thanks and recognition just as we would thank the spirits of plants or animals that we eat as food or whose hides or bones we use for our spiritual and magical objects. The spirits of the plants are living beings that can be appealed to through our words and actions. Through these acts, we build our connections with the spirits and relate more easily to them, growing ever-deepening roots in the earth. Thanks can be given in songs or chants that you learn or create as you develop your practice, or simply in quiet or silent prayer with heartfelt words that come to you as you prepare and light the herbs. They may also be found in the traditional materials from Ireland and Scotland, offering authentic practices for ritual harvest of sacred plants.

When moving the smoke around yourself, focus on bringing that energy into your body. Feel it purify you of all negativity and drive away any challenging energies or unwelcome spiritual entities. Feel the vibrations of the plants you burn filling you and giving you energy and strength. Understand that the songs you sing and the prayers you make are feeding the spirits of the plants that you request aid from. Focus on the idea that your task is a sacred act and that you are preparing yourself and the space around you for important spiritual work. In spiritual and magical contexts, attitude is everything.

Glannad, though, doesn't have to be solely a function of smoke and wind. It is any act of cleansing and purification. Asperging with water and herbs is just as effective and may be necessary in places where nothing may be burned. Working with water for purification is an excellent way to deal with issues that rise from asthma or allergies as well. It is the intent to do *glannad* that counts, not the exact form it takes. Saining and purifications are done with water and other substances in the Gaelic tradition as well as with smoke.[23]

Song and the Voice of the Wind

Song is an extremely important aspect of early Celtic life and worship. Most of the poems found in the collection called the *Carmina Gadelica* were set to music when initially collected by Alexander Carmichael.[24] Most of these tunes were not preserved, but the poems can easily be adapted by modern *Filid* and set to music, or used as models for our own original songs and prayers. Songs were sung for all the purposes of life to ring them with protection and ritual, from lighting the home fires in the morning from the coals of the previous day to covering the fire at night to preserve the spark for morning.

There are songs for gathering herbs, for milking cows, for healing charms, for taking omens from the first thing seen in the morning, and for almost anything one can imagine in daily life. We can carry this practice and this attitude forward as a part of modern CR *Filidecht*, for music is inseparable from poetry in the early Pagan traditions of Ireland and Scotland, and as such it is a deep and necessary part of CR as practiced by modern *Filid*.

Such songs can be used for divination and for healing work, based on ogam imagery, or through singing the names of individual *feda*. Songs you compose incorporating the kennings or word ogams can focus a *fid*'s energies for a specific magical or ritual purpose, and can be woven into poetry that is then used over and over again for your work, adding depth to the energies called forth.

---

[23] Campbell, 2005, 136-137 and 211-215. A sain (*seun* or *sian* in Scots Gaelic) was any charm or talisman that purified or protected, though it seems to refer far more often to protective than purifying rites or items. The *sop seile* or "spittle wisp", usually translated as "saining straw", was used to sprinkle doorposts and houses to purify and protect them, and also on new cattle when they were brought home. Horses, harness, and plough were also asperged in this manner in the spring before ploughing. Campbell says, interestingly enough, "The liquid used was menstruum." Saining with water was also used as a baptismal rite for newborns. *Seun* might also be a string wrapped around a cow's tail, or an item given to a loved one to protect them in battle. The idea of purification and protection covers a great deal of territory and can take many forms.

[24] This six-volume collection was published by the Scottish Academic Press over a period of nearly 40 years, with the final volume published in 1971. The original volumes are in both Gaelic and English. The most commonly available edition is currently in print as a single volume from Floris Press, but contains only the English and is not to be considered a complete rendering of the material.

It doesn't matter if you have a great voice or if you can't carry a tune. The purpose of the song isn't a professional level performance, it's used to express your gratitude to the spirits and to let you put emotion into your ritual in a very direct way. Song is also used to bring focus and mindfulness to your work and your divination. Remember that you're not on stage. You're singing for you and the spirits to make requests and offer thanks. Your songs don't have to be perfect; they merely need to be sung.

While for many CRs the use of a Celtic language is an important aspect of practice and having a working vocabulary of technical terms is very useful, it isn't absolutely necessary to sing or pray in Gaelic for the work to be effective. I use certain stock phrases in Irish and Scots Gaelic when I pray, though I do not speak either language fluently. In my personal interactions with my deities, they have asked me to speak Gaelic to them, but each person following a CR path will need to decide if they want to use a Celtic language in their prayers to their deities, and how much of those languages are practical and appropriate.

Understand that your songs are an offering to the spirits and the deities, rather than an evocation. CRs don't demand or order the presence of spiritual beings any more than we demand or order the presence of a respected and beloved guest in our home. We don't threaten spirits unless they are causing problems and can't be constructively dealt with in other ways. Our attitude isn't one of ordering the deities and spirits around, nor is it one of "using" them for different purposes. One may appeal to greater powers as one might appeal to a friend or a relative, but if "using" people is considered an affront to them, how much greater is the offense of "using" spirits and deities?

As with human beings, spirits and deities have different talents, gifts and abilities, and if they like us and are pleased with us, they can be asked or persuaded to use those gifts and talents for our aid and protection and that of our community. Our relationship with spirit should be familial in the best sense: cherishing each being for who and what it is and appreciating what these beings are willing to do for us in our daily lives. Powerful spirits and deities should be approached with great respect and all caution, but without an attitude of groveling or begging. The tales show us consistently that qualities such as strength, integrity, and self-reliance are greatly valued by the inhabitants of the Otherworlds. We may be flawed, but we are not inadequate. Our talents are worthy of respect and appreciation and if we don't value our own personal worth, no one else is going to do it for us.

Those wishing to practice *Filidecht* and actively use the ogam in their spiritual practice should cultivate an attitude of appreciation for the gifts given to us by the world around us and by the spiritual beings that become our patrons, friends, and helpers. These relationships should be reciprocal, with gifts offered for gifts. Offerings of food and drink should be an important part of any ritual and regularly present on the altar. The same smoke used for *glannad* can also be used as an offering to the spirits and deities as part of the exchange of gifts and energy.

It should also be understood that the Otherworld beings have their own agendas and interests. There is danger in traveling to those places and dealing with those beings. Not all deities and spirits are helpful to humanity, and some beings are what could be considered mischievous at best or malevolent at worst. Some are spirits that cause disease and imbalance, and they may need to be fought or bargained with to restore health and balance to an individual or a group. There will be times when spirits and deities present themselves to you as a danger when the underlying reality is one of testing and tempering. Never assume that what you see on the surface is the entire truth of a matter. Important lessons and great wisdom can be learned through confronting fearful events and moving through them successfully.

Proper precautious should always be taken when dealing with the Otherworld. *Filidecht*, when practiced effectively, can offer songs and spells of protection as well as appeals for aid and songs of thanks. The work of *Filidecht* at its highest is the work of aiding, healing, protecting the human community, and learning which spirits and powers will help and which will harm when they are approached by the *Fili* or encountered by the people.

The author Seán O'Boyle saw the ogam as a harp tabulature, preserving a musical method. When approached this way, ogam can aid our singing and our work with chant and sound. If each *fid* has its own note, then singing, playing, or otherwise sounding that note can help to bring its energy into our lives and rituals. Tunes can be seen as complex interweavings of energies as well as praise, focus, or magic. With mindful attention to lyrics, both word and tune can be brought to bear on the *Fili*'s task.

The ogam has another connection to the world's breath as wind through the color ogam. In the early Gaelic tradition, twelve winds are described, each with its own color and qualities. Most of those colors overlap with the color ogam, and each color word has its own emotional resonance. While some of the winds don't have an exact match, to examine the colors in reference to the winds themselves and their traditional attributes is a useful technique for deepening our understanding of what the colors might mean in terms of ogam for magic, in ritual, or for divination.

The emotional and cultural context of the hues of the color ogam can help in understanding and interpreting the traditional tales, giving a good sense of what the original authors and storytellers meant when they used them as tropes. When *ruadh* as red(-haired) refers repeatedly to anger and wrathful states in the tales, it points out the more powerful destructive resonances of Ruis in ogam interpretation. The strong links with *glas* in its green range to southwestern winds points to a certain Otherworldly energy, a connection with the Otherworld powers brought forth in healing through nGétal, and with wounding unto death that sends one to the ancestors that is the other side of this *fid*'s power.

Color is also a path through which ogam can be incorporated into energy healing work. With attention to the emotional meanings of the color words used in Gaelic, we can discern patterns that can be adapted to modern energy work or incorporated into cauldron meditations to shift the body's energy flows and levels. It holds great potential for assisting in dream or vision interpretation as well, giving a context to help sort through subtle emotional and spiritual threads within the imagery of the *aisling* state.

As with any other set of ogam meanings, color can be used as a separate definitional set, with its own context for your ritual and work. In creating your ogam *feda* for divination and ritual, you might want to dye the background of each *fid* with its appropriate color to help keep that context before you. If your set is a uniform color of stone or wood, you can draw or paint the *fid* itself in its associated color.

Ethics

Our work flows within the *dlí*, the Way or the Law of the workings of the universe. It is, if you will, similar to the concept

Erynn Rowan Laurie

of the Tao, from which all things arise. It is the guiding principle[25] that directs the flow of the streams of energy we perceive and use when we work with *Draíocht* and *Filidecht* -- with magic and poetry. As with the flowing of physical streams, energy flows better within certain channels, and to go against those flows makes things more difficult.

The creation of ethical structures is one of the ways that humanity responds to the demands of *dlí* and interprets the flow of *brí* or energy and *dán* or gift and destiny. The use of the ogam allows us a way to look into the flow of fate and interpret what we see there. Our ethical constructs give us guidelines for interpreting and living within our relationships to self and other, both human and divine. Within these structures are found *geasa* -- ritual strictures and taboos -- as well as the everyday rules we follow as we work to get along in society and our spiritual and magical work.

Defining our ethical structures helps define who we are in the universe as well as finding our place in the complex interactions of person and place. Each *fid* of the ogam illustrates a different principle within that framework of magic and spirit. The ogam gives us patterns for beginnings and endings, for the attainment of right livelihood and the achievement of right relationship. It illustrates ways in which energy and objects are used for good or ill, and the way in which our actions generate reactions in our relationships and our life.

In meditating upon Tinne, the ingot, we learn about right relationships with money and expressing our creativity in the physical world. We find ways to express our gifts through the crafts of our hands and how we come to create the physical aspects of our spiritual realities. We discover ways in which we relate to the path of the warrior and the appropriate and controlled use of force in our interactions. We learn how the use of money and exchange can help or harm society and influence our relationships with others.

---

[25] *Dlí* is modern Irish, with meanings of "binding principle," "divine precept", "law/legality", "scientific principle" etc. It goes back to Old Irish *dlíged*, with a somewhat broader range of meaning -- "guiding principle, law, or theory", "principle, rule, norm", "dictum, authoritative statement", "reason, argument", "reckoning, computation", "nature, condition, kind, manner", also law in a wide sense of those things based on tradition which one must follow, and implications of duty or obligation, or what is right and due.

If we go with the "binding principle/guiding principle" first definitions of each word, it seems that to view it as "the way/nature of things" or "the way things are" makes sense.

Sail, the willow, offers insight into the flow of time, how our physical and spiritual ancestors influence the lives we lead now, and the importance of purifying our bodies and the flow of our breath. As we examine each *fid*, we can find guides to the ethical dimensions of life, death, spiritual work, magic, money, healing, transformation, and every other part of our existence.

Our interpretations of the ogam *feda* give us ways to approach our own gnosis and understanding of our personal and social *dlí* as we seek our way in the world. Each *fid* is a word in our vocabulary of magic and spirit, a ripple in our experience of universal and personal laws of action and reaction. They are reminders of ways of being in the world. Speaking the name of a *fid* makes a ripple in the flow of time and space, and the use of poetry creates patterns with those ripples, making magic possible. Meditation and attentive focus on the *feda* attunes us to the energy of each of these particular ripples and patterns, and exercising our ethical judgment aids us in following the flow in ways proper to our time, spirit, and place.

In a CR context, there is a sense of rightness and wrongness that accompanies the practice of magic and spiritual work. This sense is often expressed through the appreciation of human virtues like strength, generosity, and eloquence. Rather than a list of commandments regarding what must not be done, *Filidecht* embraces an ethic of those things that should be pursued in a positive sense -- an ethics arising from the active practice of virtues. We should be kind to those who are weak, generous to the impoverished, and gentle to the young and the elderly. We should embrace the value of knowledge and wisdom and their eloquent expression in our words and deeds. We should act from a place of strength, and build community together whenever possible, taking pride in our accomplishments, rather than acting in ways that fragment that strength in individuals and common causes or bring shame and disgrace upon ourselves and those closest to us.

In divination, truth is of great importance and in the early Irish tales the lack of truth in judgment and speech is linked to the downfall of individuals and societies. We must truthfully express what we see, but we must do so in ways intended to help and nurture rather than harm or destroy, acting with honor in our dealings with others and with the realms of deity and spirit. In healing, we must seek to restore the proper balance of our physical, spiritual and emotional being. Our pursuit of vision should be undertaken with an attitude of respect and gratitude.

The use of ogam can teach us how to live within the proper tides of time and season, of ebb and flow.

When we act as an oracle for others, we speak with the voice of deity, and the vessel of that voice is bound to act with honor and honesty. As healers, we are agents of healing deities and should seek to embody their forces in the world, empowered but not seeking power. In both of these cases, we are vessels or conduits, not the flow itself. We can help guide and shape that energy, but we aren't that energy in and of itself. If we act against our *dlí*, we obstruct that flow and create the potential to bring harm to ourselves and to others. Those who act against the natural flow of things often burn out quickly both spiritually and emotionally. The forces expressed by the ogam *feda* are far greater than the fragile vessels of our bodies, and as with anything of great power, caution is necessary in the harnessing of it.

Spirits in the Material World

Our consideration of the forces invoked when working with the ogam must include an understanding of spirit and deity within the framework of the early Gaelic linguistic and cultural background that gave rise to the ogam. This includes a continuum of spirit that reaches from human ancestral spirits to the spirits of place and creature, leading into the greater powers that are most often understood as different deities. There apparently aren't firm dividing lines between these different kinds of spiritual entities. Rather, they flow into one another based on their connections with individuals, places, and patterns of power. It is conceivable that an ancestral spirit might, over time, develop the power and presence of deity, or that an animal spirit might in some families be considered an ancestor.

Beliefs surrounding selkies or seal-spirits in Ireland and Scotland are an example of animal ancestors and the relational connections between humans and spirits of land and place. The attachment of *bean sídhe* or fairy women, the spirits that traditionally herald death to different families is another example of the interweaving of spirit and the human realm. In some cases, humans might take spirit lovers, called *leannan sídhe*, who may give the individual powers of poetry, music, or prophecy and discernment of otherworldly realities.

Some families are believed to descend from deities as well, giving us a divine connection within our human bodies. The overlapping of human, ancestor, animal, deity, and spirit of place is profound and the weaving of this can be expressed by the *fid* Nin, which is the fork that supports the weaver's beam. It is a network of profound spiritual value, a weaving of flesh and spirit that connects us to each and every thing in the universe in a way that is similar to what is expressed in the Lakota phrase *mitakue oyasin* or "all my relations." Because of the way our energies are woven together, we are related to each thing in the universe around us, from sparrow to star. The Arthurian tales' understanding of the union between the health of the king and that of the land is a late Celtic expression of this deep and subtle belief. A modern manifestation of this belief is expressed in the 1981 John Boorman film *Excalibur*, where it is stated that the King and the Land are One. In Ireland the idea was called *Fír Flatha*, the King's Truth, and the truth of the king's judgment was directly and intimately linked to crops and the fertility of the land.

Deity and the Call to Service

Some people find themselves called by Celtic Gods and Goddesses. They are brought to service by something Otherworldly that compels them to a spiritual life. This call transcends categories of place and time and genetics, speaking directly to the heart. Encountered in dream or vision, the numinous bursts forth in the lives of different people in different ways, and some people experience that call in their encounters with Celtic music, tales, or language. Others may visit Ireland or Scotland and feel a connection with the land and the waters there, and through that find their connection with Celtic deity.

In modern western society such calls to service are often misunderstood or misinterpreted by those not called. They may be rejected as deluded roleplaying or deliberate and malicious cultural appropriation. People who receive such a call and who view deity and spirit as real and manifest are often considered eccentric, or even insane. There is, however, a difference between pathology and spiritual experience, and just because it isn't generally accepted in society doesn't mean our response to spirit is wrong or should be medicated into submission.

Sometimes that call urges us to separate ourselves from society. In mainstream religions, this call often leads people to a cloistered life, in spiritual retreats or into monasteries or abbeys. When someone outside of the spiritual mainstream receives such a call, that urge to isolation may be viewed with suspicion. In traditional indigenous societies, there were places for people whose call led them to contemplation and isolation, and they were respected and sought out for their skills and their vision. People going through a process of disintegration and spiritual rebirth were supported by colleagues and taught traditional techniques for integrating these experiences into their own lives and that of their society.

Unfortunately, those of us who receive such a call today may instead end up living in isolation without community or resources to support us. We have to negotiate the difficult path to wholeness using modern tools that are not entirely suited to the creation of a fruitful life of spirit and service to the community in oracular, healing, and ceremonial roles. One of the dangers of listening to the call of deity is that we may lose those things our society values -- home, family connections, or everyday work. We may be utterly transformed and that transformation, while it makes us useful vessels for spirit, may change our entire identity and make us in many ways unrecognizable to family and friends, unable to entirely function in modern western culture as it is currently constituted. Our vision of ourselves may change, and that shift may include a different understanding of our sexuality, the paths of energy in our bodies, and our place in the universe, as well as gaining a sense of focus and guidance in our lives.

In part this happens because we end up giving control of many aspects of our lives to the deities and spirits we communicate with. This vulnerability is viewed with suspicion in modern western culture, but if we are to be effective conduits of vision and power from the Otherworlds, our bodies are, in some ways, no longer our own. Divination and magic strip away our illusions, leaving the bare bones of our spirit, raw and wild and connected with things and places that transcend the boundaries between worlds. To see through Manannán's mists, our eyes must become the eyes of spirits. To walk the Otherworld paths, our bodies must be remade. Ogam can be a powerful guide and tool to successfully navigating these transformations.

Issues of Race and Ethnicity

For some people, a search for early Celtic spirituality is a way to seek connection with the lineage of their family in a personal way. There is a desire to trace lost roots, to discover ways of thinking and being that feel more satisfying and more connected with our origins than what western commercial culture provides. To seek these connections is a natural human desire, and reverence for the ancestors is a profound and important part of early Celtic spirituality. Visions were sought in the places where the dead were buried. The spirits of the ancestors were consulted in divination and appealed to for protection and aid by the living.[26] Some ancestors were seen as related to deity or as being among the *sídhe*, both powerful and dangerous. Their favor could be given or withdrawn at whim, and contact with them was ritualized through vision seeking, the making of offerings, and through ceremony.

The potential danger of taking ethnicity as a path to any religion is the development of an exclusionary sense of tribalism and a feeling of that spirituality as the personal property of bloodlines, the sole right of those with the "right" ancestry. Taken to extremes, this can manifest itself in racism and rigid definitions of anything outside that racial or ethnic identity as wrong, or even evil, with any mingling seen as tainting or corrupting the "purity" of the blood or the family line. Every respectable scholar of Celtic history works from a definition of "Celtic" as a linguistic and cultural rather than a racial or genetic identity. The Celtic peoples were far too diverse to be defined by genetics, and too many racist groups are seeking legitimacy through affiliating with or founding "Celtic" organizations.

Seeing ethnicity and genetic heritage as the root of spirituality is usually linked with fictitious concepts of racial purity that cannot be realistically found or maintained in any pluralistic society. No culture arises in isolation, and human patterns of migration, trade and sexual interaction ensure that no group is "pure" in any meaningful sense of the word. Even if all my immediate ancestors came from Scotland (which they did not), the people of that place encountered soldiers from all over the Roman Empire, they were constantly interacting with Norse invaders and settlers, and they traded with people from all over Europe, North Africa, and the Mediterranean. These encounters would inevitably lead to children whose parents came from

---

[26] It's important to keep in mind that some of your more recent ancestors may not exactly appreciate being approached in a Pagan manner. I know people who have done Samhain rites where they contacted their ancestors and were told that they should give up the devil worship and go back to the family's religion. Just because they're dead doesn't mean they're instantly enlightened, or even tolerant. Ancestor reverence can be a tricky business sometimes.

different places and who cannot be seen as isolated from the rest of the world.

Taking up the study of ogam may be a way for some people to connect with an ancestral path, but it is in no way necessary to be of Celtic descent to work with the ogam. Its power is in language and meaning, not genetics. If you resonate with its meanings that is all that's necessary, regardless of your background and your family history. Its meanings reach into tribal paradigms of consciousness, but they are not exclusionary; they can open us up to new ways of seeing and understanding and put us in contact with the world around us by methods we may never have considered before.

Seeking Poetry, Madness, or Death

The pursuit of *Filidecht* and the life of the visionary are dangerous. If we are successful, our lives will change. If we are unsuccessful, our lives will change. It's the nature of the change that determines our success or failure. Traditionally, a person seeking the wisdom of the *Filid* after a long period of training would sit on a mountaintop, a burial mound, or in another sacred place, most likely fasting for several days. By the end of this time, it is said that they would be granted the power of poetry and vision, go mad from being unable to negotiate the power of the Otherworld, or die.

This rite of *aisling* was most likely the culmination of an initial period of training in ritual and visionary techniques as well as the social knowledge a *Fili* needed to have. It was most likely many years in duration -- traditionally the *Filid* were said to go through twenty years of training to reach the highest grades. In the end, only the deities and spirits could determine the depth of vision that any given *Fili* would experience. The process was expected to be dangerous, and it was known and accepted that some would not pass that critical test.

In a modern pursuit of the understanding of ogam and its integration into *Filidecht* it makes sense that those seeking the path might choose to recreate the *aisling* to suit our own needs and circumstances. Ogam-based chants and inscriptions can help ward us against spiritual harm during the process, and aid in our prayers for assistance from our deities, ancestors, and helping spirits.

The recovery of lost knowledge was one of the ways the *aisling* ritual was used, as illustrated in the tale of the recovery of the lost story of the *Táin Bó Cúailnge*. According to legend, the last copy of the tale was traded away for a valuable foreign book, and many years later the sage Senchan Torpeist called upon all the *Filid* of Ireland to search for remains of the lost lore. A *Fili* named Muirgen went out in search of the story, stopping one night to sleep on the grave of the warrior Fergus mac Roich, one of the tale's heroes. During this ritual, Fergus appeared to Muirgen through the mists and narrated the tale over three days and three nights, which the poet wrote down, preserving it for future generations. This mystical revelation of the story was regarded as a true and valid substitute for the lost ancient text, brought back to the people by methods respected and practiced at that time, told by the voice of one who was present at the events related.

We don't know that the ritual of *aisling* was used to seek the aid of spirit helpers in a shamanistic sense, but it is possible and it can certainly be used effectively for that purpose today. *Aislingthe* as a genre of journeywork can be put to many uses and ogam can help focus the *Filid* on their purpose and ritual. Ogam *feda* can be called or inscribed to evoke particular energies or to aid with connection to different deities and spirits as a part of the *aisling*, prior to or during the ritual work itself. Ogam can be used to set moods in preparation for visionary work as well, giving our minds mythic resonances to connect with as we seek change in our souls and the world around us.

The Three Cauldrons: Joy and Sorrow Shall Turn Them

In the Irish tradition, there is a text called *The Cauldron of Poesy* that refers to three cauldrons found within each individual. These cauldrons, *Coire Goiriath* -- the Cauldron of Warming, *Coire Érmai* -- the Cauldron of Motion, and *Coire Sofhis* -- the Cauldron of Wisdom, are equated with physical, emotional and spiritual development in each person. Whether these cauldrons are upside-down, sideways or upright, and whether or what they are brewing and seething within them help determine one's state of health and inspiration.

This is one of the central images of *Filidecht*, and the turning of the cauldrons to the upright position in search of *imbas* or inspiration is one of the great works of the *Fili*. Over the years, I've come to the conclusion that ogam can be a powerful aid to this task. Use of the ogam *feda* through magic and ritual can enhance the pursuit of the *Fili*'s spiritual path and help to interpret the results of the work. Observation and interpretation of the *feda* within each cauldron is a useful tool for self-understanding and healing, as well as a seed for transformation.

Work with these cauldrons is important in ritual for gathering and processing energy, and they are a part of the rituals of making found later in this book for those who wish to make their own set of ogam *feda*. Meditations on each *fid* within each of the cauldrons can lead to profound realizations about the meanings of the *feda* and how they relate to the body, the spiritual realm, and the world around us.

The cauldrons are also intimately involved with the work we do with our emotions. The *Cauldron of Poesy* poem says that joy and sorrow turn the cauldrons, and it is this turning that produces enlightenment and art. This strongly suggests that engaging with our emotions -- both the pleasant and the painful -- is important to our growth and maturation as human beings and as workers of oracle and magic. These emotions are not abstract. The poem mentions the joy of sexual fulfillment and the sorrow of illness, fixing the function of the cauldrons firmly in the physical realm of the body. Work with these emotional states through the passion of Ruis or the wound implied in nGétal can be very powerful for personal transformation or healing work in other individuals or the larger community. Within this context, the embrace and acceptance of a wide variety of emotions is what fertilizes growth and transformation.

It is important to note that emotions often regarded as "bad," like anger or grief, can be turned to positive creative forces through cauldron work. Embracing and working through emotions that may be seen as negative might be exactly what is needed to understand one's situation and grasp an opportunity with enough energy to turn a situation toward justice or to break through resistant patterns of behavior. It is not the emotion itself that is negative, but allowing it unnecessary and unwarranted control, or misusing it.

Understanding and working with ogam helps place the *Fili*'s work of turning the cauldrons into personal and societal context. Cauldron work helps bring the meanings of the ogam *feda* alive in the ogam student's life, embodying them and giving them voice in the physical realm.

CHAPTER 2
Weaving Word Withies: The Letters

Language and Meaning

The ogam is, first and foremost, an alphabet. It is a system of sound arranged to express the Gaelic language, following the movements of lips, teeth, and tongue through the hollow of the mouth. Language is music that plays the human body. This music is given flesh in poetry and image, flowing and vibrating through our bodies into space.

The alphabet itself served as a memory system, a mnemonic list of concepts, items, birds, trees, rivers, crafts, colors, and fortresses linked by the initial letters of each word. It was a way of ordering the cosmos by sound. In this book I use ogam and ogams to refer to the alphabet itself and to the linked lists of meanings associated with the *feda*. Traditionally, there were ogams associated with lists of birds, fortresses, rivers, tools, trades, and other concepts. *Fid* and *feda* are used to refer to an individual letter or letters within a particular ogam set. The ogams are the lists, the *feda* are the individual items on the lists.

Most of the lists associated with the ogam were unlikely to have been linked in any kind of magical or symbolic manner. In fact, the students of *Filidecht* were encouraged to create their own lists, as the fourteenth century text the *Auriacept na n-Eces* says of the herb ogam: "to take the name of whatever herb it be for the letter with which it will commence."[27] In other words, the student was urged to create a list of herbs alphabetically. If there were magical connections in these situations, they were internal and individual to each *Fili* who created their own ogam list. These lists served as fodder for poetry, but some of them may also have served a purpose in seeking oracles and omens in the surrounding world, signs from the spirits fraught with meaning,

---

[27] Calder, 1995, 299. The Herb ogam (*lusogam*) is not the only ogam where taking the first letter of a thing's name is stated as the proper way to create a new ogam list. River-pool ogam (*linnogam*), King ogam (*rigogam*), and Food ogam (*biadogam*) also begin with one or two words and the instructions to take the name of a thing beginning with the letter and continue thus.

not necessarily as objects in and of themselves, but through the letter with which they began.

Underlying each list, however, were the names of the *feda*. Each name has a set traditional meaning, just as each letter of the Norse runic alphabet has a meaning. In most popular readings of the ogam, the *feda* are each assigned to a tree. While it's true that some of the ogam letter names are the names of trees, most are not. In a few cases, the names have no easily derivable meaning at all, and in those cases, I have looked to the associated *briatharogam* or "word ogams" -- kenning phrases that were meant to illuminate some aspect of the *fid* and its meaning.

My work here is based on that of Damien McManus in his book, *A Guide to Ogam*, and the earlier explorations of Howard Meroney[28] as they sought the earliest linguistic roots of ogam names and their meanings. In cases where the meanings of the letter names were obscure or in question, I chose my own meanings and associations based on the kennings and on my own intuitions over my years of work with the system. I offer them as suggestions and departure points for your own work, knowing that these associations are meaningful for me and that they work within the complex of modern CR *Filidecht* that I've developed over the last two decades. The linguistic information for each letter refers to McManus unless otherwise noted.

The *briatharogam* or word ogams listed are originally found in the *Auraicept na n-Éces*, though McManus has a clear and comprehensive listing of them in his *A Guide to Ogam*. They are keyed below as MM for Morainn mac Moín, MO for Mac ind Óc, and CC for Con Culainn. The "additional word ogams" listed under each *fid* are all from the Howard Meroney journal article. Each of these individuals is a figure from the lore with a connection to wisdom or the Otherworld.

In every case, I urge you to examine the evidence of language and sound and to develop your own associations and meanings as you work with the ogam. As the earliest students of *Filidecht* were encouraged to create their own webs of meaning and connection, we can create and localize ours as well. Our own tree and herb and bird ogams should reflect the world in which we live. A desert ogam would not include sea birds in its vocabulary for obvious reasons. While the bird ogam of Ireland says that *faelinn*, the gull, is the bird of Fern, there are no gulls in

---

[28] Meroney, 1949 in *Speculum*, vol XXIV, Number 1, pp 19-43

the desert or the high plains. What bird would you associate with that letter if you lived in Arizona or Manitoba? What ecological niche does it fill? What does that bird bring to mind for you?

As an example of individual creation of meaning within an ogam context, I have presented my own example of a planet-ogam, based on my more than thirty years of experience with astrology. I use "planet" loosely, including several asteroids, centaurs, and "dwarf planets" recently added to the astrological lexicon to expand upon the traditional seven planets of the ancient world. In explaining my reasoning for each choice, I hope to offer a model for your own work on building webs of meaning surrounding each *fid*. I also urge you to remember not to use the ogam as some Procrustean bed upon which to base a one-size-fits-all magical system where things are stretched or clipped to fit into preconceived categories. It does damage to both the traditional understanding of the ogam, and to the other systems being forced into compliance with the structure of the ogam. It also fosters a false sense of the ogam as a mechanical table of correspondences that can be used interchangeably, one thing substituting seamlessly for another, but this is not the case, when it comes to the actual work with Ogam.

I also present the musical note ogam proposed by Séan O'Boyle in his work *Ogam: The Poet's Secret*.[29] This is another modern speculation, and if you are musically inclined you might wish to investigate ways to apply it to your ritual work. It could also be used fruitfully for tonal chanting when vibrating the names of the *feda* for magic.

Keeping in mind the importance of the three harp strains and their magical effects in the tales,[30] a musical or harp-tabulature ogam would make a good deal of sense. The question for modern musicians would be what kind of scale the original Irish harpers used, because early music was played in a different tuning than the modern Anglo-Germanic scale, which has a value of 440 cycles per second or 440 Hertz (Hz) for the A above middle C. Baroque music is still frequently played with the A as low as 415 Hz. The composer Handel was known to have used a tuning fork with A at 423 Hz in his premier performance of

---

[29] O'Boyle, 1980

[30] Gantz, 1988, 117-118. These three strains were *goltraighe*, the crying strain; *gentraighe*, the laughter strain; and *súantraighe*, the sleep strain. They were believed to have magical powers over human minds and hearts, able to heal or kill, and the strains themselves were described in the lore as the three sons of the Goddess Bóann.

Messiah, composed in 1741[31]; about a half-tone down from the modern concert A. The A tone and the intervals between each note have varied greatly over the centuries. Even in modern times the A above middle C has ranged between 420 Hz and 460 Hz. As recently as 1971 an international conference was held to standardize the pitch for A, without much success.[32] There is no way for us to know with any certainty the scale to which pre-Christian Irish harps were actually tuned.

Each *fid* of the ogam presents us with a set of images. As we examine the *feda* in their context of culture and meaning, we can begin to pick out patterns and enlarge our understanding of the world and its workings in our own contexts of divination, magic, and healing. The *feda* ask us questions and offer us challenges. When we receive a difficult *fid* in a reading, the question inherent in this oracle is how will we work with the lesson this *fid* teaches? Where do we find ourselves resonating with this *fid* in the web of our lives?

The First Aicme:
B L F S N

Beith - B
Birch
Keyword: Purification
Word Ogams:
MM: *féochos foltchaín* - faded trunk and fair hair, withered foot with fine hair
MO: *glaisem cnis* - most silvery of skin, greyest of skin
CC: *maise malach* - beauty of the eyebrow

Color: *bán* - white
Tree: *beith* - birch

---

[31] The reference is found here http://www.uh.edu/engines/epi1305.htm
[32] Information on the history of attempts to enforce tuning standards can be found at http://www.schillerinstitute.org/music/rev_tuning_hist.html

Bird: *besan* - pheasant(?)

Note:

Planet: Hygieia

In the beginning, the god Ogma mac Elathan carved the first ogams on a twig of birch. Ogma is described as the "father" of the ogam and his hand or his knife as its "mother"[33] in an act of gender-transcending creation, with the third element of the triad being the twig itself as the pre-existing element of the ogam's embodiment. He carved the single stroke of the letter B seven times on that twig as a warning and a protection for Lug mac Ethlenn's wife against the magic of the *sídhe* who wished to kidnap her. For this, the old story says, Beith is the first letter of the ogam alphabet. The concept of primacy attaches to Beith because of its history as the first of the ogam *feda*.

Beith is most likely derived from the IE root word *$g^w et$*, meaning a resin or gum. This could potentially link it with incense, used in many cultures for purification purposes. Beith is related to the Welsh *bed(wen)*, meaning birch tree(s) and is also related to the Latin *betula*. The word ogams confirm this meaning, describing the visual qualities of the tree itself. Most varieties of birch have bark ranging from white to a light grey -- describable as faded, withered, silvery, or grey -- and their leaves turn a beautiful light yellow-gold color in the autumn, leading to the "fair hair" description.

Welsh tradition links the birch with love; bowers for trysting lovers were frequently made under birch trees or within birch thickets. Birch twig wreaths were often given to lovers as tokens.[34]

Birch was traditionally used for cleansing and purifying the home and the body. Its twigs were used as the brush for brooms and its aromatic wintergreen-scented oil made chewing birch twigs for cleaning the teeth fairly pleasant. The extracted oil is a mild analgesic, used for relieving pain.

---

[33] Calder, 1995, 273. This passage also says that "sound and matter" are the father and mother of ogam. This suggests the deep importance of proper pronunciation and the use of sound in *Filidecht*.
[34] Mac Coitir, 2003, 24

Birch sap was often tapped from the trees in northern Europe to make birch beer and birch syrup, which has a cool wintergreen flavor.[35]

In the sauna rituals of Scandinavia, birch was used to stimulate the skin for its purifying properties, by wiping away sweat and striking the body to encourage blood flow in the skin. Birch twigs were also used as switches for discipline and correction. Self-flagellation has been used as a method of spiritual purification and trance induction in many traditions throughout history, and such stimulation can trigger the release of endorphins into the bloodstream, helping the seeker reach ecstatic states.

Birch wood was used in Ireland and Scotland to make cradles that were believed to have protective qualities against illness and bad luck for the child held within, and so it is also associated with protection and infancy, particularly the protection of children. Birch boughs were also put over cradles in Scotland to protect the children within.

On Imbolc or *Lá Féil Bríd* -- February 1st -- birch rods or crosses are laid in Brighid's beds beside the Brídeog or Brighid-doll in hopes that she will come and sleep in the beds, blessing the house. In some areas, the beds themselves are made of birch twigs.[36] This could easily be read as a purification of the ritual bed in preparation for the presence of the Goddess or of the saint. Birch branches are also peeled and presented to the Brídeog on that day.[37]

The color *bán*, white, carries connotations of purity and the sacred that resonate with these associations. The wind of the south is associated with this color, though instead of *bán*, a natural-white color associated with milk, the specific color-word associated with the south wind is *geal*, which can also be read as clear, bright, radiant, or glistening in Scots Gaelic or as translucent, fair or happy in Irish. It's also a word used to describe emotional fondness and it has Otherworldly connotations in that many deities are described as white, bright, or radiant.[38] In the tale of *The Settling of the Manor of Tara*, the south is described as a place associated with music, knowledge, poetry, fertility and waterfalls, among a long list of other

---

[35] Milliken & Bridgewater, 2004, 57
[36] Mac Coitir, 2003, p 22
[37] Darwin, 1996, 85
[38] Wright-Popescul, 1997, 45

attributes.[39] We will find the color white again with the *fid* Idad, where the color is called *irfind* or "very-white" and is intensified and brightened in its associations and meanings.

In my modern planet-ogam, the asteroid Hygieia was chosen for its association with the basics of health, hygiene, and the purification of the body. Its connection with Beith is through an emphasis on physical and ritual purity. This cleansing can be seen as a protection from disease and from negative spiritual or psychic energies.

Magically, Beith is a good *fid* to use for rituals involving purification or self-discipline. Invoking its energy clears the working space and cleanses the energy fields of the body. When using Beith in healing, it can be used for purification of the space and the body and for cleansing the energies around a wound or infection. It is also useful for easing pain and encouraging the discipline to stick with a healing practice or treatment regimen.

In divination, Beith's appearance may indicate a need to purify yourself or your intentions before beginning a new project or phase of your life and work. It can be a hint that clarity and discipline are required, and that caution and preparation are necessary as you make your plans. It could indicate a young child involved in the situation.

Beith's chthonic current is found in the hidden depths of the origin of things. It is not the force and energy of creation itself but the first thing created out of a situation or in response to a need within the physical world. When it appears, it establishes precedence and helps determine what is most important, or what must be done first in a situation. Sometimes it functions to warn you of hidden dangers or of a loss of self. In the physical realm, Beith may indicate the presence of a child in the situation.

The oceanic current of Beith is expressed through creativity, writing, and eloquence. These are the chaotic processes through which deep meaning is expressed and by which you indicate what is important to you. Finding and expressing your creativity through words may be necessary here. Beith distills meaning from underlying chaos, helping to bring about order. By working with words, origins can be expressed and mysteries explored.

Its celestial current suggests that purification is needed, and that discipline is necessary to achieve clarity or follow

---

[39] Rees & Rees, 1990, 123

through with your regular spiritual practices. It hints at the presence of the deities as creative forces, and as givers of spiritual protection from chthonic forces that may be dangerous to you on a spiritual level. It is the purification that takes place before one comes into the presence of deity, preparing you for an encounter with the sacred. You may [...] ppeal to them for [...] rder to the chaos [...] ? Where do I need [...] edence, warning,

MM: *lí súla* - delight of eye, luster of eye i.e. flame
MO: *carae cethrae* - friend of cattle
CC: *lúth cethrae* - attraction of cattle, sustenance of cattle

Color: *liath* - grey
Tree: *leamhán* - elm, *caorann* - rowan
Bird: *lachu* - duck

Note:
Planet: Vesta

Lus most likely derives from one of two different IE roots; *leuk-*, "to shine," from which the meaning "flame" is derived or *leudh-*, meaning "to grow", which leads to the potential meaning of "an herb." Welsh *louber*, light or splendor, is related to the Irish Lus. I tend to read flame as the primary meaning and herb as secondary, though for you it may be the other way around. Its word-ogams draw associations to both fire and lush herbs as sustenance for livestock.

Fire is one of the central sacred things in Celtic spirituality. Inspiration is expressed with the image of fire arising from water, or blazing light within the sacred well. Poetry and inspiration are described as a fire in the head, and enlightenment is its expression in the world.

The Goddess Brighid is often associated with sacred fire and is the patron of smithcraft, poetry, and healing, all of which are associated with the use and expression of flame. With these associations, fire is also a deeply magical thing, and all three of Brighid's domains are places of deep magic. The smith transforms ore into metal, and a prayer attributed to Saint Padraig asks to be protected from the magic of "druids, smiths, and women." Among the Siberian tribes, smiths are regarded with the same awe as shamans, and it is said that smiths and shamans are "from the same nest."[40] In Irish and Scottish mythology, poetry is seen as the root of magic, and words are transformative. Healing is accomplished through poetic magic and fire as well.

The work of the herbalist is part and parcel of the work of the healer, but herbs can also be strong aids in the search for enlightenment, bringing inspiration by aiding dream and visionary states. Herbs are often prepared through the agency of fire, boiled and brewed to create healing infusions or distilled for tinctures and other tools of the healer's art. Indeed, healing often aids in the search for enlightenment and inspiration, both of which are a search for wholeness in our bodies, our minds, and our lives.

With *caorann*, the rowan tree that is frequently associated with this letter, we additionally bring in associations of magical protection, particularly of animals, from malignant magic. Rowan twigs were bound into equal-armed crosses with red thread and twigs were tied to the horns or tails of cattle to protect them from illness and harm.[41] This links nicely with the word-ogam that tells us Lus is a friend of cattle.

Elm, *leamhán*, is the other tree associated with Lus. From a strictly alphabetical standpoint, it would make more sense to assign this tree to the *fid* in keeping with the traditional pattern. In Scotland a twig of elm was placed in the churn to make sure the butter would not be stolen by the *sídhe*, giving the elm an

---

[40] Eliade, 1974, 470
[41] Evans, 1957, 273

association with magical protection and connecting it with cattle through two of the word ogams. Elm branches were also sometimes used as divining rods in dowsing for water.[42]

Liath, grey, is the color associated with this *fid*. It is found in the northwest on the compass rose of the winds in Irish and Scottish tradition. *Liath*'s meanings in Scotts Gaelic include grey-haired, moldy, lilac-colored, or pale, while the Irish *liat* adds meanings of hoary, bright, and white as well as moldy and grey. Grey is one of the otherworldly colors also associated with the color-word *glas*, which ranges in meaning from grey through green into blue. The collection of texts called the *Hibernica Minora* associates the northwest wind with dearth and the fall of blossoms[43] -- one would need the fiery energies of Lus to counter this influence. Stretching the meaning, we know today that molds like penicillin can be used to heal and are strong antibiotics, affording us a modern link between Lus and the healing arts of Brighid and Airmid.

Vesta is an asteroid associated with dedication to fire and the spirit, and a separation from the mundane world through spiritual service. Vesta seeks inspiration through meditation on the flame and guarding it from desecration, as the Vestal virgins of Rome guarded the flame in the temple of Vesta. Brighid also had an eternal flame guarded by nineteen of her priestesses, and later by the nuns of Kildare, tending the flame in twenty-day cycles. On the twentieth day, Brighid herself was said to tend the flame. This flame was extinguished in 1220 when the Archbishop of London ordered it put out because it was linked with superstition, and then again during the reign of king Henry VIII (1509-1541) as a part of the persecution of Catholics by Protestants, when abbeys and monasteries were closed and clergy murdered to further political aims.

The practice of flame tending is kept today by people around the world both within and outside of CR. After several hundred years of darkness, her sacred flame was re-lit in Kildare by Catholic lay sisters on Imbolc, 1992. On the same day, Casey June Wolf of Daughters of the Flame in Vancouver, British Columbia, Canada also re-lit her flame and founded a nonsectarian group for Brighid's devotees all over the world. Traditionally kept in an enclosure away from prying eyes, today Brighid's eternal flame is kept in the town square in Kildare and

---

[42] Mac Coitir, 2003, 130, 133
[43] Wright-Popescul, 1997, 59-60

given to anyone who comes in pilgrimage to bless all those in need of her touch.

When Lus appears in divination, it may be an indication that inspiration will strike, or an instruction to seek inspiration or enlightenment in the issue surrounding the question. Being open to inspiration from the world around you may be particularly important right now, so look to your environment for signs and omens that can guide you in the way you should go. It may suggest a need for healing through herbal means or by prayer to Brighid, or to Airmid, the Irish Goddess of herbalism.

The chthonic current of Lus is associated with food and sustenance, with animals, and the healing of animals. These are the physical aspects of the *fid*, embodied in the world and reaching into the primal energy that sustains life in the body. Here we also find herbs and plants of all types, and physical fire that warms the body and enables the preparation of herbs that act on other levels within us.

Lus's oceanic current deals with the energies and acts of healing with herbs, and with the brewing and distillation of herbal remedies. It is where magical protection from within the Otherworlds can be tapped and directed for both people and animals, though it is particularly associated with the protection of the animal world. Herbal charms for protection, particularly from malevolent magic, can also be a part of this current.

With the celestial current, Lus may indicate Otherworldly animals that bring aid and assistance to us in our spiritual work. It is a *fid* of inspiration and enlightenment, manifesting a spark of Brighid's flame within us as we seek *imbas* and walk our spiritual paths. With its link to Brighid's flame, Lus can also call upon an urge to devotion and may suggest taking up a regular spiritual discipline in the pursuit of inspiration.

Magical and spiritual teachers are also a part of the celestial current, both in person and those found through books and correspondence. Whether it suggests finding a teacher or being one, the spark of a mentor's guidance is here.

Magically, Lus can be used in rituals for seeking inspiration, or for protection from negative magic and energies. You might meditate upon Lus for help in understanding oracles and omens and sorting out images found in dreams or through vision-seeking rituals. Wearing something engraved with Lus can be helpful in warding off negative magic.

In healing, Lus may be useful in reducing fever or in warming someone with chills due to its association with fire, as well as for adding strength to herbal healing work. I also use it when doing healing work for animals.

Question: What inspires me? How do I use that inspiration?

Linked Concepts:
Sustenance, food, herbal healing, magical protection, animals and their protection, magical or spiritual teachers and teachings.

Fern - F
Alder
Keyword: Protection
Word Ogams:
MM: *airech fian* - shield of warrior bands, vanguard of warrior or hunting bands
MO: *comét lachta* - guarding of milk, milk container i.e. a bowl
CC: *dín cridi* - shelter of the heart, protection of the heart

Color: *flann* - blood red
Tree: *fern* - alder
Bird: *faelinn* - gull

Note:
Planet: Pallas

The word *fern* is related to the Welsh *gwern(en)* or alder-tree(s) and the letter value for it is V as well as F. This *fid* is the alder tree, and its wood was often used for shields. This is why its keyword is protection. Its association with shields makes this a *fid* linked with warriors and the military, and by extension with people who use force to protect, like police and fire fighters, or those who act as shields for others -- for instance workers at women's health clinics, political protestors placing themselves in harm's way, or eco-activists chaining themselves to trees or interposing themselves between whales and whaling ships.
   The wood of alder was also often used for making buckets and bowls, reflecting the word ogam that is translated as guarding of or a container for milk. In a herding society, milk is a

large part of the diet and dairy products were important as a main staple. The warriors in Celtic society were often cattle-lords who owned and protected the herds that were the source of this food, and cattle raids were a common activity. Many of the tales in the Irish lore revolve around raids made on other tribes, including the *Táin Bó Cúailnge* or Cattle Raid of Cooley, one of the most famous Irish tales of all.

With *flann* or blood red for a color, the *fid* has associations with hunters and hunting, and an alternate translation for the word ogam "shield of warrior bands" is "vanguard of hunting bands." Old Irish *fland* is the red of freshly shed blood, and so deals with the shedding of blood and the death of animals to sustain human life and society.[44] *Flann* here suggests that Fern may share some properties with Ruis, another type of "red" in the color ogam. In all these cases, Fern suggests the need for being prepared to defend oneself or others, and the making of preparations for difficulties lest blood be shed.

Fern is also a *fid* that implies emotional shelter and protection. The warrior protects what is loved, and the container protects what is held within it. The word ogam "protection of the heart" powerfully links this *fid* with emotional strength and guarding yourself or others from potential emotional harm. When found in divinatory readings with difficult *feda* like h-Úath or Ceirt, it may suggest a need to be cautious emotionally, or to guard against emotional abuses and manipulation.

Fern as the asteroid Pallas represents Pallas Athene, the great patron and protector of the city of Athens. She is the spear and shield with which we guard ourselves and what is dear to us. Willing to shed blood in defense of what is hers, she is also a Goddess of wisdom and engages in this violence only when it is wise and necessary.

In readings where it is surrounded by positive *feda*, it can suggest that you are protected emotionally, or that you are insulated against harm. Perhaps your emotions are hidden and therefore not as vulnerable to manipulation as they might otherwise be. It implies shelter and a sheltered space where you are emotionally safe.

Fern's chthonic current can manifest representing warriors or the military. It also points to issues surrounding physical shelter and protection. Police, firefighters and others who physically protect people and places may also be indicated here.

---

[44] DIL, 309

Whether those interactions are positive or negative will depend greatly on the other *feda* nearby.

Its oceanic current is more emotional, inferring emotional protections or vulnerabilities, suggesting a need for autonomy or the ability to maintain an emotional autonomy. This current is where Fern is connected with hunters and hunting, for in a proper ritual relationship, hunter and hunted are one and joined at the heart. In many traditional societies, the death of the hunted animal is considered a willing sacrifice by the animal manifested through hunting rituals for the benefit of the tribe. The relationship in its ideal form is one of love, need, gratitude, and mutual respect.

In the celestial realm, Fern deals with the containment or even the sublimation of energies and emotions. It suggests a thorough examination of emotions and working with them in the crucible of the internal cauldrons on the path to *imbas*. Fern enjoins us to look ahead and be prepared for defense when necessary, and also is a protection from illness, particularly those that are emotionally based or exacerbated by emotional stresses and intensity.

This *fid* can be used magically for protection and creating emotional walls, particularly for situations where there are bad feelings and a danger of being emotionally abused or damaged. It can help reinforce personal and emotional autonomy in times when you're feeling overwhelmed or dominated by others. It can also be used for protection of people in dangerous places, like troops in a battle zone, fire fighters going in to burning buildings, or activists facing government sanctioned violence. It is also useful for hunting magic.

Fern in healing can be used for protection from disease and to ward off illness. Because of its emotional resonances, the *fid* can be used to aid in stabilizing emotional imbalances and clearing emotional pain. It can also be useful in situations having to deal with physical heart problems.

Question: How do I shelter myself? What do I contain?

Linked Concepts:
Physical and emotional protection, walls, containment, warriors or the military, hunters and the hunt, preparation and being prepared.

Sail - S
Willow
Keyword: Flow
Word Ogams:
MM: *lí ambí* - hue of the lifeless, pallor of a lifeless one, delight of the dead
MO: *lúth bech* - activity of bees, sustenance of bees
CC: *tosach mela* - beginning of honey

Color: *sodath* - "fine-colored" (pale yellow or bone)
Tree: *sail* - willow
Bird: *seg* - hawk

Note:
Planet: Moon

Sail is the willow tree. This tree often grows at the edge of streams. In places where it doesn't grow on riverbanks, its presence frequently indicates the existence of an underground water source, and so its keyword is flow and it has associations with all those things that water is linked to. The tide is a function of water, so time is another implication of this *fid*.

The word Sail derives from **sal-*, the same root as the Old Irish word for "dirty," *salach*, therefore there are some mild connotations of impurity with this *fid* for me. This may be in reference to the color of its leaves or bark, as Meroney suggests might be the case for the word ogam "hue of the lifeless". Sail is also related to *salyx*, the Latin for willow, as well as being cognate with the Welsh *helyg(en)*, also meaning "willow(s)". Where Beith is a *fid* of purification, Sail indicates what needs to be purified or what is being resisted or denied.

In some areas of Ireland and Scotland, willow is considered a tree of bad luck, while in others it is regarded as good. It was very commonly used in basket weaving because of the flexibility of its thin branches. The Scottish poet William Ross called the willow "vile" and wrote of being stranded on an island once because the boatmen refused to use willow to repair a broken oar pin.[45]

Its word ogams indicate a connection with death and the ancestors, and the link with time and timing can also be conceived as a connotation of the past. Coffins were often woven of willow wicker in the Highlands of Scotland where timber was scarce.[46] I have come to see this *fid* as an indication that the ancestors are sending messages in some way. It might be through the voice of falling water or through song and music. Willow wood was used as the sound box for harps, and this links the *fid* with music and poetry as well, for poetry was originally accompanied on the harp in early Irish culture.[47] The famous Brian Boru harp of Ireland is entirely constructed of willow.

Because the willow's blooms attract bees it is called "activity of bees" and "beginning of honey." Mead is made from honey and both are linked with inspiration, which connects it to music and poetry as well. Music, sweetness, and pleasure can be indicated by this *fid*.

The Moon's rulership of time and tide make this the obvious planet of choice for Sail and its deep connection to water. The moon's dance with the sun determines the tides of the sea and the measure of time in months, and its waxing and waning are intensely symbolic of all cyclical movement.

The color *sodath*, translated as "fine-colored", does not have a wind associated with it. The word itself consists of *so-*, a prefix that implies goodness and is linked with good luck,[48] and *dath* meaning color. In using the *dathogam* or color ogam, this would be a *fid* of good luck and good fortune. In Ireland, willow rods were carried for good luck on a journey. Like alder, willow was also associated with bringing the butter into the churn and warding away bad luck and the loss of the butter.[49]

In divination, Sail can suggest a need to connect with or listen to the ancestors or to honor them in some way. It might mean that the dead are speaking, but it can also be living ancestors such as grandparents. The *fid* may also tell you to pay attention to timing in your endeavors. Ask yourself if you are moving with the tides or trying to struggle against them. The idea

---

[45] Milliken & Bridgewater, 2004, 149
[46] Milliken & Bridgewater, 2004, 187
[47] Breathnach, 1986, 65
[48] DIL, 553, meaning 2(a) of *so-* is also found as a particle of the name *coire sofhis*, the cauldron of "good wisdom".
[49] Mac Coitir, 2003, 40

of struggling against the proper timing has, in some readings I've done, led to the concept of denial -- insisting you are ready when you're not, or vice versa.

When reading the chthonic current of Sail, the emphasis is on its associations with the ancestors and death from the word ogams. Being associated with the ancestors, I also see the *fid* as being linked with the past in a more general sense. Where this aspect appears, you may need to listen more closely to the voice of those who came before. Being from the same root as *salach*, the Irish word for "dirty", I sometimes find it associated with impurities, whether ritual or personal, which will need to be cleansed before a task can be completed or a ritual begun. Another aspect of the implied potential impurity is a sense of denial, particularly a denial that something is wrong in a situation. Careful and honest assessment of your situation is needed.

The oceanic current is affiliated with water and all things that flow. The tides are a part of this current, whether they are lunar, oceanic, or seasonal. If this *fid* appears in concert with difficult *feda* in a reading, it may indicate the blockage of a flow in your life, or an impending delay. Music is found here, as the body of the harp was made of willow wood. Honey and mead are linked to the willow through its word ogams "activity of bees" and "beginning of honey", and through Sail's connection with mead it inspires music. Music inspires dance, and willow was thought to inspire one to dancing, perhaps even uncontrollably, by some in Ireland.[50]

Proper timing is a celestial aspect of Sail. I associate it with the art of reading astrological influences when working out the right time for action. Work with this *fid* can help bring your timing into harmony with the flow of astrological tides just as the oceanic current is related to the tides of the sea. Considering the willow's folkloric link with good luck in some places, this *fid* suggests that the observation of proper timing will bring lucky results. This level of Sail is the one I associate with poetry that is expressed through music, and with song.

Sail can be used for magic having to do with flow or anything to do with water. It is good for working with timing and tides so that you know the proper moment for action. Both the

---

[50] W. G. Wood-Martin's *Traces of the Elder Faiths of Ireland* is cited in Mac Coitir regarding the custom of placing a rod of willow over the door to make those who enter dance the night away.

aspects of water and tide suggest that Sail would be good for magic linked with the moon and its phases.

For healing, this *fid* can be used in work for cleansing or encouraging blood flow, and for anything having to do with menstruation. Willow's inner bark is a source of salicylic acid, which we know best as aspirin, and so it can also be used to help relieve pain.

Question: Where am I resisting the flow of my life? Am I listening to the world around me?

Linked Concepts:
Ancestors and messages from the ancestors, death, the realm of the dead, time, tides, knowledge of time and proper timing, denial, impurity, music, honey and mead.

Nin - N
Letters - Support
Keyword: Connection
Word Ogams:
MM: *costud side* - checking of peace, establishing of peace, weaving of silk
MO: *bág ban* - fight of women (the weaver's beam), boast of women, contest of women
CC: *bág maise* - contest of beauty, boast of beauty

Color: *necht* - clear
Tree: *fuinseóg, uinnsiu* - ash, *nentóg* - nettle
Bird: *naescu* - snipe

Note:
Planet: Juno

The *fid* Nin, with its keyword of connection, means both letters and a fork. McManus says the etymology of the word is unclear, but that it definitely refers to both letters generally and "a letter" specifically. The secondary meaning of Nin[51] refers to part of a weaver's loom; Meroney suggests it may mean a forked branch and McManus agrees that "fork" is another meaning for the word.

Nin then is the forked branch that supports the weaver's beam, and the letters that draw up our contracts. Weaving is the work of Nin, in both the physical sense of making fiber and in the social sense of weaving together individuals and energies into a greater tapestry of cooperation and peace. In Gaelic terms it expresses a concept akin to the Lakota phrase *mitakuye oyasin* or "All my relations." Nin is a *fid* of relationships both familial and conceptual.

Weaving is, in so many cultures, primarily the work of women and therefore Nin can be seen a *fid* of women's power and of networking and female friends. It is a *fid* of writing for the purpose of clarity and contract, where Beith is more likely to be about writing for the sake of symbolism and art. This weaving and communication implies choices and safety nets where people are found who can be supportive in difficult times and who can act as shelter when things go wrong. There are also aspects of law and legalities involved in this *fid* because of its suggestion of contracts and agreements.

Relationships with others bring obligation as well as support. Where you are supported, you are also in a place to provide support to others who need your assistance. Nin is the *fid* of the friend who lends a hand when needed, and weaves connections, creating community. It is the *fid* of family and blood relations as well as the contract of marriage, and these things carry strong resonances of support and caring within community.

The color *necht* is sometimes rendered as clear or transparent. It also means clean, pure or white, like several of the other color words in the *dathogam*. Rooted the Old Irish *nig-* it refers to that which is cleansed or purified, and Necht was one of the titles of the deity Núadha; in this case it most likely referred to his purity.[52] For me, it carries a resonance of clarity and clear sight, or of transparency.

The tree usually associated with this *fid* is the ash, though the Irish names are *uinnius* in Old Irish and *fuinseóg* more recently. Both spears and looms were made of ash, so there is some connection here. As with many other trees, the ash in

---

[51] DIL, 478 suggests this *nin* may be identical with the first.
[52] DIL, 475

Scotland is associated with the protection of milk and churns. In the Scottish Highlands, the green end of an ash branch was put into a fire and the sap that came from it was given to newborns as their first food, to give them the strength of the ash tree.[53] Three Irish ash trees were among the sacred *bile* or holy trees of the island: *Bile Uisnigh, Bile Tortan* and *Craobh Daithi*. These were regarded as world-trees, and the support of the province.[54]

Nettle, while not a tree, has a connection with Nin as well and is called a "tree" for this letter in the *Auriacept na n-Éces*, though it would no doubt fit better as part of an herb ogam. The fiber of nettle was used for weaving in Ireland and Scotland, though not widely; it was more often used to provide a dye for other fibers. Nettle cloth was regarded as being stronger and wearing better than linen, despite providing less fiber than flax.[55]

Nin's magic is that of weaving and community creation. It can be used to help bring people together for common cause, and is good for working on peace projects and other tasks that bring disparate people and communities together. Its link with letters and contracts means that it can be used in workings for clarity and understanding in written communications and to help keep legal proceedings in a clear and cooperative space.

The asteroid Juno represents women, the power of women, and the relationships between them, whether in harmony or jealousy. Juno holds temporal power as a queen and knowing her own needs and desires, she is able to express them and bring her will into manifestation. She can be seen as iconic of women in relationships and family. As the wife of Jupiter, she strives to express her own desires and power in that relationship.

Nin's chthonic current deals with weaving in many of its manifestations. It is the creative power of women making cloth as well as the weaving of obligations. Written contracts and the use of writing and letters in the service of community are found here. Assistance may be needed or given, and Nin may indicate a safety net within the situation. The word ogams suggest pride and boasting as aspects of this *fid*, both of which were seen as virtues among the early Gaelic tribes.

The oceanic Nin brings networking, negotiations, and acts of diplomacy between competing or warring parties. It builds

---

[53] Mac Coitir, 2003, 122
[54] Rees & Rees, 1990, 120
[55] *Flora Celtica* references Thomas Campbell's *Letters From the South*, published in 1837, as saying that his mother told him she thought nettle cloth was "more durable than any species of linen."

bridges and expresses choice and communication of many sorts. It can be an expression of will, and the connecting threads that join people together through emotional bonds. The flow of words between people is prominent with this current.

With the celestial current, this *fid* is one of clarity and communication. It suggests harmony and peace in relationships, and speaks of friendship, cooperation, and common cause among diverse people. In both the Norse and Greek cultures, weaving and spinning are associated with fate, and so this current may also indicate the warp and weft of what is fated to be. Nin brings connections through communication, and urges you to look for deeper meaning. Nin's link with writing and contracts by necessity brings a connection with the law and the establishment of social order through legal means.

The weaving connotations of Nin mean that it can be used for healing, broken bones, and knitting torn tissue, encouraging the healing of wounds that have been stitched together. Because it is also a *fid* of clarity, it is useful for work with the eyes and vision, and for clarity between the healer and the client. Its meaning of letters suggests its use for communication and making agreements with healing spirits and cooperation between the worlds of spiritual healing and mainstream medicine so that both interact peacefully and well.

Question: What are my obligations? How am I related to others?

Linked Concepts:
Peace, support, choices, letters and writing, contracts and agreements, weaving, harmony, women's power, networking, safety nets, a circle of friends.

The Second Aicme:
H D T C Q

h-Úath - H
Terror
Keyword: Despair
Word Ogams:
MM: *condál cúan* - pack of wolves, assembly of packs of hounds
MO: *bánad gnúise* - blanching of faces
CC: *ansam aidche* - most difficult at night

Color: *h-úath* - "terrible" (color of bruises)
Tree: *sceach gheal* - whitethorn/hawthorn, *crann fír* - test tree,
"truth tree"
Bird: *hadaig* - night raven

Note:
Planet: Pluto

H-Úath, with the keyword of despair, is perhaps the most challenging *fid* of the ogam. Its appearance heralds difficulties, the potential for harm, and emotional distress. It is associated with night terrors, fear, and physical violence. This *fid* suggests fights and frightful situations as well as being in danger.

One of h-Úath's associated trees is the hawthorn, whose thorns were used in several different ways by the *Filid*. It was primarily used for cursing and focusing malevolent magic. It is particularly associated with the *glám dícenn*, where seven *Filid* stood on a hilltop beneath a thorn tree at the juncture of seven territories reciting poems appropriate to their grade; in one hand they held a stone and in the other the thorn from a hawthorn tree.[56] Perhaps part of the reason for its connection with cursing,

---

[56] Breatnach, 1987, 140. The *glám dícenn* ritual probably had several forms. Breatnach's translation of the material says, "Probably the best known description of the process involved in a *glám dícenn* is that in MV III 155 (IT iii

death, and malevolence is that the blossoms of some hawthorn varieties smell very similar to rotting flesh.

Hawthorn is known as *sceach gheal*, literally "white/bright thorn" in Irish. Hawthorns frequently grow on *sidhe* mounds and holy wells, and in Ireland and Scotland they are rarely cut down or even pruned because of the ill luck that follows those who damage the trees. Traditionally, the blossoms were never brought into the house except on Bealtinne.

Hawthorn has its protective aspects as well, though. Hedgerows are usually composed of hawthorn bushes. Hawthorn trees are planted near the doors of houses to ward off evil. When blooms are brought into the house for Bealtinne, good luck and protection are assured for the year.

Crann fír, translated as test tree but literally the "tree of truth," is far more obscure. We have no way of knowing what species it might have been, just as the *bile*, the tree of life or world-tree of a territory could be a specimen of any of several different species. We can speculate that it may have been a purely mythological tree, never existing in the physical world at all. As such, its name suggests that it might have had a function like the cup Manannán offered to Cormac mac Airt, testing the truth of a statement. Fear often has a way of forcing us to face the truth, and this may be its link to h-Úath's meaning.

Misfortune is often found with h-Úath. As much as we may wish to avoid bad luck, it is part of life and difficulties often present us with challenges that, when faced and overcome, can make us stronger and more resilient. Part of the challenge of this *fid* is to remain strong and not give in to our fears. We must examine how fear sometimes works to protect us and decide whether this fear is functional or no longer serves a useful purpose and must be overcome.

Remember also that some fears are illusory. Watch the *feda* falling near this one for hints to the direction and reality of the fears you face. Sometimes the worst fears are the ones that never come to fruition, but only hold us back from our potential because they keep us from acting. All too often it isn't reality that is the terror, but possibility.

96-7). Amongst other things, it says that the seven grades of poets should go to the top of a hill before sunrise and, with their backs to a whitethorn, the wind from the North, and a thorn from the whitethorn in each one's hand, they should chant the satire. There is another version of this in CIH 1564.27-1565.19 ...which...has...'or a clayen image of the man to whom it (viz. the satire) is made, and a thorn from the whitethorn in each man's hand, and they piercing the image with their whitethorn thorns'."

None of us can escape from adversity. In CR spirituality, we are enjoined to have courage and to face those things that frighten us. The Celtic deities favor those who stand fast in the face of difficulty and strive to overcome their shortcomings and their fears. When pain and problems are unavoidable, our mettle is tested and we are transformed in that crucible. The act of resistance is a powerful one, socially as well as personally, and resistance is at the heart of political activism and social change.

The color of h-Úath is "terrible." Though it has no formal definition within the Irish language as a color-word, I associate it with the color of bruises because of the violence that may come when this *fid* appears. Like many of the colors associated with the ogam, it does not have a wind associated with it, though we could speculate that a whirlwind might be appropriate here, carving a destructive path across the landscape of our lives.

Pluto is a planet of subversion and transformation, bringing submerged pain and power to the surface, sometimes with volcanic force. Properly directed, Pluto can express great strength, but it is also capable of inflicting immense damage, and its energies must be used with care, just as with the energies of h-Úath. Always remember that accidents are possible and exercise due caution when working with these energies. Thinking of h-Úath's power in terms of nuclear destruction is probably the best cautionary approach to dealing with it.

In divination during ritual, h-Úath may appear as a strong negative if it's received after an offering or a sacrifice. Something critical may be missing, the offering may be insufficient, or it may be advisable to either start over or abandon the ritual altogether and examine what has gone wrong. When this comes up as a part of divination for ritual, drawing a second *fid* to help discern what has happened and how or whether to proceed is usually a very good idea.

The *fid* is often an indication that you are moving in the wrong direction, and is a thorny barrier against further movement, advising a necessary and possibly abrupt turn down a different path. It may herald the arrival of unwelcome or malevolent energies, influences, or entities into ritual space and, depending on any clarifying *feda*, may require a thorough purification of self, tools, and space before anything further can be done.

H-Úath's chthonic current is often destructive and disruptive, bringing warning of misfortune, difficulty and strife. It may refer to war and battles -- physical or metaphorical -- or to accidents or enemies. With this current, you may experience a feeling of being trapped in your situation, surrounded by thorny barriers. It can also indicate a strand of hidden or subversive power in your situation and warn you to examine everything carefully. Plans that you've made or projects you've been working on may shatter in your hands.

Its oceanic current is more emotional, bespeaking fear, despair, and anxiety in the midst of chaos. It can indicate nightmares of many kinds, leading to exhaustion from a lack of healthy sleep. You may be moving in the wrong direction, misled by circumstance, false evidence, or your own shortsightedness. Situations or people surrounding the issue at hand may bring shocks, or a severe feeling of something missing in your life or your surroundings. At its best, with highly favorable *feda* around it to mitigate its problematic powers, this current might suggest the transformation of pain through facing adversity. It may speak of the ordeal path as a potent but dangerous and difficult way of transformation.

With the celestial current, h-Úath has slightly less painful and disruptive connotations. While it can indicate loneliness or a feeling of abandonment, it can also point to breaking through a chaotic, dangerous situation or to the development of strength through facing down fears and adversaries. Resistance and activism may be necessary to move forward in your current situation. It may advise calling upon violent or dangerous powers for protection or self-defense, though this is always best undertaken with great caution, adequate preparation, and with one's strongest shields in place. When it comes up in relation to health, it may indicate a need for surgery, with the sharpness of the wolf's tooth and the hawthorn's prick bringing forth images of the surgeon's scalpel.

H-Úath can be used magically to turn negative forces against themselves, but should be used with extreme caution if at all. Cursing, while not advisable under most circumstances, is also a part of h-Úath's magic and might be legitimately used for self-defense. It may be useful to call upon the energy of wolves and the sharp spikes of the hawthorn for protection and to drive away any malevolence that may be facing us, though great care must be taken so that the harm inherent in h-Úath doesn't turn around and bite.

Like the Norse rune Thurisaz, which means "thorn", h-Úath can sometimes successfully be used to break through negative situations or to construct a powerful barrier against intrusions. Looking at this *fid* as a natural hedgerow is a very helpful image in this kind of work. Seeing oneself as Bre'r Rabbit, "born and raised in a briar patch," can also be helpful. H-Úath should be used with great caution and only after you have a good deal of experience in working with ogam for magic. I would honestly recommend that only people who are tightly connected with the energies of this *fid* use it, because it can harm even those who resonate well with it, but when used properly it can be extremely powerful.

In healing, h-Úath can be used in conjunction with techniques such as acupuncture and acupressure, or for piercing emotional wounds that have become blocked and festering. It can defeat fear and help defend against nightmares if invoked as a boundary. The sharpness of h-Úath may also be useful in breaking through the terrible barriers of anxiety and panic disorders. Used with precision and care, it can also help with stunting and removing cancers. When surgery is necessary, this *fid* may prove useful for guiding the hand of the surgeon, and making sure that everything that must be removed is taken from the body successfully.

Question: Where do my fears hold me back? How do my fears protect me?

Linked Concepts:
Fear, misfortune, loneliness, nightmares, difficulty, anxiety, destruction, accidents, enemies, war, strife, battles, shock, feeling or being trapped.

Dair - D
Oak
Keyword: Strength
Word Ogams:
MM: *ardam dosae* - highest of bushes, most exalted tree
MO: *grés soír* - carpenter's work, handicraft of an artificer
CC: *slechtam soíre* - most carved of craftsmanship

Color: *dubh* - black, dark
Tree: *dair* - oak
Bird: *droen* - wren

Note:
Planet: Jupiter

Dair is the oak tree. It has been a revered tree throughout much of Europe, and though it was not as central to the Druidism of Ireland, it still has strong associations with sacred sites, including Brighid's well and her eternal flame at Kildare (derived from *cill daire*, literally "cell/church of the oak"). Its wood is heavy and strong, and this *fid's* keyword is strength for that reason. Oak resists lightning strikes, even though it is frequently struck by this fire from the heavens.

This *fid* has deep associations with deity and sacred places. Oak is a tree of firmness and endurance, as the Gods are firm and enduring. Because it is a tree of deity, the *fid* also has connections with truth and skill, both of which are qualities of deity. Truth is one of the defining traits of the worthy king, and this aspect of rulership is part and parcel of Dair's meaning.

Truth leads to fair and righteous judgment and so this is also a *fid* of justice and the rule of law, administered by the strength of a truthful and honest leader. When the sanctity of true judgment is violated, destruction comes just as lightning strikes. In the Irish lore, kings were struck down by supernatural power for making false judgments. The earth herself would reject a king's falsehood.

Oak is valued for many purposes and used for anything requiring strength, where weight is not an issue. Doors have often been made of oak to keep out intruders. The tree itself is long-lived and working with its wood takes effort, but what is made from it is frequently exquisite in craftsmanship and long-lasting, for less talented woodworkers use softer woods to practice their arts, graduating to harder and more valuable woods as their skill grows.

For me, as for many others, Dair also has links to gateways and thresholds -- the liminal places where you are neither inside nor out, not in one place or another, but somewhere in between. It is in those edge-places where profound meetings with deity can occur. It's a place where wisdom, insight, and the understanding to provide a true judgment can be found.

Jupiter is linked in many European cultures with the oak and its strength and power. It's expansive and generous, deeply philosophical, and concerned with secular as well as spiritual power and the rule of law. Jupiter and the oak are both symbolic of stability and endurance. This planet's connections with philosophy and a love of learning also connect it with Dair's place as a conduit for the lightning strike of insight.

Dubh, black or dark, is the color associated with this *fid*. It is the property of the north wind, a wind bringing battle in the Irish tradition. The word carries associations of severity, disaster, rigorousness, moroseness, and malevolence. It brings cold, snow, and storm, and traditionally presaged plague, illness, and drought. The north wind was the ruler of all the winds, more powerful than the rest, pitying no one in its strength. Pride, strife, and assault are also a part of the lore linked with the north.[57] *Dubh*'s meaning fits most closely with the destructive spectrum of storm and lightning associations in Dair, requiring strength and endurance to negotiate its troubles. It is the misuse of strength in conflict, leading to war.

Dair's chthonic current in divination evokes stability, firmness, and endurance. When it appears, look to what is foundational in your life. It presages strength and longevity in people, institutions, and ideas, but may warn of inflexibility and stubbornness. Dair helps in building strong foundations from which to work, just as the wood of the oak is strong and abiding. In situations where a decision is called for, it is important to remain firm in your convictions. What is founded under its influence will be lasting, for good or ill.

The oceanic current speaks of great effort, pushing through with all your strength and your will. The liminal places within the mist are indicated; gateways and thresholds of all types may be in evidence in your life. Dair can also represent a sacred place or a grove, the nemeton where deity and humanity meet between the realms. Lightning and storms are found here as well, with their disruptive and powerful energies. When properly harnessed, this current can generate great power, though strength and perseverance is required to control it.

In its celestial current, Dair relates to truth and skill. It may indicate honesty in a situation, or the need for it. People and situations indicated by this current of Dair are usually trustworthy, and the circumstances around them will be reliable. This *fid* can refer to a skillful person, or to someone thoughtful and philosophical. It urges practice to perfect skill, as well as a love of learning. Dair's celestial manifestation can find expression in philosophy and theology, and can point to work

---

[57] Wright-Popescul, 1997, 65-68

with magic and prayer invoking the power of deity. One of its highest purposes is justice, true judgment, and the wisdom of appropriate jurisprudence. Attorneys, barristers, and success in legal matters may be indicated here.

Oak magic works with directing power and through storms and lightning. Dair can be used in calling upon many deities, including Brighid and the storm-God Lug. Its use asks justice and the power of the Gods into your work, so be certain that the magic you pursue is just and your motivations are true, for what you create with Dair will be enduring and difficult to change after the fact.

Dair in healing work lends strength and endurance to muscle, bone, and the internal systems. It is also good for work that helps with conditions of weakness, like osteoporosis, chronic fatigue, fibromyalgia, or other debilitating diseases. It can aid as well in regimens for strength training and physical therapy that restore the body's strength and endurance after injury or protracted illness. With those in hospital, it can be used to work for strength to endure surgery, chemotherapy, or other physically exhausting treatments.

Question: What are my greatest strengths? How do I use those strengths?

Linked Concepts:
Stability, firmness, endurance, effort, skill, truth, leadership, justice, foundations, longevity, the deities, thresholds and gateways, sacred places.

Tinne - T
Ingot
Keyword: Mastery
Word Ogams:
MM: *trian roith* - a third of a wheel, one of three parts of a wheel i.e. axle
MO: *smuir gúaile* - fires of coal i.e. iron, marrow of charcoal i.e. molten ingot
CC: *trian n-airm* - a third of a weapon, one of three parts of a weapon i.e. a bar of iron or metal blade
Additional word ogam: Today

Color: *temen* - dark grey
Tree: *cuileann* - holly, *trom* - elder
Bird: *truith* - starling

Note:
Planet: Sun

This *fid* carries a meaning of "ingot" or "a bar of metal." In early Celtic societies, metal was valuable and bars of it were sometimes used as currency. Metal held great value for what it could be worked into and so Tinne is associated not just with wealth, but with creativity, skill, and the physical mastery of arts and craftsmanship. As such, it is a *fid* of the *Aes Dána*, the people of art -- those who are skilled and talented in different ways.

Though we do not often turn to smiths today, Tinne can be interpreted as a *fid* of technology, both mundane and magical, and therefore those who work with the bright marrow of the computer or other high technology items are also associated with this *fid*. Those who are highly skilled at working magic also fall under its purview.

In its most general sense, Tinne deals with issues of creativity, work, and material prosperity. It shows us where our talents lie. The work of the smith has also been in creating weapons, and so this *fid* is also linked with weaponry, war, and strife, as well as with practitioners of the martial arts. It can indicate the military or law enforcement as well.

The trees linked with this *fid* are Holly and Elder. Holly is most often seen as Tinne's tree in the modern literature, though Elder, called *trom* in Irish, would be a better fit by the tree name.

Elder's reputation is of both cursing and ill luck, and of protection from those misfortunes. The *Annals of the Four Masters* tells a tale of a queen exacting revenge upon her husband's mistress, taking a bundle of elder rods and tying them up with nine knots to prevent her from having a quick and easy birth. Children's cradles were never made from elder, for fear the *Sídhe* would steal or harm the baby. To strike a child or an animal with an elder switch would prevent their further growth. And yet in Scotland, the elder is a powerful tree for use in charms against malevolent magic, and to anoint the eyes with its sap would allow the person to see into the *Sídhe* realm.[58]

---

[58] Mac Coitir, 2003, 108-113

Holly is named *cuileann* in Irish. In County Tyrone, to plant a holly near the house was a sign that the daughters of that house would never marry or bear children. Spears or darts were often made of holly in folktales and the literary tradition, and chariot poles were cut from holly trees. Its berries, bright red, may have been associated with blood, and in Irish lore it is sometimes associated with severed heads.[59]

The color *temen* or "dark grey" is, in Old Irish, *teimen*. It means "darkness" or "obscurity" and can refer to that which is enigmatic or hidden. Its wind is the dark wind of the northeast, also seen listed as *teimheil* in some sources. Wright-Popescul links it with Gaelic words meaning obscurity, shade, a spot, a stain, or a residual trace.[60] For me, this is the color of cold iron and this wind, being a sub-wind of the north, would carry some of its energies of strife, moderated a bit by the east's traditional links with prosperity in the tale of *The Settling of the Manor of Tara*.

I have linked Tinne with the Sun through its emphasis on wealth, value, and the brilliance of metal in the smith's forge. Though the *fid* is most directly linked with iron and the Sun is more properly connected with gold in western occultism, it is the associations with mastery and wealth that bring them together here. Other students of *Filidecht* might choose to link Tinne with Mars rather than the Sun, because of its association with warriors and with iron, and this is a perfectly acceptable alternative reading.

The chthonic current of Tinne is one of solidity, dealing with metal, money, or wealth, and with weapons. It's material prosperity and the working world, and can indicate how you deal with making or losing money. Tinne can involve a sense of immediacy or urgency, a need to move on a project right now, or a reminder to stop procrastinating. It can also indicate martial arts or their practitioners. The *fid* can refer to technologies of all kinds as well, but with this current it is normally physical technology: hardware rather than software. It's metal and blades, weaponry, and the sharp, cutting edge.

Tinne's oceanic current is more about the technical skill associated with technological items. It's the creative force that can be harnessed to manifest new inventions, or the code that drives computers. This current is also the transforming fire of the forge, and what is being forged, still brilliant and glowing. This

---

[59] Mac Coitir, 2003, 66-71
[60] Wright-Popescul, 1997, 70

also leads us to Tinne's oceanic manifestation being perceived as a matter of transformative and artistic techniques, whether used in the physical world of art or the realm of spiritual change. It's the technology and the craft of transformation more than the transformation itself, which is a function of Straif. This current may also refer to the internal work of the martial artist or the warrior's path, from attitude to energy practices.

The *fid*'s celestial current deals with issues of mastery. It's an engagement with magical technologies and the *Aes Dána* -- the deities as the People of Art. As the smith transforms stone ore into metal, so the creative artist transforms raw material into beautiful and useful objects. In a long-term sense, it can refer to one's career or vocation, whatever field that may lie within. Its appearance may herald a new level of mastery within your chosen profession or your craft. The celestial energies of Tinne are concerned with the ideals of making, and with breaking through blocks to your creativity, allowing you to achieve mastery over technologies, whether they are magical, spiritual, metaphorical, or physical.

Tinne's magical uses are many, and it's particularly useful for work where physical objects are being created or worked with. It can aid your creativity in any realm and help break through creative blocks in your projects. It's of particular aid to blacksmiths and other metalworkers, and to sculptors or jewelers. Its magic can be directed toward the study and mastery of any work with the hands, or for technological and online forms of magic involving computers and programming languages. Invoking its power can help with focus in the martial arts or the warrior's path.

Its healing associations are with the hands and arms because of Tinne's associations with smithcraft. It's good for conditions that cause difficulties with steady hands or for strengthening of sinew and work that develops hand-eye coordination.

Question: How do I express my creativity? What is my relationship with work and prosperity?

Linked Concepts:
The Aes Dana, creative force, technical skill, making, the forge, arts and crafts, wealth or money, magical technologies, immediacy (time in a divination).

Coll - C
Hazel
Keyword: Wisdom
Word Ogams:
MM: *cáiniu fedai* - fairest of trees
MO: *carae blóesc* - friend of cracking, friend of nutshells
CC: *milsem fedo* - sweetest tree

Color: *crón* - brown
Tree: *coll* - hazel
Bird: (*córr* - crane/heron)

Note:
Planet: Mercury

Coll, the hazel, is one of the premier symbols of wisdom in Irish and Scottish traditions. References to it abound throughout the lore, and the literature regarding poets. Nine hazel trees are found surrounding the Well of Wisdom in the Otherworld realms, and its nuts fall into the well to be eaten by the salmon that dwell there, each nut eaten adding a spot to their sides. The salmon themselves are the carriers of wisdom and in many tales a *Fili* or *Draoí* might spend years or a lifetime waiting for the opportunity to consume the salmon and gain enlightenment and poetic ability from this profound source.

There's so much material surrounding hazels and wisdom that an entire book could be written on that subject alone, but suffice it to say that this *fid* represents wisdom and the entirety and depth of the wisdom-traditions of the Gaelic-speaking peoples. All that is wise and creative and profound is the domain of this *fid*, and enlightenment is the end result of its proper pursuit. This is the *fid* of seeking and second-sight, of the attainment of knowledge and the wisdom to use it properly, and of true judgment and discernment.

It's easy to see how Coll and its associations with wisdom and its transmission are linked to Mercury. The planet's symbolism is inextricably entwined with medieval and modern Western wisdom and mystery traditions through alchemy and Hermeticism. In *Filidecht*, Coll is the central image of the wisdom that transforms us, and Mercury is transformative power arrived at through the pursuit of wisdom.

Its color is *crón* or brown. In Irish lore, the northwest wind is dark brown or *ciar* in color. In Scots Gaelic, *ciar* has a range of meanings, encompassing dusky, dark grey, dark brown, swarthy, roan, sable, and gloomy, while Irish *ciar* has a similar range of meanings, including a chestnut color. Most of the color meanings associated with the wind are those used to refer to animals, particularly horses or cattle.[61] In Old Irish, *crón* is brown, reddish brown, dark yellow, or possibly a shade of red. It may also refer to crimson, dun, or swarthy, with a potential meaning of perverse, and has been used to refer to the abyss of hell in a Christian context.[62]

I chose *corr*, the crane or heron, as the missing bird ogam for this *fid*. In Irish myth, the crane is a bird of prophecy, and though it's sometimes seen as an ill omen, it's also associated strongly with wisdom and magic. Manannán mac Lir possessed a crane skin bag in which he kept his treasures. The crane from which it was made was once Aífe, a woman who had been shape-shifted by a curse.[63] The God Lug did a form of battle magic called *corrguinecht* or "crane magic" that involved standing on one leg with one hand behind his back and one eye closed. This posture is one of Otherworldly power and reminiscent of the sundering of Bóand when she approached the Well of Wisdom -- the water rose and tore from her one eye, one arm and one leg, which can be read as having sight in both the mundane realms and the Otherworld.

When this *fid* is received in divination, inspiration and wisdom are at hand. Trust that you know or will find the answers you seek, and that you will be able to apply that knowledge properly and in its right place and time. The attainment may be difficult or even a long time in coming, but it already has its place in your life.

Coll has links to tradition and the wisdom found in nature and from natural sources. It suggests wisdom-seeking rituals or the search for vision and imbas or poetic enlightenment. The Well of Wisdom was said to be the source of the five senses, and so Coll is a reminder of how important the use of our senses is to our search for truth and wisdom. Use the evidence of sight and

[61] Wright-Popescul, 1997, 63-64
[62] DIL, 160
[63] MacKillop, 1998, 97-98

touch, of scent and taste and hearing, and trust yourself to understand them.

This *fid*'s chthonic current speaks of the five streams of the senses and of physical evidence used to pursue answers. Follow what your senses tell you and trust their wisdom. It may mean sources of wisdom or refer to the Otherworldly Well of Wisdom if the question involves such things. It can also refer to tradition and the passing of customs and secrets from one generation to another in living memory. Coll may be a reminder to use your observational skills when working to solve problems.

Coll's oceanic current is transformative wisdom and the ability to find answers through second sight or incubatory rituals. The use of wisdom and knowledge to spark transformation and change is found here. It can also refer to things found in the between spaces: between sleeping and waking, walking in the mist along the coast, gazing toward the stars at dawn or dusk. If you are in this place, your identity may shift between species or gender, garnering experience that leads to understanding. This current speaks to the mystery of fire rising from water, and the nine wells of Manannán mac Lir that are found beneath the sea.

The celestial manifestation of Coll indicates dealings with poetic inspiration and loss of self in the currents of the Otherworlds, called *imbas* in Irish. It can be seen as a form of emotionally engaged enlightenment often expressed in spiritually charged poetry and ecstasy. Wisdom is found in all its depths. Omen-taking and ecstatic visionary ability are indicated by celestial Coll. Using its discernment can lead you to spiritual and intellectual truth, cracking the shell of a problem to get to its substance. The ability to make wise and balanced judgments is found here. Self-knowledge and personal gnosis are also a deep part of this current.

Magically, Coll is a prayer for wisdom. It invokes our most profound abilities to change reality and perceive beyond the mists into Otherworld realms. If you want to know the proper path to pursue, use Coll to help guide you.

As a healing ogam, Coll brings wisdom and guidance for the healer and the client. It can help with making proper choices and decisions regarding treatment and the progress of the situation, as well as helping to understand the processes that are happening. It can sharpen your senses for observation in healing work as well.

Question: Where does my wisdom lie? How do I make proper use of my wisdom?

Linked Concepts:
Poetic inspiration, the well of wisdom, the world tree, sources of wisdom, tradition, the senses, visionary and creative ability, second sight, omen-taking, liminality.

Ceirt - Q
Rag - Shrub
Keyword: Misfortune
Word Ogams:
MM: *cliathar baiscill* - shelter of a hind, shelter of a lunatic
MO: *bríg anduini* - force of a man, substance of an insignificant person
CC: *dígu fethail* - worst of ornament or covering; dregs of clothing

Color: *quair* - "mouse-colored" (light grey-brown)
Tree: *cuileann* - holly, *caorann* - rowan, *crann creathach* - aspen, *úll* - apple
Bird: *querc* - hen

Note:
Planet: Eris

Ceirt, along with h-Úath, is one of the most challenging ogam *feda*. Its meaning of a rag or a shrub[64] links it in my mind with the practice of tying rags to clootie trees in Ireland and Scotland as an appeal for healing. These trees are often found at sacred wells or on fairy mounds, and are significant for being very much associated with Otherworldly beings and energies that can be fickle and unpredictable.

---

[64] McManus uses the "shrub" or "bush" definition, while Meroney suggested that the word was translated as "a rag". I found the connections between both of these suggested meanings useful enough that I have chosen to use both, though Meroney's definition is probably not correct.

This *fid* also brings to mind the story of Suibhne Geilt, the mad poet who had once been a powerful king until his courage failed him in battle after being cursed by a saint, and he fled into the wilderness to live among the birds and animals, flitting from tree to tree until he grew feathers. Its word ogam, "shelter of a lunatic," suggests both the bushes under which the madman seeks shelter, and the brokenness of mental illness itself. I tend to see the story of Suibhne as an illustration of what today we would call post-traumatic stress, sited within a magical and spiritual context. Suibhne is the sacred madman or *geilt*, who creates powerful poetry in the matrix of his madness.

At this writing, Eris is the newest named member of the solar system. It is considered a dwarf planet, and its naming heralded the controversial reclassification of Pluto and Ceres as dwarf planets, rather than a planet and an asteroid, respectively. Eris is the disruptive element of chaos, which fits in well with Ceirt's general instability and fickle unpredictability. But it should also be understood that sometimes the injection of a little uncertainty is necessary for life to move forward. Approached with an open and accepting attitude, chaos can be joyous, fertile, and creative. As yet, Eris has no formal astrological symbol, but I associate it with the eight-spoked chaos arrow -- energy without direction or focus.

Ceirt's color is *quair*, translated as "mouse-colored" in the *Auraicept*, and most field mice are a light to medium grey-brown. This color has no associated wind, but its mousy manifestation would suggest timidity and a certain amount of destruction of food supplies.

Four trees are associated with this fid. They are holly - *cuileann*, rowan - *caorann*, aspen - *crann creathac* or *chraobh chrithinn*, and apple - *úll*. The folklore and symbolism surrounding rowan and holly have previously been explored in the sections on Lus and Tinne.

Christian legend says that aspen wood was used for Christ's cross, and so in Ireland and Scotland the tree is often associated with death and misfortune. In Scotland stones and clods of earth would sometimes be thrown at the tree, and the quaking of its leaves was ascribed to its guilt associated with Christ's death. In Uist, no crofter would use aspen for his plough or tools and no fisherman would have aspen in his boat or creels.[65] So great was the taboo against the use of aspen that the

---

[65] Darwin, 1996, 161

Scottish poet William Ross told a tale of being on a boat in a storm that was driven ashore onto an island. The only trees available for wood to repair the boat were aspen and willow as mentioned above; the reputation of both trees was so bad that the boatmen chose to await rescue rather than use the wood of either tree to replace the broken thole pins that held the oars.[66]

Despite this, aspen wood is used for herring barrel staves, milk pails, tables, and chairs. It was sometimes used for house carpentry but is subject to rot and so keeping the wood dry is imperative.[67] Like the rowan in North America, aspen is sometimes called "mountain ash" in parts of Scotland, illustrating how reliance on folk names can cause difficulties in identifying plants and trees that are of distinctly different species but called by the same names.[68]

The apple, on the other hand, is often associated with the Otherworld in its most positive aspects. In fact, one of the Irish Otherworlds was named *Eamhain Ablach*, the Realm of Apples. It is one of the favored mythological foods throughout the Celtic islands, not unlike hazelnuts. Found on magical branches and eaten in Otherworldly feasts, the apple looms large in insular Celtic myth.

The warrior Cú Chulainn follows a wheel and a rolling apple across the Plain of Ill-Luck on his quest to find the home of Scáthach, a great woman warrior who taught him many of his most powerful battle-feats.[69] This is not its only link with divination; it was frequently used for divining games at Samhain all throughout Ireland and Scotland.[70]

The complex of meanings surrounding this *fid* often point to intense frustration and even self-destructive activity. When it comes up in a reading, be careful of sudden changes in fortune or capricious individuals. It's associated with bad luck and with psychological problems, but because of its linked association with clootie trees, there can also be an element of hope to this *fid* that h-Úath lacks. In divination, it can point to a situation of poverty or illness that is temporary, or to setbacks in a person's life or situation.

Retreat rather than advance may be necessary when this *fid* appears, so approach the situation with caution or leave it for

---

[66] Milliken & Bridgewater, 2004, 149
[67] Milliken & Bridgewater, 2004, 95
[68] Milliken & Bridgewater, 2004, 120
[69] Rees & Rees, 1990, 254
[70] Darwin, 2004, 150

another time when energies and emotions are more stable and you're in a better place to cope with what's happening. The message of Ceirt is that there is a light in the darkness, and to have the fortitude to pursue that hope, even when it's faint.

Misfortune, frustration, poverty, illness, and bad luck are part and parcel of Ceirt's chthonic current. A need for caution or retreat may manifest here, reflecting difficult physical or emotional circumstances. You may be approaching a situation with timidity, damaging yourself in the process. Look to the surrounding *feda* for clarification of your situation. When dealing with difficult people, malice may be involved; be sure it is not your own. Be very careful that you are not acting as your own worst enemy.

The oceanic current of Ceirt signals the potential for or presence of madness or mental illness. Situations may change without notice and you may feel like nothing is stable. Disruptive chaos can inject itself into your life with incredible rapidity. This may be simple impulse, but it could also be caprice or malicious fickleness. Care is necessary any time this *fid* appears.

Ceirt's celestial manifestation is not quite as harsh as its other currents. Here, the frustration and bad luck are most likely temporary. Where illness is found, there is hope of healing, though recovery may be slow. This current exhorts you to press on through difficulty. Your situation may call for sacrifices to be made, whether physical or metaphorical. If all other indications are favorable, Ceirt's celestial current may suggest that negativity is being bound and harm is in some way being mitigated. There is a light at the end of the tunnel that might not actually be a train.

Ceirt's magical effects can be used, with due caution, to bind, entangle, or hinder negative influences or cause the retreat of malevolent magic or energies. If you wish to use it in magic, I would advise invoking it in combination with strongly positive *feda* to contain its energies and direct them in ways that will not bring the more difficult aspects of its influence down upon you. As with h-Úath, dealing with this *fid* in magic is best done only when you have experience with ogam, you know your shielding and protective techniques, and you're working from a solid, positive mental and emotional state. Like h-Úath, working with this *fid* without proper preparation and understanding is just asking for trouble.

While I do not ordinarily consider this a healing *fid*, it can be used in careful combination with Straif and nGétal for help with mental illnesses or to transform scattered and damaging emotional states into more stable ones in times of great need. Even Suibhne Geilt had a period of lucidity after his madness.

Question: Where in my life am I frustrated? What traps me in cycles of self-destruction?

Linked Concepts:
Poverty, illness, fleeing, retreat, madness, insanity, ill luck without total loss, psychological issues and problems, the hope for healing from illness or madness.

The Third Aicme:
M G Ng Sr R

Muin - M
Love - Esteem - Trickery
Keyword: Communication
Word Ogams:
MM: *tressam fedmae* - strongest of powers i.e. the desire or affection for another, strongest of effort, strongest in exertion
MO: *árusc n-airlig* - condition of slaughter, proverb of slaughter
CC: *conar gotha* - path of the voice
Additional word ogam: Back of an ox
Additional word ogam: Desire of a man, affection of man

Color: *mbracht* - variegated, speckled (many-colored)
Tree: *finemain* - vine
Bird: *mintan* - titmouse

Note:
Planet: Venus

This *fid* is the center of a constellation of meanings that all center around communications. Muin is a *fid* of love and esteem, but it's also the *fid* of trickery, lies, and deceit. Intuition and other nearby *feda* in a reading will help determine which meaning fits best into the situation, but because Muin represents the throat -- the path of the voice -- it's essentially about finding your voice and the ways in which you communicate.

Muin is a tapestry of emotion and its threads encompass many of the ways in which emotions are expressed. So often, talking about emotion is as much a matter of interpretation as it is of expression. Learning to understand emotion and its subtleties is one of the underlying lessons of this *fid*.

Its word ogam "the back of an ox" offers another view of Muin: there is effort in expressing yourself clearly and understandably, and effort in discerning the truth from lies. Sometimes this communication can be a heavy burden, but the results are necessary and worthwhile.

The vine, *finemain*, is not a tree in any traditional sense but it is listed as the tree associated with this *fid*. Grapes are made into wine, producing conviviality and pleasure, but also inclining a person to drunkenness. Grapevines are not native to Ireland and barely grow in its climate. They were a much later import and even in the warmest historical periods were difficult to cultivate. Wine was never a native beverage and was imported from the continent long before viniculture was brought to the islands. Although this import was a high-status drink, it's likely that its listing here is a nod to the importance of wine to Christian ritual; the alcoholic beverages most associated with insular Celtic ritual are mead and ale, neither of which is brewed with grapes.

Venus is a planet associated with love and pleasure, but in its negative aspects it can also be associated with the misuse of those things for manipulation. Venus can express envy, jealousy, and fickleness as well as generosity in love. Just as Muin has connotations of voice and speech, Venus can be associated with a pleasant voice and harmonious communications as well as its more traditionally sensual and sexual meanings.

Mbracht, the color associated with this *fid*, is usually defined as variegated or multi-colored, though *brecht* means speckled in Old Irish. Given Muin's wide and varied array of meaning, this seems quite fitting. Plaid, multicolored spotted, or striped might be a way to conceptualize this "color" in your work, combining the influences of many shades into a tapestry of understanding. Several ogam *feda* are associated with speckles or spots, and speckled things are often associated with the Otherworld or have an Otherworldly origin. There is a "speckled" wind, but its color-word is *alad*, the term used for the color associated with the *fid* Ailm.

Muin's chthonic current covers a number of meanings. It's the physical labor of work and bearing a burden suggested by the word ogam "back of an ox." Its subterranean implications may suggest a truth being denied, buried by a desire to see the world differently than it actually is. It may be the physical manifestation of sexual desire or physical affections. Under some circumstances it might refer to sexual magic. Bodily pleasures and hedonistic attitudes are found with this current.

The oceanic current is one of concealment -- flattery, persuasive words, deception and the concealment of truth for good or ill. Lies, half-truths, insincerity, manipulation, and misinterpretation dwell here, along with fickleness and jealousy. A depth of emotion may be indicated, but it may be disguised for any number of reasons. When this current appears, be very careful about meaning and intention. Be sure you're getting to the root of the issue.

Self-expression, finding and using one's voice, listening, and clarity in communication come with Muin's celestial current. Discernment is found here, and the ability to tell truth from lies and to uncover the hidden aspects of a situation. This is where love, respect, and esteem manifest, fostering genial relationships between friends, family, lovers, and deities. These feelings are different from the physical urges of Muin's chthonic current, being less involved with the body and more with the mind and the finer emotions.

When this *fid* appears in divination, look to the others nearby and listen to your spirits to decide which direction its energies flow. It indicates depth of emotion, regardless of the presence or absence of the physical passions of Ruis. Desire and affection may be indicated, but often there is a hint of caution to watch the words of others. In concert with Nin, another *fid* of communication and contracts, be sure to express yourself clearly and fully on the topic at hand in order to receive a fair hearing.

If Muin is surrounded or touched by challenging *feda*, like h-Úath or Ceirt, beware of lies and manipulation. Watch for flattery used to insincere ends. Be ready to speak your truth and call things as you see them, for misinterpretation may be easier than you think. Be careful also of half-truths that conceal larger lies.

Muin used for magic can be a powerful aid to self-expression. It can assist those who have difficulty with public speaking or help you give clarity to your words when you are under stress. It can also help where you suspect untruths and wish to uncover them. In terms of love-magic, it can help you communicate your affections effectively, though I would strongly advise against the use of magic in any effort to "make" someone love you. These workings inevitably seem to backfire somehow, and no one will be happy with the situation. Muin could be used to enhance magical workings where sexual energies are brought to bear, intensifying those workings and focusing them to positive purposes.

The *fid's* connection with the neck, throat, and the voice suggests healing powers for the mouth and throat, and for the ears that hear messages as well. Lungs, back and shoulders are also connected here and Muin can be useful in treating problems arising there.

Question: How do I communicate with others? How do I interpret what they are saying to me?

Linked Concepts:
Work, effort, carrying a heavy burden; falsehoods, tricks, lies, concealment or denial of facts or truth; love, respect, desire; speaking, persuasion, flattery, finding your voice.

Gort - G
Garden
Keyword: Growth
Word Ogams:
MM: *milsiu féraib* - sweeter than grasses, sweetest grass
MO: *inded erc* - suitable place for cows
CC: *sásad ile* - sating of multitudes, satisfaction of multitudes
Additional word ogam: *glaisem gelta* - greenest of pastures
Additional word ogam: *med n-ercc* - counterpart of heaven
Color: *gorm* - blue
Tree: *edeand* - ivy, *finemain* - vine
Bird: *géis* - swan
99

Note:

Planet: Ceres

Gort is the safe haven. It's the garden where things are protected so they can flourish and grow. It is the *fid* of cultivation and patience that leads to abundance. Gardens must be protected from anything that would destroy the plants, from deer and slugs to disease and drought, but the places so protected are oases of peace and pleasure. This *fid* can imply hard work, as tending a garden can be filled with days of weeding and dealing with pests, but the beauty of gardens fills our souls. For some, a garden is as close as they ever get to wild nature, growing flowers in window boxes or in pots on a balcony. Even then, they can be tiny places to center and ground, giving green space to breathe, to rest and refresh our eyes, minds and spirits.

The word ogams "suitable place for cows" and "greenest of pastures" suggest that this is not just the vegetable garden, supplying human larders, but it's also the protected pasture space where cattle graze, bringing plenty to animals as well as humans.

This *fid* of gardens and pastures is about nourishing and feeding yourself or others, physically, emotionally, and spiritually. It speaks to plenty and fertility, and points to places in your life where there is abundance. It is a *fid* of generosity and hospitality.

Ceres is an asteroid connected with the Roman Goddess of grain and harvest, making it the perfect link with the protected field of Gort. Ceres is linked with the acquisition of sustenance and security through patience, and in its fullest expression this *fid* can bring those energies to fruition.

Gort's trees are *finemain*, the vine, discussed above in the section on Gort, and *edeand* or ivy. In Scotland, ivy was twined into a wreath with honeysuckle and rowan to place over the lintel of a cow byre or under the churns in the dairy to protect cattle from disease and the evil eye. It was also used for a number of different medicinal preparations, from burn treatment and skin problems to astringents and diuretics.[71] Ivy was also used in Scotland for love magic. Three leaves of ivy were pinned onto a girl's nightgown to help her dream of her future husband, and as late as the 1940s in Rosneath, schoolgirls would take ivy leaves

---

[71] Darwin, 1996, 72-73

from a wall near the church, placing them inside their blouse and sing "Ivy, ivy, I love you, in my bosom I put you, the first young man who speaks to me, my future husband he will be."[72]

Gorm, the color blue, is one of the most soothing colors. Most people perceive it as being restful and restorative. The color of one of the southwest winds is translated as blue, though the color word used for it is *glas*. The word *glas* covers a variety of shades including the spectrum of blue, green, and grey. Because the color for nGétal is *nglas*, the specifics of that term will be dealt with in that section. Like *glas*, *gorm*'s range of meaning is also very flexible, covering deep blue, blue-black, and cerulean with a secondary meaning of verdant green like rich grass in pasture. This is a logical definition for a color associated with fields and gardens. It can also be used for dark, swarthy, or black colors. When used in referring to weapons or heroes, it can mean illustrious or splendid.[73]

The chthonic current of Gort speaks of fields, pastures, gardens, cultivation, and fertility in the natural world. Brought into the world of culture, it carries implications of hospitality, the safety of enclosed places, food, and feasting. It may point to a need to weed out negative influences or the process of doing such winnowing. If the chthonic current of Gort is afflicted in a reading, it could indicate the risk or presence of cancerous growths or the growth of negative situations.

Gort's oceanic current deals more with energy than the physical world. Here you find restorative rest, sheltered growth, incubation, meditation, gestation, and spiritual retreat. It is quiet, subtle movement and development like a seed growing within the embrace of the earth, or a sense of hibernation as a bear sleeps sheltered within a hollow in the winter.

Celestial Gort is abundance and harvest, showing the rewards of patience. Generosity, blessings, peace, and thankfulness are found here. There is a general air of gratitude and plenty, with an assurance of ease in the situation, though it may have been long in coming. Happiness is possible where this current is found.

When Gort appears in a reading, it may indicate that a period of prosperity is coming, and a little more patience is required to get there. It can suggest that you look to the blessings in your life and be thankful for them. It frequently indicates a happy situation or a place of safety.

---

[72] Milliken & Bridgewater, 2004, 136
[73] DIL, 368

Sometimes Gort suggests that you pull back from your activity and find yourself a safe and sheltered place for rest, particularly when it appears with nGétal. This is the place for incubation and restoration, a need for peace and quiet and nurturance.

In magical work, this *fid* is good for prosperity, fertility, and growth. Properly used, it can bring abundance and foster a generous and giving environment. It can also be used in creating a space of safety and peace in combination with other *feda* in a healing context, or for rest in a difficult time.

For healing work, Gort can be used to bring peaceful, restorative rest to those who need it, and to aid with wasting diseases. I would suggest avoiding the use of this *fid* in cases where cancers and other disorders of growth are present, as encouraging growth where it is already out of control is not necessarily wise. It can be useful for pregnant women to help with the growth of the child in the womb and to encourage and protect a difficult pregnancy, particularly in concert with other *feda* connected with children and birth.

Question: Where is my safe space to grow? How do I cultivate my highest self?

Linked Concepts:
Fertility, plenty, wealth, abundance, generosity, happiness, patience, waiting for fruition, cycles and cyclic time, sanctuary or a place of safety and peace.

nGétal - Ng
Wound - Charm
Keyword: Healing
Word Ogams:
MM: *lúth lego* - a physician's strength, sustenance of a leech, physician's cry
MO: *étiud midach* - robe of physicians, raiment of physicians
CC: *tosach n-échto* - beginning of murder; beginning of slaying

Color: *nglas* - green
Tree: *giolach* - broom, *raith* - fern

Bird: *ngéigh* - goose

Note:
Planet: Chiron

NGétal is the primary *fid* of healing. The name itself means both a wound and the charm that is sung over it. The wound and the healer have an intrinsic relationship, for without the wound or the imbalance, the healer is unnecessary. In some cases, as with a broken and badly healed bone, the healer is called upon to open the wound, to re-break the bone so that it may be set to heal properly.

An important aspect of traditional healing in Celtic cultures was the making of charms and the singing of poems over healing herbs and the person who was injured or ill. Such charms and songs are recorded in medieval Irish manuscripts and in living Scottish folk practice, carrying on a tradition from the Middle Ages into the early twentieth century. This aspect of Celtic tradition seems not unlike that of Dine or Lakota healing, where song and prayer play as important a role as herbs and surgery in dealing with disease.

Healing was the bailiwick of many deities in Irish culture, each seeming to have their own area of expertise. Airmid was associated with herbal healing, Miach with surgery and Dian Cécht with healing charms. Dian Cécht is the father of Airmid and Miach, and they, along with Ochttríuil, tended the healing well named Sláine or "Health" in the tale of *The Second Battle of Mag Tuiredh*. The wounded and dead of the Tuatha Dé Danann were immersed in the well and rose from it whole and unhurt.[74] Brighid is another Goddess who is profoundly linked with healing in the Irish and Scottish traditions. Even the hero Fionn was able to heal by giving the wounded water he'd carried in the palms of his hands.[75]

Chiron as the wounded healer is a profound expression of both of the opposing energies of nGétal. In astrology, it symbolizes where one is most deeply wounded and how one wounds others, as well as how we heal ourselves and those around us. This celestial centaur was the link that led me to consider assigning astrological bodies to the ogam feda as a planet ogam, and its initiatory power gave me the inspiration to

---

[74] Gray, 1982, 55
[75] Rees & Rees, 1990, 283

bridge two disparate systems of thought as a catalyst for transforming my understanding of both.

As with Gort, nGétal's color is associated with one of the southwest winds, though the color word for the green wind used is *uaine*, usually a brighter and more verdant green than the misty green of *glas*. In Old Irish, though, even *uaine* is used to express a similar color range as *glas* -- greens moving through blues and greys. Both words are used of vegetation, the sea, and eyes.[76] The southwest is strongly associated with death and the ancestors. *Tech Duinn*, the House of Donn, is located to the southwest of Ireland. It's considered the dwelling place of the dead and its physical location is one of the large sea stacks off the southwest tip of Ireland.

The southwest's "blue" wind uses the world *glas* as its identifier. Blue and green became separate color words very late in the history of most languages, and Gaelic is no exception. The color associated with nGétal is *nglas*, one of the variants of green. Its spectrum of meaning deals with an oceanic range of colors, from the grey of mists through the blue of sky reflected in sea to the deep green of the ocean in storm.[77] The color itself has strong Otherworldly associations and has many links with things set apart and sacred. The nature of both wind color words is one of liminality and the blurring of boundaries.

Fern and broom -- *raith* and *giolach* -- are the two "trees" associated with this *fid*. Several varieties of fern were used in Scotland for medicinal purposes as a tonic or applied for sprain.[78] It would often be used for bedding, being plentiful and easily replaced. Bracken ferns, the sort most often used, had insect repellent qualities, though fern was considered inferior to heather for bedding.[79] Bracken was excellent for thatching though, and could provide a suitable roof for as much as thirty years with one well-cared-for thatching. It was considered quite valuable for that purpose in Scotland and the right to pull it for thatch was enthusiastically pursued.[80]

Broom had uses as a disinfectant and was sometimes burnt to purify and fumigate homes.[81] Along with birch or hazel, it might be used as the peeled white wand for Imbolc's Brighid

[76] DIL, 620
[77] Wright-Popescul, 1997, 50
[78] Milliken and Bridgewater, 2004, 230
[79] Darwin, 1996, 61
[80] Milliken and Bridgewater, 2004, 89
[81] MacCoitir, 2003, 101

rituals. Its flexible branches were used as the brush of brooms, and it was used medicinally as a narcotic and as a tonic for kidney, liver, and heart afflictions. Overdoses of broom can be toxic, so caution was necessary in its use, as with so many other herbs.[82] Broom was also associated with weddings and fertility in some parts of the north of Scotland. A bridal staff made from broom wood was kept in the bride's house overnight to enhance fertility.[83]

The chthonic current of nGétal is a mixed bag. It may signify doctors and other healers as physical individuals, or healing technologies in and of themselves. It can indicate the place where one is wounded emotionally. It's also physical wounding and death, injury, and the possibility of accidents. Healthcare should be a priority and preventative and precautionary measures taken when this current appears.

With the oceanic current, we deal with the concept of health imbalances because of the current's fluctuating nature. These may be hormonal imbalances or other types of problems caused by being physically out of balance in some way. Changes in health may be imminent. Chronic illness may be indicated. Regeneration of many kinds can be a part of this current as well. Magical healing through chant and charm is found here, along with the mysteries of the wounded healer. Initiatory illness and healing as a process of initiation speak to the spiritual component of nGétal, carrying powerful lessons for anyone who would do healing work.

In its celestial current, nGétal points to the presence and work of healing deities in one's life. Balance, good health, wellbeing, and recovery after long illness are found here. The alignment of healing energies comes into play, as does striving for the ideals of healing, fitness, and health. This is the place where illness and injury are ameliorated and the body brought into balance. In a difficult situation, this current brings hope after struggle and sickness.

When nGétal appears in divination, it suggests that health is or should be a priority now. It may indicate the danger of injury when paired with h-Úath or other challenging *feda*. In positive readings, it may suggest that an injury or illness is healing, or that a course of treatment for a chronic health problem may be going well. It can be a reminder to watch your health or to get something checked on that you might otherwise

---

[82] Darwin, 1996, 112
[83] Milliken and Bridgewater, 2004, 138

consider minor. It is a very hopeful *fid* to draw for those who are ill, as it implies active and progressing healing and the restoration of health and wellbeing.

Magically, this *fid* is excellent for all types of healing work, and useful for healers to call upon when doing any work with their clients. I have an image of this *fid* surrounded by calligraphy of its word ogams in Old Irish and other meaningful symbols that I put on my altar when doing healing work to remind me of the power of this *fid* and invoke its healing qualities.

In specific healing work it can be useful to anoint the afflicted part with blessed water, colored body paints or healing substances like herb powders or oils to aid with the flow of energy by drawing this *fid* on the skin. This anointing can bring the energies of the *fid* into the client's body energies in a very powerful way, augmenting their healing process.

Question: Where am I wounded? What in my life requires healing?

Linked Concepts:
Wounding, death, beneficial magic, healers and doctors, good health, wellbeing, regeneration, hope.

Straif - Sr
Sulfur
Keyword: Transformation
Word Ogams:
MM: *tressam rúamnai* - strongest of red, strongest reddening dye
MO: *mórad rún* - increasing of secrets, increase of secrets
CC: *saigid nél* - seeking of clouds i.e. its smoke above it

Color: *sorcha* - "bright" (brilliant white or yellow)
Tree: *draighean* - (sloe) blackthorn, *saildrong* - willowbrake
Bird: *smólach* - thrush

Note: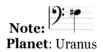

Planet: Uranus

Straif is sulfur, linked in western history with alchemy and transformation. It was used as a mordant in dyeing to create a wide variety of colors inexpensively, and so transforms cloth in dull natural colors to brighter, more valuable shades. The word ogam "seeking of clouds" seems, in my mind, to suggest divination through the seeking of omens, through *neldoracht* (interpreting the shapes of clouds, or possibly astrology), or through watching the smoke rise from fires or incense and interpreting its shapes and movements.

"Increasing of secrets" also strongly suggests occult work and a link with all things hidden and mysterious. Much of what the Druids did was held secret to those within the Druidic schools, taught only by word of mouth. Shape-shifting is one of the mythic characteristics of Druidic ability. This physical mutation leads to a total change of perception, transforming a person from one basic nature to another, as sulfur is a part of the alchemical process seeking to turn base metals into gold.

Straif is a *fid* of secrecy and mystery, but also of exploring those mysteries and revealing them. It offers us a model of transformation and transcendence, using knowledge developed and nurtured through practice with others to transcend difficulties and bring forth the potential that lies within each of us.

The sloe or blackthorn, *draighean*, is one of the trees associated with this *fid*. Blackthorn staves are often used as walking sticks, and are also strong wood traditionally used for the Irish club or *shillelagh*. In *The Destruction of Da Derga's Hostel*, Da Derga is accompanied by "three fifties of warriors" each carrying iron bound blackthorn clubs. Its wood was used for protection from the malevolent and trickster energies of the *Sídhe*, carried or kept by the bedside. Despite this, the wood was often considered unlucky to cut or bring indoors and, like other thorn trees, was protected by the *Sídhe* as well. In the *Mesca Ulad* warriors were compared to blackthorn bushes, and blackthorn is associated with the ability to hold even the fierceness of wild boars in check in the tale of the *Wooing of*

Étaín. Blackthorn sloes are edible and are also a component of sloe gin.[84]

Uranus is the first planet beyond the last of the classically known planets, Saturn. It is seen as a boundary-breaker, leading the way into the unknown and that which is beyond the visible world. Uranus transcends the visible solar system, revealing what was previously hidden and profoundly transforming our understanding of the universe around us. Like Straif, it's dynamic and spiritually charged, and the pursuit of the mysteries it reveals may be considered eccentric by mundane society.

The color *sorcha*, in Old Irish rendered *sorchae*, is translated as "bright" in the *Auraicept na n-Éces*. It carries meanings of bright, luminous, radiant, brilliant, and light, and is associated with legitimacy of birth in some legal texts.[85]

Straif's chthonic current speaks of secrets and the preservation of secret knowledge. It can refer to magical or occult mysteries and to a depth of magical and spiritual practice. Sulfur burned for intense purification and exorcism may be a part of this current. Practical magic may also be indicated in the form of spellwork for everyday things.

The oceanic current deals with alchemy in all its forms: spiritual, psychological and laboratory. Straif in this current reminds us to expect the unexpected. When it appears, things are in flux and changing in potentially unpredictable ways. Sudden reversals of fortune are possible. Shapeshifting and transformation are a part of this current, as is initiatory experience that induces profound change.

Revelation and transcendence are part of Straif's celestial current. Intense spiritual work often comes with this *fid*, along with important shifts in perception. Divination by astrology, or through freeform associative means like watching the shapes in clouds or smoke may be useful as a part of the spiritual direction being taken when this *fid* appears. Allow the imagination to lead and look at things with new eyes.

When this *fid* appears in a reading, change is on the way. Nothing will remain the same. It suggests a need for spiritual work and development, shifting your shape from an old form to a new one. The change implied is total, and it may be a complete reversal of fortune, but whatever is in the wind, it will be utterly different than what has come before.

---

[84] MacCoitir, 2004, 102-107
[85] DIL 558, "*mac soirche*, son of light, i.e. of legitimate (or legitimized) birth."

Prepare for the unexpected with Straif's appearance. Such changes may be guided and predicted, given enough study and a depth of practice with firm intent. As alchemy is a deep discipline, change can be managed through spiritual work when Straif is an influence. Straif gives the ability to transform attitudes in healing. Despair can become hope. This *fid* is good for work with the emotions and for transforming deep seated issues that have strong roots in the past, changing things without destroying the vessel.

Question: What part of my life requires total change? How am I being transformed?

Linked Concepts:
Spiritual work, secrets, magical or occult mysteries, mutability, shape-shifting, divination, taking of omens, transcendence.

Ruis - R
Redness
Keyword: Passion
Word Ogams:
MM: *tindem rucci* - most painful of shames, intensest of blushes, most intense blushing
MO: *rúamnae drech* - redness of faces, reddening of faces
CC: *bruth fergae* - glow of anger

Color: *ruadh* -"red-haired"
Tree: *trom* - elder, *mónóg* - bogberry, *raith* - fern
Bird: *rócnat* - rook

Note:
Planet: Mars

Ruis, redness, is the *fid* of intensity and passion. It deals in emotions that may either help or harm, depending on their use. It can indicate anger, shame, or embarrassment, calling up those things that arouse guilt and frenzy. Ruis can also be a loss of control, whether enraged or ecstatic.

The *fid*'s passionate nature can manifest in sexuality and eroticism, whether for pleasure or in an attempt to control others. It can be obsessive and abusive as well, leading to danger and extremes of action. Like passion itself, Ruis can be joyful or steeped in hatred, and its energies are turbulent and unpredictable. Jealousy and rage are part and parcel of this *fid*'s energies, but they can be tempered and turned to passionate love as well.

Mars expresses the energies of Ruis very well, ruling unbridled rage and anger, as well as passionate sexuality that moves beyond the beauty and sensuality of Venus. When Mars is appropriately understood and controlled, passion and power can be directed for intense and positive results. As with Ruis, if it is unrestrained and badly aspected destruction and terrible pain can result.

Rúad in Old Irish is literally translated as red, generally a brownish or dark red and may refer to the color of dried bloodstains where *fland* implies the red of freshly shed blood. *Rúad* could be the russet of autumn foliage. It also has a secondary poetic meaning of strong, mighty, or formidable.[86] The warrior in battle frenzy is sometimes described as being surrounded by a red halo and is supernaturally strong, as is so often seen in the tales of Cú Chulainn. In modern Irish, *ruadh* is often used as a descriptor for red hair and sometimes associated with temper and ill luck.

In the compass rose of winds, one of the southeast winds is red, though the word used is *dearg*. This is a more commonly used word for red in the Gaelic languages. In Scottish Gaelic, the word's meaning palette includes crimson, flaming, red-hot, real, intense, violent, notorious, severe, bitter, and impetuous.[87] As with *rúad*, these color meanings point to the intensifying and destructive sides of Ruis.

Fern, one of the "trees" of Ruis, is described under nGétal. Elder, another tree associated with this *fid*, is treated in the entry for Tinne. The bogberry, *mónóg*, is a shrub more commonly known as the wild cranberry, a plant related to heather. It was a common food plant but has become quite rare in its original environment in modern times, supplanted by the larger North American cranberry as a food source.

---

[86] DIL 512
[87] Wright-Popescul, 1997, 433-44

The chthonic current of Ruis is a difficult one. Most of its meanings are emotions that are hard for people to face. Shame, embarrassment, guilt, envy, and jealousy are often indicated. Obsession and rage are possible. I have often seen this current appear when a client has a history of sexual abuse, or deals with the abuse of sexuality and sensuality in their lives. There may be blocked sexual expression or an inability to experience eroticism and sensuality in a positive way. There may be closeting or denial of sexual orientation. If this current appears but is surrounded by positive *feda*, it may indicate a deep appreciation of sensuality and eroticism or perhaps an intense and positive hedonistic streak.

Its oceanic current is equally intense. It can indicate a loss of control, or a fear of that loss. Ecstatic trance and practices may be a strong part of spiritual practice. The warrior's frenzy described in the Irish tales manifests here, with all the intensity and loss of control that this implies. Intensity of emotion that turns the cauldrons through joy and sorrow is a part of this current as well, and can be a strong positive force for growth and the development of maturity and wisdom. This is the current of lust and sexual arousal. It may potentially indicate an interest or involvement in alternative sexual practices such as BDSM[88] and other manifestations of the kink community. With the help of oceanic Ruis, it is possible to transform traumas in healing ways.

Positive passions are found with this *fid*'s celestial current. Love of life and of all life forms, deep devotion to deity in a manner akin to *Bhakti* yoga within Hinduism, and sacred sexuality may manifest when this current appears. There may be anger, but it's turned to cleansing and constructive purposes through emotional work within the cauldrons, or through self-reflection and examination, often generating involvement in social activism and a deep desire for justice, or expressing that anger through healing work. The celestial current of Ruis gives powerful focus and energy to overcome difficulties.

Where this *fid* appears, there may be a deep seated fear of loss of control that can lead to challenging and difficult interactions with others, particularly in group situations where control may be the object of great struggle.

In a more positive vein, Ruis can also suggest that there is love and positive passion surrounding the situation. Rather than

---

[88] The acronym BDSM can stand for a spectrum of activities; bondage and discipline, domination and submission, and sadism and masochism are the most common readings of the term.

obsession, it may indicate a useful focus that gives power to pursue difficult tasks and bring them to completion. When danger arises, anger can be channeled to protective action. Anger itself can be cleansing and a powerful incentive to work for justice in the situation, so take care not to read anger as a solely negative phenomenon.

Ruis can be used for healing work in situations of recovery from sexual abuse, rape, and sexual trauma. Tempered with other *feda*, it can be helpful in work with emotional extremes, helping to redirect anger and rage to more useful and constructive channels. The erotic and sexual energies of this *fid* can also be helpful in healing work with reproductive organs, in cases of sexually transmitted diseases, and in healing work on sexuality and sexual self-identity.

Question: What am I passionate about? How do my passions help or harm me?

Linked Concepts:
Shame, anger, embarrassment, jealousy, the warrior's frenzy, loss of control, obsession, sexuality and eroticism or their abuse, guilt, ecstatic trance.

The Fourth Aicme:
A O U E I

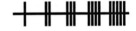

Ailm - A
Cry
Keyword: Inception
Word Ogams:
MM: *ardam íachta* - loudest of groanings, loudest of groans
MO: *tosach frecrai* - beginning of an answer
CC: *tosach garmae* - beginning of expressions, beginning of calling

Color: *alad* - piebald, speckled (spotted black & white)

Tree: *giúis* - fir, *ochtach* - pine
Bird: *aidhircleóg* - lapwing

Note:
Planet: Astraea

Ailm is the "ah!" cry of birth and death.[89] It is a *fid* of initiation, where birth and death are one, a passage from one state to another. Its keyword is inception and it indicates beginnings. Where Beith indicates primacy and the importance of what comes first, Ailm is beginning in its purest form. It is origin and creation. As birth results in a new life in the physical world, death is considered a birth into the Otherworld and the realm of the ancestors.

The *fid* also suggests the rush of epiphany; the "a-ha!" moment of discovery that Coll's search for *imbas* leads us to. It is the beginning of understanding and the beginning of an answer, implying that there is much further to go before a fullness of understanding and the wisdom of Coll is achieved. Initiation is a process of incubation and birth, both hazardous and rewarding. Like labor and birth, if something goes wrong in the process, death may result, whether physical, psychological or spiritual.

The *fid* is also associated with pregnancy and birth, similar to Beith's links with children, but this *fid* is more closely related to the actual physical process of conception as the initiation of life. It also deals with the period between conception and birth, and so is a *fid* of deep incubation and hidden growth that bursts forth in a blaze of inspiration. It is the danger and necessity of labor that results in the birth of something new, even if that labor is painful and exhausting.

Astraea is an asteroid that manifests in following things through stubbornly to their conclusion, for good or ill. Both birth and death are inexorable processes; both of them are painful and both must be followed through to completion. The initiatory birth/death cycle of Ailm is aided and pushed by the tenacity of Astraea, giving the strength to hold on and see the transformation through to its logical and necessary conclusion. It is a reminder that Ailm's initiatory energies sometimes require enough stubbornness to hang on until the bitter end.

---

[89] McManus, 1991, 38 says that the word Ailm's meaning is uncertain, though all the word ogams point to a meaning of the "ah" sound itself, hence my use of "Cry" for its definition.

The color *alad* means speckled and is translated as "piebald" in the *Auraicept na n-Éces*. One of the northeast winds is speckled, *aladh*, as well. According to Wright-Popescul, the Scottish Gaelic word *àladh* carries a variety of meanings including speckled, variegated, nursing a child, wisdom, skill, craft, malice, and lie. In Irish, *álad* can also mean wound, spite, or ill-feeling,[90] though *áladh* also refers to the color but is not much used now.[91] Old Irish *alad* is much more specifically piebald or variegated, without as much of a broad range of meaning.[92] Piebald is usually a color associated with black and white spotted horses.

The evergreen conifers pine and fir -- *ochtach* and *giúis* -- are listed as the trees for this *fid*. They appear to be seen as interchangeable in a linguistic sense and in the lore, and the Old Irish word *giús* seems to apply equally to both tree species. Old Irish *ochtach* is also used interchangeably, with additional associations to spears or lances, and the poles that support houses. Conifer resin was used to pitch and seal seams between boards in boats or anything else that needed waterproofing. It was sometimes burned as a fumigant or incense.

Saining or purifying mothers and newborn babies was done in the Orkneys by whirling a flaming pine candle three times around their bed. The wood was so resinous that slips of it burned brightly like a candle, and such pine candles were in use until oil lamps became more economical. The needles and buds of these trees are high in vitamin C and have been used in the past as part of a tea for scurvy. Healing ointments were also made from the pitch of pine or fir.[93]

The physical processes of birth and death are indicated with the chthonic current of Ailm. Pregnancy can be indicated. If there is a serious or terminal illness involved, death may be near, particularly if Úr also appears. Children and the cycle of life are a part of this current, along with an emphasis on the origins of things. If children are not specifically indicated, this current may refer to a family as a whole, and a new addition through adoption or other less traditional methods.

Ailm's oceanic current is the brink of discovery, waiting on the threshold of something new and vital. While it is a part of a process of initiation, this is the dark time of incubation between

[90] Wright-Popescul, 1997, 72
[91] Dineen, 1927, 34
[92] DIL, 36
[93] Darwin, 1996, 64

conception and birth. It may indicate a long process of labor, or hidden growth moving beneath the surface. When the oceanic current appears, you may be in the midst of a passage from one place or state of being to another. This passage cannot be rushed, but must be waited out patiently and doggedly, even if the wait is difficult, painful, and challenging.

The celestial current refers to beginnings of all kinds. It may be the inception of a project or a business, the start of a new path in life, or the beginning of a new cycle of experiences. It is the pure force of creation, and the epiphany in moments of blinding revelation. Spiritual enlightenment may happen in an instant, but remember that you'll still have to do the dishes tomorrow. The work of maintaining spiritual realization and developing it into wisdom takes time and patience. Remember that an initiation is only a beginning, now matter how energizing the experience.

When Ailm appears in divination, a new thing is coming into being. Someone may be pregnant or about to give birth, or you may be starting a new project, full of energy and the initial spark of enthusiasm. Your creativity is strong here, and you may find yourself on the brink of discovery, an epiphany waiting to happen.

Spiritually, you may be at the point of initiation, waiting in pregnant pause for that step over the threshold into a new life. It is possible that you are being presented with opportunities for new knowledge and understanding, or beginning a course of study, whether spiritual or mundane. An idea you've received may be at a point where incubation, persistence, and endurance are necessary, nurturing its growth for the birth to come, or it may be ready now to bring forth into manifestation.

Ailm is a good *fid* for healing work with children, and to help with labor and giving birth. With Gort, it is a good *fid* to use for dealing with pregnancies in all their phases. Its energy can also help with expulsion of things that have been blocking healing, and it is useful to work with this *fid* when beginning new phases of treatment of longstanding problems.

Question: What work am I starting? How am I being initiated?

Linked Concepts:
Birth and death as beginnings, the cycle of life, origination, inception, conception, creation, children, pregnancy, initial understanding, epiphany.

Onn - O
Foundation - Wheel
Keyword: Movement
Word Ogams:
MM: *congnaid ech* - helper of horses i.e. the wheels of a chariot,
wounder of horses; hastener of horses (horsewhip)
MO: *féthem soíre* - smoothest of work; smoothest of
craftsmanship
CC: *lúth fían* - desire of the fianna i.e. heather, sustaining
equipment of warrior or hunting bands

Color: *odhar* - dun
Tree: *aiteann, conasg* - furze, whin, gorse, *fuinseog* - ash,
froach - heather
Bird: *odoroscrach* - scrat

Note:
Planet: Urania

The name Onn may be derived from the Old Irish word *fonn*,[94]
referring to the sole of the foot, a foundation -- for instance the
base of a chariot, -- or a wanderer. As such, it is both a
foundation and the motive force. Its meaning of "wheel" is based
on its word ogam of "helper of horses" with its gloss of "the
wheels of a chariot." Onn is anything in motion. It is the journey
we take in our lives, and the journeys we make through the
Otherworlds as part of our spiritual pursuits. It is travel in the
physical world as well.

This *fid* addresses the paths we take and the choices we
make as we move through life. It concerns our direction and our
intentions as we decide what to do and where to go. It is also

---

[94] McManus, 1991, 38 gives Old Irish *onn* as meaning "ash," though DIL, 491 says
it may be pine or furze, and ash is given as a questionable tertiary meaning. This
is another case where I side with Meroney, 1949, 33, who feels that the name Onn
is derived from either *fonn*, a foundation, or *fonnad*, the frame of a chariot. In
DIL, 325, *fonn* is the sole of the foot, a foundation, and soil or ground. *Fonnad*, as
well as being the frame of a chariot, also refers to swift motion and movement in
DIL 326. With all this in mind, foundation or wheel both seem to be reasonable
interpretations and I felt no need to use the questionable definition of ash.

those things that help make the journey easier or quicker, as a goad urges a horse to greater speed when properly applied.

Urania is the muse of astrology, and as an asteroid it represents the ability to discern and understand the patterns and movement of the skies. It apprehends the great wheel of the stars and interprets their motion as the journey of every life. The planets were called "wanderers" by the Greeks to contrast them with the fixed stars, and Urania expresses the energies of Onn as the wanderer, ever in motion, ever exploring, ever seeking understanding through the spectrum of experience.

Odhar or dun, a dull yellow brown color, is associated with this *fid*. Its color definition ranges through pale, yellowish, khaki, drab, sallow, and brown. This color is associated with the west wind in the compass rose, and in the tale of *The Settling of the Manor of Tara*, Fintan mac Bóchra says the west has "her learning, her foundation, her teaching, her alliance, her judgment, her chronicles, her counsels, her stories, her history, her science, her comeliness, her eloquence, her beauty, her blushing, her bounty, her abundance, her wealth..."[95] Foundations are a part of the core meaning of Onn, and so the lore about this wind and its color fits well with the *fid*.

Three different "trees" are associated with Onn. Ash was covered in the section on Nin. Furze, gorse, and whin are all names for the same thorny shrub. It was a valuable source of food for horses and cattle and it was considered of such value that one Irish folk saying states "gold under furze, silver under rushes, and famine under heather." In some parts of Ireland the furze was used as a May bush rather than the hawthorn, and in parts of County Claire it was preferred to the hawthorn for that purpose. Furze burns furiously when dry, and was used as part of the purifying fires between which cattle were driven as they were sent out to the shielings at the beginning of grazing season.[96]

Heather, despite its great usefulness in many areas of life, is frequently associated with poverty. It grows on over-grazed and deforested land where little else will establish itself. Heather was often used for thatching roofs, but it was heavier than many of the preferred materials, and caught fire easily. It tends to be very durable, however, and some thatchers say that a good heather thatch will last up to a hundred years.[97] Heather roots were used to make very strong rope, however, which was used for

---

[95] Wright-Popescul, 1997, 56
[96] Mac Coitir, 2003, 92-93
[97] Milliken & Bridgewater, 2004, 86

many purposes. Straight young heather shoots were used to create beds that were said to be softer and more pleasant than feather beds, and the scent of their flowers was believed to induce a good sleep. Heather was also used to flavor ale and mead, and was used as a tonic for coughs, consumption, depression and other ailments.[98]

Like the sole of the foot or the platform of a chariot, chthonic Onn is a foundation in motion. There is stability within even when the outside world is moving at breakneck speed. Swift motion or vehicles may be a part of this current; tend to your car or truck if you haven't done regular maintenance on it recently. Travel is often indicated with this current, whether local or foreign. There may be a long stay in a distant place. Movement meditations such as yoga and martial arts are also found with this current, centering the mind and spirit while the body is in motion.

With the oceanic current, Onn's travel becomes pilgrimage -- journey undertaken for emotional and spiritual reasons. Being the seeker is a part of the pilgrim's task in journeying to the holy places. These journeys are not mundane, but affect the traveler spiritually. A change of heart or profound realization may result from a journey taken. This current is about movement and what is in motion in a person's life.

Onn's celestial current can indicate a need for or regular engagement with spiritual and Otherworld journeying. Control and confidence in Otherworld situations is suggested. The *fid* may also point to a need for contact with guiding or guardian spirits, like the white stag or hart who leads the traveler through the mists and into the Otherworld realms beyond. If you are unfamiliar with which spirits aid you, this may be a call to find them and learn from them. What is learned on these voyages may vary, but the need is certainly there.

When Onn appears in a reading, it can indicate that you need to examine the direction of your life. It may mean you may be about to take a trip. The *fid* may also indicate internal motion or journeys; changes of mind or of heart, turning thoughts over to examine them, or the use of active and physical methods of meditation such as yoga, walking, or martial arts forms. I have also often seen it suggesting a need to turn within for a spiritual journey, moving through the mists into the Otherworlds with the aid of deities and spirits.

---

[98] Darwin, 1996, 105-109

Onn can also indicate confidence when it appears, as the warrior in the chariot is confident in her balance and her ability to control the situation. The warrior's charioteer is able to guide the horses on the path and do her tasks with great skill as she moves swiftly and efficiently in her purpose.

Magically this *fid* is a powerful influence for physical travel, to begin or protect a journey, as well as being useful for Otherworld journeys. Its implications suggest using it to work for smooth and trouble-free travel, even in difficult situations. It can aid in bringing movement to stagnant places and help shift blockages in your life.

As a healing *fid*, Onn is good for work with feet and legs, as well as for moving energy. It can aid in breaking blockages and getting things flowing physically and emotionally. In situations where limbs or joints are stiff, it can help smooth out movement and improve range of motion. If you need encouragement for exercise to aid your health, this is a good *fid* to use.

Question: Where is my journey taking me? How do I follow my path?

Linked Concepts:
Travel, journeys, movement in static situations, spirit journey work, Otherworld workings, guidance and guiding spirits, foundations, the founding of new projects.

Úr - U
Soil
Keyword: Death
Word Ogams:
MM: *úaraib adbaib* - in cold dwellings
MO: *sílad cland* - propagation of plants, seeding up of plants, growing of plants
CC: *forbbaíd ambí* - shroud of a lifeless one, shroud of the lifeless i.e. soil
Additional word ogam: *gruidem dál* - most prompt of meetings
Additional word ogam: *guiremh dál* - nearest of meetings

Color: *usghda* -"resinous" (amber)

Tree: *sceach* - thorn, *froech* - heather
Bird: *uiseóg* - lark

Note: 𝄢 ♩

Planet: Earth

Although Úr doesn't come at the end of the ogam[99], it is the *fid* of death, fate, and finality. It is a *fid* of endings and represents the knowledge that all endings are simply doors to new beginnings. The early Continental Celts were said to believe that death was the middle of a long life, and so death held little fear for them. Our culture regards death as something to be dreaded and avoided at all costs, but ultimately it comes to everyone, regardless of talents, rank, or station.

This *fid* deals with issues of death and grieving, as well as the cycles of life and death, but it also deals with deaths that are more metaphorical and the passing away of circumstances or situations in life. It suggests anything that is inescapable or inevitable, anything that cannot be cheated, finessed, or gotten around.

Because Úr is the soil, it can also be taken as the physical body and the physical world around us in all its imminence. It is the embodiment and physical manifestation of spiritual principles and practices. Úr is the land itself, the earth upon which we walk every day, and the place in which we bury our dead. Its link with the land also brings it into close accord with the local land spirits of the place you live.

Úr is quite literally the Earth and as such it's both the ground of being from which we arise, and the place of our ultimate rest in death. It's the substance of our bodies and their disintegration back into the cosmos to continue the cycles of life and death. Psychologically, death is central to our spiritual understanding of bodies as mortal. Astrologically and emotionally, Earth is the center of our cosmos and our understanding of ourselves as human.

In Old Irish, the world *úscada*, rendered as *usghda* in the ogam tracts, means greasy, resin-colored, or resinous. It is not associated with any of the winds, but from "resinous" we can infer an amber type color. Resin is the thick, sticky sap of

---

[99] The vowel sequence of this *aicme* is determined by the position of sound in the mouth, moving from the back of the tongue with AH (Ailm) to the front with EE (Idad). The OO of Úr falls in the middle of this sonic sequence.

coniferous trees or other plants, and many incenses are made from resins. These include frankincense, myrrh, amber, dragon's blood, copal, and pine or fir. Most conifer resins, at least when wet, tend toward the same range of colors as amber, encompassing yellow-browns, yellows, reddish browns and creamy colors. I feel that defining *usghda* as "amber" within the color ogam is not unreasonable.

Both heather and thorn trees have been addressed in the material on other *feda* -- heather in Onn, whitethorn in h-Úath, and blackthorn in Straif. These multiple associations once again give the ogam student broad permission to interpret a local tree ogam as they see fit within the boundaries of traditional insular Celtic lore and local folk ways.

The chthonic current of Úr can be taken quite literally as caves, graves, burial, and the earth. It is soil and physicality, bodies, and corpses. If a spirit is unable to detach from its body after death, a haunting may be suggested. It's also the idea of our mortality and limitations, humanity, and the endings of things, whether relationships or ideals. Land spirits are a part of this current. Physical offerings and flesh for sacrifice may be indicated when this fid is the oracle for a ritual. Because of earth's heaviness, stagnation within a situation may be indicated. This current emphasizes the need to let go of what has passed and move forward. It is important to remember that physical deaths are not the only kind -- relationships die, as do businesses, institutions, hopes, and ideals.

The process of dying is associated with Úr's oceanic current. Grief, disintegration, and release are often found here, as they are worked through after loss. Ghosts and spirits of the dead or the ancestors may be indicated, though why they are a part of the situation may require a look at the surrounding *feda*. The cycles of life, death, and rebirth express themselves through this current, with the hope of reunion or of movement through different bodies and forms in an afterlife or through reincarnation. This current emphasizes the need to let go of what has passed and move forward.

The celestial current brings a sense of inevitability to a situation. A situation may seem inescapable or fated, for good or ill. Finality and endings of all kinds are found here. Memories of the dead may be heavy on the mind, or they might instead be bringing helpful and hopeful messages to the living. In some cases, this current suggests an embodiment of spiritual principles, bringing them from a realm of intellectual theory to physical practice and grounding them in daily life.

In divination, Úr may signal a death, but most often it means the end of something, or a necessary letting-go. It may be a physical object, a relationship, or a way of viewing the world. Rather than the transformation of Straif, this *fid* suggests that the issue is ending, its energy and physical presence passing out of your life rather than becoming something else. It may advise leaving behind a difficult relationship or presage the death of a hope you have cherished.

When drawn as part of divination during ritual, it may indicate the need for some kind of flesh offering, some fragment of animal life-energy. This could indicate anything in a range between a bit of meat, fowl, or fish from your meal to a few drops of your blood from a pinprick given to fire or water. In the wilderness, it could easily entail the offering of found feathers or bones, returned to the earth in some way.

This *fid* is powerful magic for ending things and for cutting away what is unwanted in your life. Its power is finality and laying things to rest. It can also be used to aid communication with the land spirits in hopes of gaining their favor or cooperation or when clearing land or planning new construction in an undisturbed place.

The presence of the spirits of the dead, in each of this *fid*'s currents, takes different manifestations in each one. The chthonic current suggests a spirit's continued clinging to the body, unable to accept death. In this case Úr itself may be used to lay the spirit to rest. It's also suitable in situations where restless spirits inhabit a place, sending them on to where they belong rather than allowing them to disturb the living. The oceanic current manifests more in a spirit who may need to pass on a final message before departing. The celestial suggests a living person clinging to the spirit of the dead, unable to let go of them and fully grieve the loss. This situation might be dealt with using Gort's connection with healing rest, and the passion of Ruis to help the person accept the intensity of their grief and move through it. The celestial current may also refer to a spirit who returns sometimes years later to act as a guide during times of need.

The image of body as clay gives this *fid* a powerful use for healing skin and flesh and for working with muscle problems. Its death-associated energies can aid in killing cancerous cells. It's also a good *fid* for working with those who are dying, allowing them to go peacefully to their rest. Hospice work can be aided by Úr's energies, and it can be strengthening for those working with the dying and those left behind.

Question: What in my life is passing away? What must I leave behind?

Linked Concepts:
Graves and graveyards, burial, grieving, cycles of life and death, ghosts or hauntings, the end of cycles, inevitability and the inescapable, the body, physicality, embodiment of spiritual principles, the land or the earth, land spirits, caves or caverns, memories of the dead.

Edad - E
Amanita
Keyword: Vision
Word Ogams:
MM: *érgnaid fid* - discerning tree, distinguished wood
MO: *commaín carat* - exchange of friends, synonym for a friend
CC: *brátahir beithi* - brother of birch
Additional word ogam: *aercaid fer no fid* - plant or tree of harm
Additional word ogam: *erchra fer* - plant of destruction
Additional word ogam: *clesach uisce* - tricky in water, i.e. *éiccne*,
a variety of salmon
Color: *erc* - red-speckled
Tree: *iúr* - yew, *crann fír* - test-tree, *crann creathach* - aspen
Bird: *eala* - swan

Note:
Planet: Neptune

Edad is a word that has no meaning in Irish, but the word ogams and color ogam can be used as a guide to potential meanings. Because there is no actual traditional meaning, I have chosen to associate it with the *Amanita muscaria* mushroom, also called the Fly Agaric. This is the very easily recognizable red mushroom with white speckles on its cap, and the color ogam associated with the letter translates as "red-speckled." Additionally, *A. muscaria* grows in a symbiotic relationship with the birch tree, and can thus be interpreted as a "brother of birch," which is one of the word ogams. This fungus is well known for its association with vision seeking, being used by Siberian shamans and other spirit workers throughout its circumpolar range around the globe.

Seen in this light, the *fid* can be associated with divination and dreaming, and the altered states of consciousness in which communication with spirits occurs. Rather than being the Otherworld journey itself, like Onn, it is the tool set used to make the journey. Edad is the *fid* of enlightenment and the things needed to find that state.

The *Amanita* is used as a tool for discerning truth by those who ingest it in ritual and it produces a profound intoxication if used properly -- but can be destructive or even deadly if used improperly. Without proper training in its use, ingesting any entheogen can be dangerous. Don't take the use of it as a metaphor in this book as any kind of encouragement or permission to experiment with the fungus physically. With this *fid*, the *Amanita* is a metaphor for any vehicle that brings you to the Otherworld, where information can be gained from the *Sídhe* or similar spirits or Otherworldly beings. It is the coracle or skin boat for the *immram* or the sweathouse where visions are sought. Meditation, dream incubation, sensory deprivation, and other methods can be used with much less danger to person and psyche, but the message remains the same when Edad appears.

Erc, the color associated with this *fid*, is translated as "red-speckled." The Old Irish word itself, however, has a wide range of meaning. Along with red-speckled, it can mean dark red. It refers to red or red-eared cattle. It is also a reference to speckled fish like trout and salmon; both the cattle and the speckled fish point to an Otherworldly link, as these fish are the vehicles of wisdom in many insular tales, and red-eared cattle are almost always supernatural in origin. *Erc* can refer to heaven or the heavens, perhaps for the mottling of clouds in the sky. *Erc* is sometimes defined as a lizard, a reptile, or a bee. It may also be defined as falsehood or deceit.[100] This last offers a caution against the illusory aspects of this *fid*.

Neptune is the planet that rules trance and intoxication. It rules illusion and the skills to discern one's way through the

---

[100] DIL, 278

mists. It moves beyond the impetus to explore mystery found in Uranus and takes us into the oceanic depths of the psyche and the Otherworlds just as Edad aids us in our journey, giving us a vehicle for our voyage. Improperly used, both Neptune and Edad can lead us down false paths and into addiction, destruction and death. With wisdom and moderation, they help us on the path to enlightenment.

Iúr, the yew, is one of the trees associated with this *fid*. The yew is very frequently found in old graveyards throughout Ireland and Scotland. It is one of the longest-lived trees in the world, and is thus often associated with immortality and perhaps because of this with the hope of eternal life after death. The tree itself is very toxic, and its wood is used for making bows -- another practice that links it with traditions surrounding death. It is yew wood that was used in the practice of *fidlanna*[101] or "divination by wood" in the *Tochmarc Étaíne*, after Étaín was kidnapped. Ogams were carved on four yew rods and used to determine where she had been taken.

In *The Settling of the Manor of Tara*, the ancient shapeshifter Fintan mac Bóchra planted a yew berry and lived so long that he saw it grow to shelter one hundred men before it died of old age.[102] The Yew of Ross was one of the five great sacred trees of Ireland, immortalized in a poem from the *Metrical Dindshenchas* praising its strength and value. It is called "best of beings... a stout, strong god... beauty's honor... spell of knowledge" in this poem.[103]

The other tree associated with Edad is the aspen. It is discussed under the entry for Ceirt.

Edad's chthonic current suggests caution about interpretation or practice. It may counsel an examination of the tools and techniques you use for your visionary work. Careful discrimination between illusion and reality is suggested. It can also refer to the tools of divination, or the vehicles used in your journeying work, whether they are physical, psychological, or spiritual. Vision inducing rituals may be a necessary part of your situation, particularly where vision work has practical applications in daily life.

The oceanic current cautions against the dangers of visionary work: illusion, intoxication and addiction. Approach trance and altered states of consciousness carefully when they

---

[101] From *fidlann*, "a piece of wood used in divination", DIL, 305
[102] Mac Coitir, 2003, 140
[103] Mac Coitir, 2003, 144-145

are necessary, for they can be dangerous as well as enlightening. This *fid*'s appearance may indicate a need for work within trance or altered states, and can mark a point where dissolution of self becomes part of ritual for good or ill. Seeking visions may be advisable. Oceanic Edad may refer to the process of divination itself.

Celestial Edad suggests the possibility of enlightenment through the applied practice of vision seeking and dream incubation. It can refer to the influence of the *Sídhe* and similar Otherworldly beings -- the presence of deity within an Otherworld setting may be strong. Communication and establishing relationships with spirits through Otherworld journeying, trance, dream, or vision work can be indicated here.

In divination Edad often appears when you are being enjoined to examine the tools you use to access Otherworldly wisdom. Perhaps it is time to learn a new skill, or to pay closer attention to your dreams or those moments when you receive impressions from spirit or your inner self. It is also a call for caution and discernment, for discrimination between illusion and reality. Examine your insights and work to understand new ways to make them useful in the physical world.

While there is no firm evidence that *A. muscaria* was used in Ireland or Scotland,[104] there is enough to suggest that Edad in magic can be used to aid in creating relationships with the *Sídhe* and other spirits, and for the blessing and proper use of tools for vision seeking practices. It can be used to enhance dreamwork and meditation as well.

As a healing *fid*, Edad is important in work where the healing is done through dream incubation and the interpretation of dreams and visions, as well as healing on a spiritual or soul level, when wounds go deeper than the physical body. It can also be useful in work where the healer makes journeys into the Otherworlds as part of the healing process.

Question: How do I see the world? What gifts do my insights bring?

Linked Concepts:
Divination, dreams, contracts, and relationships with spirits, vision-seeking, intoxication, discernment, enlightenment and the

---

[104] The literary evidence is discussed at length in the *Shaman's Drum* article *Speckled Snake, Brother of Birch:* Amanita Muscaria *Motifs in Celtic Literature* by Erynn Rowan Laurie and Timothy White, 1997, issue 44, pp 53-65.

tools used to reach it, communication with the *Sídhe* and Otherworldly beings, connections with the Otherworld.

Idad - I
Age
Keyword: Memory
Word Ogams:
MM: *sinem fedo* - oldest of woods, oldest tree, oldest letter, older than letters
MO: *caínem sen* - fairest of the ancients
CC: *lúth lobair* - energy of an infirm person
Additional word ogam: *crinam feada no cláinem* - most withered of wood, crookedest of wood
Additional word ogam: *cáined sen no aileam áis* - lovely wood, most pleasant of growth
Additional word ogam: *claidem* - sword.

Color: *irfind* - "very-white"
Tree: *iúr, ibar* - yew, *crann soirb* - service tree, *edeand* - ivy, *aiteal* - juniper
Bird: *illat* - eagle

Note: 𝄢
Planet: Saturn

The word Idad has no translation in Irish, but it is most often associated with the yew and with concepts of age and longevity. I associate it strongly with the ancestors, history, and tradition, and for these reasons I interpret it as Age and its keyword as memory. The elders in our society are our link to the past, whether that past is of our personal family, our land, or our culture. We too will age and someday become elders ourselves. Idad is the *fid* that teaches us the lessons of age.

Aging does not always or necessarily imply infirmity. When you are old, it means you've survived and endured where many others haven't. Wine aged is wine ripened to fullness. Idad is a *fid* of permanence, survival, and endurance as well as of lore and tradition, for tradition and culture survive beyond the physical bodies of their carriers. To me, it also carries a connotation of reincarnation, and of remembering or bringing things back from life to life as we pass from form to form. Idad links the generations, from elders to infants, over and over. It is the *fid* of legacy and inheritance, and an expression of what we hope to leave behind when we die.

As Idad expresses age and the wisdom of cultural stability and the ancestors, Saturn rules tradition, history, and the wisdom of age. Saturn sets boundaries for propriety and structure, just as tradition plays this role in societies. It defines and supports individual, family, and cultural strength through the unchanging depth and endurance of connection to the past, for good or ill. Where Idad is the end of the ogam sequence, Saturn was the end of the visible solar system, defining the boundaries of the ancient cosmos.

The color *irfind* or "very-white" is an intensification of Beith's *bán*. White is often associated with deific presence or with purity and great supernatural power. *Find*, a word for pale, white, or fair, is the same word from which the name of the hero Fionn (fair) is derived.

There are several trees associated with Idad, just as there are with many of the other feda. Yew was discussed under the entry for Edad. The ivy was described under Gort.

Juniper or *aiteal* is a tree very strongly linked with purification. It was used in Ireland and Scotland for fumigations and purifications of homes and cattle. In the *Carmina Gadelica*, charms are given for ritual harvest to use juniper ("mountain yew") as a charm against drowning, danger, and fear. It was believed that no house where juniper was kept could catch fire.[105]

Crann soirb, the service tree, is a European fruit tree related to the rowan, with oblong or pear-shaped fruits and leaves that are grouped very like rowan leaves. It is native to southern Europe, North Africa, and western Asia, but frequently planted in central Europe for its fruit. The fruit is very sour but edible, particularly after frost, and is sometimes used to make beer.[106] It's extremely uncommon in North America, and virtually unknown. One rare and unique variety, the Arran Service Tree, grows only in Scotland. It's possible that this is the variety referred to in the tree ogam.[107]

Age, longevity, and immortality are all expressions of the chthonic current of Idad. Things that are permanent or have

---

[105] Mac Coitir, 2003, 148
[106] Phillips, 1978, 198
[107] Milliken & Bridgewater, 2004, 28

deep cultural roots are found here. Endurance is also strongly indicated by this current. Elders of different kinds may be involved when this current appears: grandparents, spiritual elders, or older authority figures. There may be a physical inheritance of some sort. This current can also show you where physical boundaries lie, marking the ends of a place or time of influence. Illness and infirmity can also be indicated by this current of Idad, particularly those illnesses that come with aging.

With the oceanic current, we see an expression of the bond between generations. This may be through lore passed from elders to children, the oral traditions of a culture, or a study of the lore by students in academic or other situations where learning is important. Transmission of tradition and sharing of lore manifests with this current. Maturation and ripening are a part of the shifting oceanic current of Idad as well. If other influences support the reading, there may be a reference here to past lives or reincarnation.

The celestial current speaks of memory and history and of the gifts these things give us. It's the survival of tradition, and the positive structure given by traditional beliefs and societies. This current can refer to the ancestors generally, or to specific individual ancestors; in either case, these are ancestors who have passed into the Otherworld, not elders who are still living.

When Idad appears in a reading, it may be pointing you to older sources of information, whether stories from your elders, books of lore, or links drawn in previous lives. It challenges us to look at our past as we determine our future, and to lay foundations of wisdom for the generations to come. It can indicate the permanence or endurance of a condition or situation that you have created or that has been forming around you. There are both positive and negative implications to this, and it may be that advice is needed from others who have gone through similar situations before you.

Magically, Idad can help you link with the spirits of the ancestors, or with your own ancestors, whether physical or spiritual. It may be of assistance in doing past life work, examining previous turns on the wheel for the lessons they can impart to our current lives.

The healing energies of Idad are good for working with the elderly, and for helping people prepare for the end stages of their lives. Its use may aid memory in those whose minds are failing. It can also help those who are aging endure the inevitable breakdown of bodies with dignity and grace.

Question: How does my past make me who I am today? How do I understand my past to decide whom I become?

Linked Concepts:
History, lore, tradition, old tales, venerability, the past, age and aging, elders, the ancestors, endurance, permanence, reincarnation or past lives, survival.

The Forfeda
The Extra Letters

Since I don't work with the *forfeda* but some people do, I've included some notes about them here. The information given above on the original ogam can set the pattern for your own personal work and research about this *aicme*, should you choose to pursue your studies in this direction. Information in the popular Pagan press regarding these letters varies wildly, and scholarly and traditional sources should, as always, be given precedent when working out divinatory meanings and magical or ritual associations.

Some ogam students find that using the *forfeda* enriches their experience with the ogam. Many of them would never dream of doing an ogam reading without them. Others find them problematic at best. These additional letters are not found in any of the stone inscriptions, and were only rarely used in the manuscripts. While they were added one at a time at a much later date than the original ogam letters were developed, they were certainly a part of the medieval ogam tradition and are a legitimate part of the system. The *Auraicept na n-Éces* includes them in some of the ogam lists, but ignores them in others. It appears to me that even the medieval ogamists didn't agree about their use.

It is my hope that those who work with these additional letters will offer their experiences and knowledge regarding them to the community as they become more comfortable with their use.

Ebad - Ea/Ch (É)
Salmon

Tree: elecampane, woodbine, aspen
MM: *snámchaín feda*: fair-swimming letter, best swimming letter
MO: *cosc lobair*: admonishing of an infirm person, correction of a sick man, desire of an invalid, feast of an invalid
CC: *caínem éco*: fairest fish, most lovely of salmon
Other word ogams for this fid: most bouyant of wood, "that it is a kenning for the great *bratan*, for *é* (salmon) is a name for *bratan* (salmon)"
Meanings: carrier of wisdom, vehicle of inspiration, spiritual nourishment

Ór - Oi/Th (Ó)
Gold

Tree: spindle tree, heather
MM: *sruithem aicde*: most venerable substance, most venerable of materials
MO: *lí crotha*: splendor of form, hue of ruddiness
Meanings: worth, value, wealth

Uillend - Ui/Ph (Y)
Elbow

Tree: ivy, woodbine, honeysuckle
MM: *túthmar fid*: fragrant tree, fragrant wood
MO: *cubat oll*: great elbow, great cubit
Other word ogams for this fid: juicy wood
Meanings: flexibility, change, measurement

Pín or Iphín - Ia/Pe (P)
Honey

Tree: pine, gooseberry
MM: *milsem fedo*: sweetest tree
MO: *amram mlais*: most wonderful taste
Meanings: sweetness of life, divine influences

Emancholl - Ae/X (X)
Twin-C, Twin Hazels

Tree: witch hazel
MM: *lúad sáethaig*: groan of a sick person, expression of a weary one "ach!"
MO: *mol galraig*: groan of a sick person
Meanings: illness, intensification of other fiodh

CHAPTER 3
Working with the Feda

Each *fid* of the ogam has a variety of meanings like the range of color in a spectrum. The meanings of the names themselves are the basis of our work and interpretations, but they are shaded and informed by the word-ogams or *briatharogam* -- the phrases associated with them in the traditional materials. Each *fid* also has personal meanings that are influenced by our own developing associations that gather in complex webs as we learn to work with them over time.

Before we can successfully perform divination or magic with the ogam, we need to learn the meanings of the *feda* and understand how they relate to each other and to our lives. Understanding requires study and meditation, working with the ogam regularly to fix the basic meanings in your mind, and examining your impressions about the traditional meanings and associations for their resonances in your life and the world around you. All of the exercises I present here are useful for gaining understanding so that you can use the ogam for any purpose; divinatory, magical, or spiritual.

Achieving understanding is important before starting to work actively with the ogam. With a flawed understanding, you may be calling upon powers and energies that you don't intend to call on or completely comprehend. Some of the *feda* must be approached with great caution and a solid understanding of which of their several meanings is the center of your focus to avoid mixed signals and unintended magical or ritual results. In divination, an incomplete understanding isn't dangerous so much as potentially confusing. The greater your understanding of the shades of meaning of each *fid*, the clearer your work will be, and the easier it will be to focus on your goals in ritual and magic through their agency. Greater comprehension will bring more clarity in divination as well.

In *Filidecht* the meaning of words is of utmost importance and because the ogam is one of the *Fili*'s tools, a thorough understanding of the meaning of each *fid* is crucial. Words are the root of magic in this tradition and anything less than complete understanding can bring results that are unanticipated or unwanted. Always strive to know precisely what you're working with and why. When you have that depth of understanding, reversing or unweaving an unintended result is much easier to accomplish.

An easy first step toward understanding for most people is to make a series of flash cards out of whatever is available. These are not sacred tools as your working *feda* will be, but are aids for your memory and can be carried with you anywhere and played with in any way that helps you to learn the shapes, names and meanings of each *fid*. They don't have to be anything fancy. Half of a 3x5 card with each *fid*, its name and meanings and its keyword are all you really need. So long as you can read the writing on it, you don't need to worry about how neat it is. If you want to play a little, you can do calligraphy or use paints if that will help fix things in your mind.

Choosing one each week to focus on is a good start with this system. It's best to go in order, from the first of the B *aicme* to the last of the A *aicme*. Don't make all the flash cards at once and don't try to rush the process. Treat each one as a separate learning experience with the *fid* you're working on. Devote some time to looking at the *fid*, understanding where in the sequence of the ogam series it fits, and repeating its Irish name. Say the name aloud as you draw the *fid* on your card. Pronounce it carefully as you write the name and its corresponding English letter beneath the *fid*. Write down its meaning or meanings beneath that, and then its keyword in capital letters. On the back, draw only the *fid* itself, and its corresponding letter, so that you can use it to test your memory as you learn the meanings.

Carry the finished card around with you and look at it frequently during the day to refresh your memory. Repeat its name when you look at it, and tell yourself what its letter is, what it means, and what its keyword is. An additional practice to fix its shape in your mind is to use a whiteboard or other surface to repeatedly draw the shape while intoning its name. Writing the *fid* over and over as you repeat its name fixes it mentally and helps you remember the order of the *feda*.

Sound is another vital aspect of working with the ogam, and this practice should accompany the creation of your *fid* cards. Oral magic is accomplished through proper pronunciation, and the lack of it can turn one word into another, skewing your work in unexpected ways. The words *heal* and *heel* may sound identical, but their meanings are quite different, and this is the sort of thing that can easily happen in an unfamiliar language.

Punning and wordplay are also important parts of magic in Gaelic, and the early Irish were noted for their love of wordplay. To know and understand what words mean helps you avoid magical traps and pitfalls -- Cú Chulainn's *geas*[108] against harming or eating "dog" is a strong case in point. He was named after a dog -- *cú* -- but *madra* is another Irish word for dog. In a late version of the Cú Chulainn cycle of tales, when he accidentally killed an otter, "*madra uisce*" translated as "water dog," he violated that *geas* and it ultimately led to his death. Here you can see the importance of knowing words and their exact meanings, and the importance of their sounds.

To learn the proper sounds of the ogam, work with the pronunciations offered in the glossary. Sing or chant the names, vibrating them strongly, and push their energy outward from the diaphragm. As you do this, visualize the shape of the *fid* you're chanting. Repeat it on long, drawn out notes so that each intonation of the name takes a full breath. Visualize that energy piercing the mists between our world and the Otherworlds, carrying the *fid* with it on your voice. Your work with the Stone on the Belly exercise in chapter 5 will help you prepare for this practice, giving your breath the strength to carry the sound deep into the Otherworlds.

Vowels carry longer, further, and more easily than consonants, though some of the nasals (nGétal, Muin, etc) can vibrate well in the sinuses. When you're vibrating them properly in your head, it may tickle at first, but you can feel the buzz in your skull very clearly. Deeper notes will make your chest vibrate and rattle. This is what you should strive for -- the sound moving powerfully through your body should remind you of standing in

---

[108] A *geas* is a ritual injunction, magical stricture, or taboo that is imposed or practiced for ritual reasons. In many cases, *geasa* are imposed upon someone by outside forces -- this might be a deity, a spirit, or a druid. Violation of *geasa* in the tales is usually, but not always, fatal. In modern practice, some people feel called to take *geasa* upon them. These may be dietary or other ritual taboos that they feel their deities or other spirits are asking them to undertake to maintain magical power, or to purify themselves over a long term for ritual purposes.

Taking on *geasa* is serious business and should not be done by anyone just starting on the CR path. These obligations are taken very seriously by the spirits and deities, and by the community and can have life-changing results. *Geasa* can't be taken and dropped like tastes in music or clothing styles. They're more like getting a tattoo on your spirit -- the mark is going to be there for a lifetime, removing it after the fact is extremely difficult, and the attempt to remove it will probably leave scars. You need to be certain that it is what your deities want. It's very important to consult with others in the CR community as well as with the spirits through divination.

front of a big speaker at a concert, with the drumbeat and bass notes pounding through you. This work is called "vibrating" in many other magical disciplines for exactly this reason.

This creation of sound, in and of itself, is a powerful magical technique for focusing energies on your goals. If you work with music and the suggested tone equivalents from Seán O'Boyle's *The Poet's Secret*, you can sing the names on their note as well, to give added depth to the practice. Playing the note on an instrument can help fix the tone and vibration in your mind, and singing it will fix it in your body physically as well, as the cavities of your body are vibratory chambers within your chest and your head.

It's important to ground those energies after you work with them sonically. Singing them like this puts that energy into your environment, and it's best not to have that vibration around on a long-term basis you unless you are doing specific magical or spiritual work with particular *feda*. To ground the energies, you can imagine the vibrations fading away as sound fades into silence.

An extremely important thing to remember is that O'Boyle's reading of ogam as a harp tablature and musical notation is a system personal to him, as is the scale of notes he worked out. It may or may not be useful to you and can't be described as traditional. If you're a musician, you may find or even create another tonal scale that works better for you than O'Boyle's. The concept is a good one and is a great springboard for other explorations.

Ultimately, whether or not you can carry a tune is immaterial to the process of sound vibration. It's not so much the particular note that you hit in this process that's important as the ability to cause the name of the *fid* to vibrate powerfully somewhere comfortably within your vocal range. The individual notes themselves will only be important if you're a musician and you decide to work with ogam in concert with music as a magical system.

As you create each card and vibrate the *fid's* name, remember to keep reviewing the ones you made before. Give yourself time to go through the whole set of twenty *feda* slowly. It may take six months to a year to really get deeply into your studies; remember that learning to work with the ogam took many years for the original *Filid*. Rushing the process won't help you learn and it might actually impede your progress and lead to confusion. Move at a speed that's comfortable for you, and keep up with the reviews of each previous *fid* as you add a new one. It won't take long before you're able to associate all of the *feda* and their names with their meanings and keywords, and you'll be able to advance to the next level as you seek understanding.

As you go through the process of drawing the entire series of ogam *feda*, start to examine them together and consider how each of them relates to the others around it. What stories do they seem to tell with each other? How does one *fid* influence another in meaning or emotional hue? Does one intensify or mute another? How do they balance one another's extremes? What patterns do you see working between them? Does the sequence of each *aicme* suggest any particular flow to you?

Keep a notebook or other record of your meditations and the connections you draw between the *feda*. Record your emotional responses to them, what you see or sense when you meditate on them, and what happens throughout the day that seems to connect with that *fid's* theme or meaning. Write down the answers to the questions you ask yourself about each *fid*, and contemplate the key questions from this text as well. You'll find that as your understanding increases, the information you gather in your notes will be very useful when you start working with divination, ritual, and magic. Different patterns of meaning emerge as different *feda* combine and your notebook will give you a feel for how to interpret them as they appear.

A useful kinesthetic tool for learning the ogam was invented by the British poet, Robert Graves, in his deeply flawed book, *The White Goddess*. This is his interpretation of the traditional *basogam* or "palm of the hand ogam," where the palm was used as a baseline for indicating a letter, most likely by the number and angle of fingers held across it. Other sources based upon Graves list it as the "finger ogam," but it is not found by that name in the traditional ogam tract lists in the *Auraicept na n-Éces*. He equated each letter with a segment of one of the fingers. The first *aicme* is on the tip of each finger, the second in the initial pad above the first joint, the third *aicme* is below the first joint and the fourth *aicme* below the second joint of each finger above the palm.

Painting each *fid* in its place on the hand with henna or other coloring will make learning easy as you go through and touch each letter, reciting the order of the feda in each *aicme*. Depending on the positioning, most fingers will be touched with the tip of the thumb, but the thumb can be touched with any fingertip that is most comfortable for you.

This modern adaptation of ogam could also be used as a form of finger spelling or to indicate concepts in private communication with other ogam workers. Shapes made by the fingers to indicate a *fid* can be used to direct energy for gesture work in ritual and meditation as you progress in your ogam work, much as *mudras* are used in Hinduism and Buddhism to convey ideas and focus energies. Your choice of fingers and positions in doing this type of work could be used to indicate more than one *fid* at a time for a combination of energies or meanings. When drawing a *fid* in the air or on the body for energy work, try using the finger on which that *fid* is found for a clearer, more precise focus of that energy.

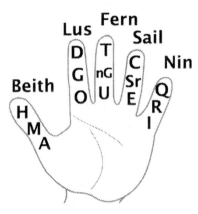

Robert Graves's "Finger Ogam"

Illustration by Bob Daverin

As you practice these exercises and faithfully note your results, your understanding will begin to deepen. In time, you'll want to broaden your work beyond just the basic sounds, shapes, and interrelationships. The energies of the ogam can be useful for healing work, for instance. To fix the ogam's healing associations into your mind, try drawing each *fid* on your body in water on the parts that each *fid*'s energy affects. Intone the name of the *fid* as you do so, and project its energy into your body there, observing its effects. Try to feel how the activity changes your body's energy flow and its emotional state. Is it warming or cooling, energizing or enervating, comforting or irritating? Do those reactions change with the time of day or the season of the year? Do they change depending on what you've had to eat or drink? Do some things intensify your reactions to this exercise or the individual *feda*, while others decrease or dull them?

After you have done any energy flow exercise, it's very important to let the *fid*'s power drain away, just as water drains from a sieve. This is particularly necessary with *feda* like h-Úath, Ceirt, and Straif, whose vibrations can be dangerous or disruptive if they are not properly contained and controlled.

Even helpful and healing *feda* can have their challenging or dangerous manifestations; nGétal is a strong healing *fid*, but its other root meaning is wounding or slaying. Remember that as you work, and act with caution and common sense. Until you understand the energies very well and know how they work in your body and your psyche, you need to remove everything that you put into yourself.

Grounding energy is a basic form of magical and spiritual hygiene, just like washing your hands or doing regular purification work. To maintain disruptive energies within your body can lead to not just psychic distress, but to confusion, disorientation and, potentially, physical illness. Playing with energies like these without properly grounding them when you're done can destabilize or aggravate already existent health or psychiatric problems. While Straif as transformation might not seem particularly problematic or dangerous on the surface, do you know exactly what transformation that energy will bring? There are dangerous transformations as well as safe and healthy ones.

Glannad is a good way to begin the grounding after your work, as it disperses what has been gathered and purifies your energies. Visualize and feel the specific energies taken on during your work with the *fid* flowing out of you like water. Breathe them out into the air and feel them swirl away with the motion of your breath. Feel the earth beneath you taking those energies in through your feet and legs and neutralizing them. If need be, you can touch the earth with your hands, or lie on the earth, letting the energy settle into the ground that way. Washing your hands in salt water is also an effective grounding technique. Work with any or all of these methods until your energy is clear and the energies taken on during your meditations with the *feda* are gone from your body.

Remember that these study exercises are not meant to shift anything in you permanently, but only to give you a grasp of what the *feda* energy signatures feel like. Know that long-term work with the ogam, like intensive work with any magical system, *will* change your life, your energies, and your sense of yourself. It's vital that you understand what you're getting into before you start invoking those changes deliberately.

The art of *Filidecht* is transformative, certainly, but the original *Filid* knew there were dangers involved -- hence their repeated warnings about seeking poetry, and the potential for the process to end in madness or death. Tradition has it that the

Filid took twenty years of training to become masters of their art, so this should give some indication of the rigorous nature of the path. It also serves as a reminder that none of us becomes an expert by reading a single book or working our way through a system for a couple of months. All these things are just beginnings.

Basic learning exercises are not the time to dance at the edge. If all you want from the ogam is a divination tool, then you may never end up risking this at all. Don't start along the way of the *Fili* until you're well prepared and you know that *Filidecht* is a path you wish to pursue. Becoming a *Fili* will change your life in ways you can't predict, and you must understand and accept that if you do this work. A study exercise is not the time to carry these energies and incorporate them into your body or your soul, and it's never wise to deal with them without set parameters and controls.

As you advance in your understanding of the ogam, it becomes increasingly important to read the Irish and Scots Gaelic myths and folklore to see how different concepts or principles found in the ogam are illustrated. This includes working through the traditional Ogam lists from the *Auraicept na n-Éces*. These lists cover an incredible variety of material, some of which may be inspiring to you while other lists may not resonate at all. It's not necessary to memorize all the lists, but having an idea of what they contain will be useful when you're reading the lore.

Not only does this information provide you with the cultural and linguistic context of the ogam, it also gives you a lexicon of stories and images to work from when you're trying to understand or explain how a particular *fid* works magically or in divination and ritual. Are the objects or concepts seen in positive or negative ways? Is their presentation varied depending on circumstance? Do they have stagnating or transformative effects? How are they viewed within the Irish and Scottish Gaelic literary traditions? What are the emotional resonances when cranes appear in a tale and how do they change from story to story? What does fire evoke when it is central to a story? Which forces or objects are strongly linked with particular emotions, with creation, or with destruction? What events and emotions are associated with particular colors and how are they described? Which deities, spirits, or heroes seem to embody the essence of particular *feda* to you?

The other aspect of this reading and research is that it plants the Gaelic context in your subconscious. The more you read, the more your mind can explore the meanings in dreams or visionary states. It gives your mind and spirit time to let the information steep and brew within you, just as doing internal cauldron work steeps the energies in your body. Even though you may not immediately start seeing connections with the ogam *feda* in the stories, as time goes by and you re-read the material your mind will begin to grasp the emotional resonances and ways of seeing that the tales present.

In time, you'll find yourself having "a-ha!" moments when an obscure passage becomes clear, allowing you to see past the surface of the action and figures in the tale and into the underlying lessons. A salmon will no longer be just a fish, but a manifestation of the action of Coll's links to wisdom and tradition. The red fury of Cú Chulainn in battle is not simply a color, but a reflection of the dangerous passion and power of Ruis. Brighid at the forge works her creative brilliance with Tinne's iron ingot, bringing wealth and protection to those who use her tools.

When you feel more confident with your grasp of the meanings, begin working with basic divination study, drawing an individual *fid* to get a feel for the tone and flow of a day, or drawing three *feda* to assess your physical, emotional and mental/spiritual state. When interpreting the *feda* you draw, look beyond the immediate and obvious meanings and into deeper levels, drawing associations from many different directions. Observe what happens and how you feel during each day, seeing if any of it connects with the *feda* you've drawn. Keeping notes on this can help you observe patterns as they develop, and you'll be able to draw personal meanings and associations from those occurrences.

Keep an eye on the world around you as well. If you draw Lus one morning, do you see ducks flying overhead that afternoon? Did you draw Coll on a day when cranes or herons were wading in the shallows of a lake nearby? Which birds or animals in your environment resonate with different *feda* for you? This is particularly important in places where the species from the Irish bird ogam don't exist for you locally. Seeing non-native species in a zoo or a bird identification book may be a fun and interesting exercise, but it's an entirely different experience to learn about the behavior, habitats, and preferences of the birds that live near you and integrate them into your own local bird ogam. This is one way to develop a basis for omen seeking through the use of ogam.

We can create our own ogam lists of other types as well, just as the original *Filid* did. In the *Auraicept na n-Éces*, students of *Filidecht* were instructed to create their own herb ogams by making a list of plants starting with each letter. You can proceed that way yourself or you can take a more symbolic approach and study herbalism, basing your personal herb ogam on how a given herb affects the body and the mind, or through its role in the environment. Given that these instructions date back to the 14th century, the activity can certainly be considered traditional. The creation of one's own ogams is also a legitimate part of modern CR practice.

As an illustrative exercise, I created a planet ogam, included in the section on the *feda* and their meanings. The logic of my choices was based in part on my more than thirty years of experience with traditional astrology, and in part on intuitions about some of the newer recognized members of our solar system. I looked at each body's established meaning and symbolism and meditated on whether and how they resonated with the *feda*. This is in no way an attempt to impose western astrology on CR, nor is it the creation of a modern "Celtic astrology." Instead, it's an exercise in looking at the *feda* and a very different system of esoteric knowledge in an attempt to see where they might successfully overlap and interact. In this way, we help keep the ogam tradition alive and in motion, giving it added relevance to our modern daily lives.

In order to create a twenty-*fid* planet ogam, I had to reach beyond the traditional seven planets of classical astrology and into the newer fields of work with the influence of asteroids, centaurs, and dwarf planets. The 2006 naming of the dwarf planet Eris seemed particularly appropriate in both its chaotic influence on the definition of our solar system -- embodied in the simultaneous demotion of Pluto from planet to dwarf planet and the continuing astronomical controversy about the definition of 'planet' -- and in how well it fits with the frustrating and chaotic energies that are often associated with the appearance of Ceirt in a reading.

Some of the *feda* had more obvious planetary associations than others. Chiron, a centaur, with its strong mythology of the wounded healer, seemed a natural fit for nGétal, the *fid* of wounding and healing. It was the spark for the rest of the exercise and inspired me to look further into the potential for parallels of meaning. Venus, with its sensuality and smooth speech, felt appropriate for Muin, the *fid* of love, esteem, and the voice. The legendary fickleness of love fits well with the flip side of Muin's meaning, in tricks and deception. Other *feda* and planets were more difficult to discern. Should I assign Mars to the fierce passions of Ruis or the smith-forged iron of Tinne? Both would certainly fit very well with different aspects of Mars's meanings in astrology. In some cases, like my assigning the Sun to Tinne, the associations are tenuous, stretching the edges of the definitional field of both *fid* and planet.

The object of defining your own ogams is not to create a "table of correspondences" that all interlock and can be substituted for one another in a ritual or magical sense. Sail's tree ogam of willow and its bird ogam, the hawk, don't both have direct lunar associations, though I assigned the Moon to that letter. It's important to understand that you're not trying to derive a set of connected grids filled with things that are seen as magically or spiritually "the same," nor will they all mean the same thing -- one symbol in lockstep with another. Rather, they are a collage of images that might bring similar themes to mind, either in terms of poetry and myth or of personal power and transformation. Remember that most of the Irish ogams "correspond" only insofar as they all start with the same letter as the *fid* with which they're associated. They were primarily intended as mnemonic devices for a catalogue of alliterative images in poetry. Loose fields of meaning and a sense of play are very helpful in this exercise.

In the case of the willow and the hawk, their Old Irish names are *sail* and *seg* and, as far as I can tell, the alliteration is their only traditional connection. The beauty of the tradition's permission to create your own ogams is that you, as a modern ogam-worker, can draw any links you like between the two within your own psyche and the personal mythology of your life *if you don't find anything specific within the insular Celtic spiritual and cultural context*. Where links exist in the traditional lore, they should be given precedence because they are most likely what was originally intended. Personal meanings take a back seat to the tradition when working in a CR context.

You also need to understand that another person studying the ogam may derive entirely different resonances between the images of a given *fid*, or no association at all, and this is perfectly acceptable. Developing your own associations and webs of meaning is not an exercise in putting the *feda* into unyielding boxes and grids. It's a way of developing an organic understanding of a wide variety of symbols, some of which were intended for coding and cryptographic work, others of which were meant to have mythic resonances.

It is situations like these where the distinctions between Unverified Personal Gnosis, Shared Gnosis, and Tradition are important. Your personal work can be entirely valid for you, but meaningless to others. Meanings arrived at by different ogam workers in different places may in fact overlap, but that doesn't make them traditional -- it makes them a useful modern addition to the CR traditions surrounding the ogam. Traditional sources may not always resonate for you as an individual, but they are and remain a part of the vital cultural context that makes CR a Celtic path rather than a part of eclectic, Wiccan, or Ceremonial Magic-based Neopaganism. The differences between personal validity and traditional authenticity should be clearly understood and articulated.

When you're comfortable with the basic meanings of the *feda* and how they relate to one another, you can begin to work with the ogam glyph called the *Féige Find* (FF), commonly translated as "Fionn's Window" but which also translates as "Fionn's Ridgepole/Rooftree." This mysterious five-ringed image appears in the *Auraicept na n-Éces* or Scholar's Primer. It consists of five concentric rings with the ogam feda including the letters of the *forfeda* drawn in groups around it. At the top is the Beith *aicme*, to the right is the h-Úath *aicme*, at the bottom is the Muin *aicme*, and on the left is the Ailm *aicme*. I believe that this figure ties in to certain aspects of Irish myth and cosmology, though

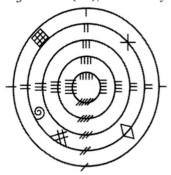

Feige Find

Illustration by Bob Daverin

there is no proof of this. For me, it works as a cosmological mandala and as a gateway into the Otherworlds. Whether it is conceived as window or ridgepole, in both cases it is a metaphor for reaching into those Otherworldly places. The window is obvious in modern western culture, but the ridgepole requires a bit of explaining.

In round huts, there is often a central post that holds up the roof of the building. It is called the ridgepole or roof-tree. In some cultures, this is seen as analogous to the world-tree, and is considered a bridge between our world and the world of spirits. The *Féige Find* can be imagined as the tree that the poet climbs upward into the center to reach *imbas* and the Otherworlds. The glyph itself, with its five concentric rings, can be seen as the roof of the hut when you lie on your back looking up to the rings of thatching and the central smoke-hole. The ogam *feda* themselves are like the bindings that hold the thatch, and the stars spinning in the night sky around the central post of the world tree, or the north star that is the nail about which the heavens revolve.

Filid were said to climb the ogam as a tree, and the highest ranks of poets inhabited the top of that tree. Sometimes one who was well versed in the lore and taught at the highest level was called the *clíath*, "the top of the ridgepole of learning." In this way, the FF glyph can be conceptualized as a pathway of achievement for the student of ogam and of *Filidecht*, moving from the outer rings toward the center.

The five rings motif shows up again in the Emain Macha archaeological site in Ireland. The structure there is far older than the fourteenth century book the FF glyph is found in. The structure was made of oak posts, filled in with stones, and then burned to the ground for ritual purposes, probably standing for only a few months at most. Five rings of protection show up in a tale, *Scéla Éogain*, concerning the birth of king Cormac mac Airt, when the Druid-smith Olc Aiche draws them around the infant king to keep him safe from every form of harm. These recurrences of five concentric rings may be coincidental, but to me they're quite suggestive of magical or spiritual significance.

The arrangement of the *forfeda* in between the main *aicme* is suggestive as well. We find two of these *feda* in the lower left quadrant. Whether or not this had any significance to the medieval Irish monk who drew the diagram, its positioning is interesting to me because it's suggestive of a gateway that would, on a modern map, be located in the southwestern part of the drawing; this assumes that the top of the glyph correlates to north, which is not generally the case for medieval maps. More often, the top of the map was equated to the east.

Be that as it may, in insular Celtic, and specifically Irish cosmology, the land of the dead is often considered to be located in the southwest. *Teach Duinn*, the House of Donn, is off the southwest coast of the Bearra Penninsula, and is said to be where the dead go on their way to the Otherworld lands beyond. This is also the place where it's claimed that Cessair landed, the first person ever in Ireland. Even without an ancient correlation between the *aicme* placement in the FF and the directions, modern minds can use it as a potential gateway for travel into the land of the ancestors. This connection is a piece of shared modern gnosis among many ogam workers in CR.

It's important to note that the four primary *aicme* themselves don't seem to have any particular "directional" qualities of meaning to them as articulated in *The Settling of the Manor of Tara*[109]. Nor are the *aicme* or directions associated with the four treasures of the Tuatha Dé Danann. For people coming out of mainstream Neopaganism and Wicca, it's very important to remember that the Celtic cosmological system did not appear have a concept of the four classical elements until after the arrival of Christianity, and so the directions, the four treasures, and the *aicme* do not have "elemental" associations either.[110] It's critical not to force traditional quaternities within Celtic mythology into this later, alien system. If you feel the need to work with those patterns, understand clearly that it is your own gnosis, and not a part of the CR tradition.

The FF glyph can be used for more in depth work with the *feda* as a gateway into the energies of each *fid*. The concentric rings work very well to produce a tunnel effect when the focus is softened as you gaze at it, particularly in dim lighting. As you focus, regulate your breathing to go into a light trance state and visualize the *fid* you're working with in the center of the glyph. As you feel yourself going into a meditative state, you can push yourself "through" the tunnel and into the *fid* itself, to see what lies within its internal energetic and spiritual landscape.

Be open to impressions on any level. What does the energy feel like? Do you see anything with your mind's eye? Can you hear anything around you? Does scent or taste come into it at all?

---

[109] These directional qualities can be greatly condensed to battle in the north, prosperity in the east, music in the south and learning in the west.

[110] The four treasures of the Tuatha Dé Danann are the Stone of Fál, the Spear of Lug, the Sword of Núadha and the Cauldron of Daghda. Some Neopagans and modern magicians equate them with the directions, the four elements, and the four suits of the Tarot. This is not how the original Irish Pagans would have seen them. In the tale of their origins, the treasures are all said to come from the north, or a direction that appears to translate as "the north-above." This can probably best be read as coming from the sky, which is the realm of some of the deities. The origin of the four elements as a formal system is found within Greek philosophy and would have been imported into Irish and Scottish lore much later.

What impressions do you get about the *fid* or about where you are? Give yourself enough time to explore this Otherworldly space. Be sure to make notes when you return, as well. The sooner you write down your impressions, the more information you'll be able to retain. It's profitable to visit these ogam Otherworlds many times, building on your knowledge with each return. Pay particular attention to recurrent patterns and images, as these are very likely to be important associations for you in your personal magical work.

What you learn through this process should, like the results of any other form of ogam meditation, be checked against what you can find in the Irish and Scottish lore and through discussions with others who understand and work with the ogam. Working with others is an excellent way to help deepen your understandings and sort useful impressions and information that fit within the CR tradition from individual material that works for you, but may not apply to others. These distinctions are important, because tradition and context are what make the difference between the personal and the genuinely Celtic. The excitement of discovering that a personal inspiration is confirmed in the lore is hard to describe, but knowing that you've linked into the current of the tradition in that way is a great feeling. It can give great reinforcement to the work you do, and sharing those insights helps to develop the CR ogam tradition.

Meditations with the FF can be applied to dream work as well. In Irish, the group of tales based on dreams is called *aisling*. Many dream tales are recorded, ranging in topics from the comedic to the Otherworldly and dramatic. Developing dreaming rituals linked with your ogam work is one way to carry the *aisling* tradition forward into modern CR.

Setting up a bedside altar with an image of the FF and items associated with the *fid* you're working with can be a focus for you as you prepare for sleep. The FF could be drawn or painted on a small round mirror or the surface of a black mirror to serve as a physical gateway. *Glannad* should be done before bed, along with some basic warding work to keep yourself and your space safe while you're doing guided dream work. A candle with the *fid* in question marked on it could be used as a meditative aid as you focus on the mirror while going into a trance state. Be sure to put the candle out before you fade into sleep.

Once again, keeping a journal or notebook of this work is a good idea. Your notebook and a pen should be kept on the dream altar by your bedside, and written or drawn in immediately upon waking to help you recall your dreams and their images. It takes practice to get consistent results with dream work of this sort, but once you've conditioned yourself, the dream world is a rich field for exploration of the ogam and your own personal internal landscape as it relates to the images of the ogam system.

For those working with the tree ogam paradigm, a popular method of learning about the *feda* is to find local trees of the appropriate species. Take time to acquaint yourself with the tree or shrub, observing it through the course of a year and making notes about its progress and growth. Note when it buds, when it blooms, when the leaves fall -- if they do -- and when its seeds or berries ripen. What is its average lifespan? How tall does it get? How many trunks does it usually produce? What do the leaves look like? What color and texture is its bark? What does its sap and its bloom smell like? What scent do its leaves or bark have if they're burned as incense? How does that incense feel to your developing Otherworld senses?

What is the wood of the tree used for in traditional Celtic cultures? What are its folk names? How strong is its wood? What qualities was it valued for? Was it considered safe to bring indoors, or was its presence a danger or *geas*? What magic was associated with it? What did it ward against or attract? Is it toxic, edible, or never used as a food species because it doesn't provide anything that can be used that way? What colors of dye does it produce? If it's a non-toxic species, what does the sap taste like? What are the qualities of its fruits or nuts or sap? How was it used medicinally?

Observe the birds, insects, and animals that frequent the tree. What eats its fruit or nuts? What pollinates it? Who lives in the tree or shelters there? What damages the tree through its activities?

Spend time each week in meditation with the tree, sitting at its roots with your back to it, or sitting within the branches of a shrub. Reach out to the tree with your energies and feel its life force. Feel yourself merge with the tree and its energies. Strive to understand the life cycle of the tree through its seasonal rounds and how that cycle relates to its *fid*. If the tree isn't traditionally considered bad luck to bring inside, try keeping a few leafy or blooming branches in a vase on your altar as you work with its energies.

Even if you're not working with the tree ogam, this method works exceptionally well for learning about those *feda* that are named for trees, like Dair, Coll, and Beith. If you don't live in a place where these trees or shrubs grow wild, study photos and tree identification books. Better still, go to nurseries or arboretums and spend time with them as ornamentals. If you have land and the ecology will support these trees, you might consider planting one or more on your property, tending them as you learn about their energies and habits. Some people who are blessed with land and patience have planted sacred groves of ogam trees, or gardens of healing herbs based on their personal herb ogams. [111]

It should be noted when working with these ogams that some plants associated with the ogam *feda* are invasive and can be devastating to non-native environments where they have been introduced. In the Pacific Northwest where I live, English Ivy (associated with Gort, Idad, and the *forfeda fid* Uillend) and Scotch Broom (associated with nGétal) are particularly destructive, strangling out native plants and overwhelming native habitats for wildlife. English Ivy can literally choke the life out of a tree or break down the brick face of a building it climbs. Local wildlands and watershed restoration organizations make frequent pleas for volunteers to root these invasive plants out of parks and from the banks of salmon streams so that the local balance of nature can be restored. Despite this devastating problem, both species are still commonly planted as ornamentals in the region. *Please do not plant Irish ogam plants and trees on your land if they are known to be aggressively invasive foreign plants in your area.*

If you work intensively with a particular ogam plant and you wish to keep a specimen, consider keeping it potted inside where it can't escape into the environment. Also, even if the species is invasive, you may feel better not volunteering for invasive plant eradication programs if they deal with your

---

[111] The best and most extensive information about working with the tree ogam can be found at http://paganachd.com/articles/treehuggers.html -- *Tree Huggers: A Methodology for Crann Ogham Work (a.k.a. Raven and Kathryn Get Lost in the Woods)* by Raven nic Rhóisín and Kathryn Price NicDhàna. The essay covers a wide range of ideas and techniques, dealing in depth with the material mentioned in this book and far more. They are experts with CR techniques in ogam studies and I cannot recommend their article and their approach highly enough for those working with the tree ogam.

particular plant allies. There are other ways of helping the environment without having to volunteer your time destroying what may in fact be the physical embodiment of your helping spirit.

The invasive plant situation is a very important example of when it really is usually better to find a local native equivalent for your personal ogam study and work with that plant or tree. Respect for the local environment and sensitivity to its needs are essential to *Filidecht*, and making the local land spirits have to fight off intrusive invaders isn't a good way to build a relationship with them. We have so many options open to us that bringing in plants that will destroy the local environment can't be considered a positive spiritual act. Exercising your imagination and your spiritual insight to find appropriate alternatives is a healthy and creative way to address these issues.

CHAPTER 4
Basic Ogam Divination

Approaching Divination

There are several ways to approach divination with ogam. Ogam *feda* made with twigs or tiles present more flexibility than *feda* drawn on cards because they can be used not just for formalized layouts, but also for a random casting of part or all of the *feda*.

Drawing one *fid* each day to meditate on is a good way to familiarize yourself with the meanings and symbols associated with them. If you can find an image that brings each *fid* to mind, to place on your altar while you're doing the meditative work, so much the better. That image might be the physical object described by the name of the *fid*, like a lump of sulfur for Straif, or the bark of a birch tree for Beith. For a concept-*fid* like Muin, something that brings love or esteem to mind might be appropriate, or perhaps you might find taking something from one of its other associated ogams to be a useful approach; for instance a picture or figure of an ox to remind yourself of the word ogam about the ox's back and its association with strength and perseverance.

Working with an individual *fid* each day, or over the course of a week or a month at a time, can lead to a deeper understanding and appreciation of the *fid's* meanings in magic and healing, as well as divination. Both magic and healing work using the ogam will deepen your understanding of ways to read the feda in your divinatory work. The web weaves together in fascinating ways, each fiber added to warp and weft strengthening the fabric of your understanding and ability.

Divination with ogam is not like working with the Tarot -- a much more familiar method for most people. Though ogam decks are available, they aren't traditional in any sense. They also force the deck designer's concepts about the ogam and their cosmology onto the reader. This in itself isn't a bad thing, but if you're working with the symbolism and methods in this book, you'll find that the commercial decks clash with some of the information here and may make it more difficult to focus on any system that is not symbolized by the imagery on the deck's cards themselves.

All of the available decks that I know of work from the tree ogam paradigm, and while this is a very common way of using the ogam it isn't, as has been emphasized throughout this book, the only approach. For me, it isn't the best approach either, though whether to use the trees, this system, or any other as your primary paradigm is up to you and should be determined by which system works best for you. Just because it's not my preferred system doesn't mean it won't be yours.

Because the B and H *aicmí* are mirror images of one another, it isn't really possible or advisable to read "reversed" ogam meanings the way one reads reversals with the Tarot. The meaning of a *fid* doesn't change because it has fallen upside-down or on its side; the *fid* is still itself and expresses the same energies. *Feda* that fall face-down in a random toss might not be read because they are not an influence on the situation at hand; not every thread of energy will appear in every reading. If they are read, they will more often express latent or hidden aspects of a situation and will have less immediacy. When working with twigs, it may not be possible to tell if a *fid* is face up or face down unless they are shaped so they can lay flat on their face. I have used a set cut onto twigs that are triangular wedges so that the feda are carved across a corner. This set doesn't have any way for a *fid* to appear face down.

Reading all twenty *feda* in a random toss is certainly possible, if a bit complex, but I wouldn't recommend that method for a beginning reader. That method is addressed in the chapter on advanced divinatory techniques. A better technique for someone just beginning with the random toss method is to pull a certain symbolic number of *feda* and use those for the random toss, narrowing the focus of the reading to a more manageable field of potential meaning. Three or nine are both good, traditionally significant numbers to work with.

Divinatory readings are derived from the traditional associations of the *fid* and its name, the word ogams associated with the letter, the relationship of one *fid* to another, and with the help of your guiding deities and spirits. The word *divination* itself derives linguistically from the idea that the divine influences the way the lots fall so that they relate to the matter being asked about.

Layouts and random tosses are read in different ways, and the length and shape of your *feda* will be an influence on how many *feda* might touch or cross each other in a given random toss. Keep this in mind, as these interstices are often important in determining shades of meaning or relative importance. Long twigs might potentially fall across a dozen or more of the other *feda* in a random toss. Smaller *feda*, made with small stone or bone cabochons, may only be able to touch or cross one or two other *feda* at a time. Tumbled stone or glass "jewel" *feda* will be able touch each other but it may not be possible for one *fid* to cross another because their shapes might prevent such interactions.

A selection of commercial ogam systems is shown on the left. Top and bottom left are by Liz and Colin Murray. Upper left sticks are a Caitlín Matthews set. Far left is by Gerry Maguire Thompson. The author's hand made ogam sets are in the center and on the right.
From the author's collection.

Many people who first learn divination with Tarot or other deck-based systems tend to fall into a pattern of believing that reading "reversals" is necessary to take advantage of the full depth of a system. This isn't the case. Each ogam *fid* has a range of meanings and should not be looked at in a dualistic fashion. The *feda* do not have "positive" and "negative" meanings per se. Within the CR worldview, a triadic basis for interpretation serves a more functional purpose and doesn't carry the baggage of the dualism that modern western culture applies to everything. Rather than categorizing the meaning of each *fid* into positive and negative traits, consider that each *fid*'s meanings can express as part of any of three currents within the context of ogam work: chthonic, oceanic or celestial. It may be internal, external, or liminal. It might be physical, emotional, or spiritual. It may have expressions in the three realms of land, sea and sky, or the three cauldrons of warming, motion, and wisdom.

Even *feda* which might be read at first glance as "negative," like h-Úath's "terror" or Ceirt's air of misfortune, can potentially have useful and transformative aspects in divination, ritual, and magic. They may be a warning against involvement in a given situation or with a particular person, or a strong 'no' from deity or spirit. H-Úath's association with "a pack of wolves" means that it could possibly provide a useful and necessary point of contact with wolf spirits or the defensive power of the wolf's tooth, but only if approached with great caution. It can sometimes be used for the breaking of barriers between you and your goals, or as a strong protection against enemies -- though use for these purposes is not without risk and definitely not recommended to beginners.

Preparing for a reading is a ritual in itself. While pulling a *fid* every day is an excellent way to help meditate upon and fix meanings in your mind, the act of doing readings is different from the work and play of your everyday life. It's an invocation of spirit into your presence and your consciousness. Consider it a way to ask advice from your deities and spirits; you don't randomly call your friends every five minutes to ask their opinion on what to have for dinner or what color shirt to wear this morning (or if you do, you shouldn't), and you should treat the ogam and the deities and spirits you call upon in your divinatory work with similar respect. The divine surrounds us and permeates the world, but it often takes a certain focus to see it. Ritual preparation for divination is a way of tuning yourself into that constant presence.

This isn't to say you can't practice -- practice is absolutely necessary for learning. But treat your time working with your ogam *feda* in divination as something special. Set aside a place in your room or on your altar for keeping your ogam *feda*. You might store them in a special bag or box, or have a particular cloth you use only for casting your *feda*. Perhaps you'll have particular oils or incenses like juniper oil, leaves, or berries you use for purification in preparation for your work and study. If you have a particular tutelary deity, it's good to offer a prayer to him or her, and to call upon any spirits you work with to aid you in your task. If you don't have a special deity you usually work with, Ogma as the creator of the ogam is a very good place to start. His wisdom and eloquence can guide you as you learn his secret arts. Brighid the poet and prophet is another deity whose influence is important for divination and who can be helpful to the student of ogam.

Preparatory ritual doesn't have to be elaborate. It might just be a moment of focused meditation with your bag of *feda* between your palms, asking for the help of your deities and spirits to find the truth and imbuing your *feda* with their power and wisdom. If you prefer more formal ritual to help you create a divinatory mindset, you might set up an altar with deity and spirit images, light a candle, and make offerings of food and drink to the powers that aid you, passing your *feda* through the smoke of juniper to clear away influences from previous readings.

Don't feel that either extreme is the right one for all occasions. It might be that some days all you have time for is a short prayer, but if you're doing divination for a public ritual after an offering to determine its acceptability, a more elaborate setup will most likely be desired. Listen to your deities and spirits and they will help you find the right level of preparation for each situation.

This said, I do think there is a bare minimum of ritual preparation that should be observed. My feeling is that it's necessary to at least focus for a moment on what you're doing and why you are doing it, with a request to your deities and spirits for their aid. Ritual is an important signal to your mind, your spirit, and to the forces of the sacred that something important is happening. The word divination is from the same root as "divine"; it is an appeal to the sacred beings to reveal to us what is hidden. Without it, "divination" is no more than a game.

Preparation helps open your mind to the possibilities of what is before you. With practice, it moves you into a slightly altered state of consciousness where you find yourself closer to the realms of deity and spirit, able to see their movement and influence more clearly. Divination opens a doorway within, and you step into the mists where our world and the Otherworld intersect. Time bends in that place, and past, present and future become one. You are, in that moment, at the center where all worlds meet and the world-tree passes through. You sit at the edge of the well of wisdom and it infuses your spirit and sparks *imbas* within you, the inspiration that brings poetry and prophecy.

During this preparatory time, you will need to formulate the question or phrase the issue you wish to address. The more precise you are when you focus on the issue at hand, the better your results will be when the *feda* are tossed or laid out. Focusing on your question or issue during your preparatory ritual sends out your intentions and your inquiry to the world, helping to create a synchronic moment in time that allows the influence of deity or spirits into your reading. The moment your question is asked is the seed of the answer. The universe unfolds around it to demonstrate how the situation is developing.

In *Filidecht*, divination is more than a rote reading of symbols. It's the art of taking in hand the connecting thread of poetry that joins all things. To perform divination is to gaze into the preserving shrines of nature and memory and come away transformed and renewed. Not all you see will be pleasant, nor will it always be what you want to see, but there will be truth in it. It's necessary to listen creatively, observe carefully, and speak from the heart.

The practice of divination reaches into the heart of all life, showing us the possibilities as we stand on the brink of a decision or action. Very little that we see is inevitable, for the very act of divining offers us options and potentials: futures to strive for or fates to avoid. By practicing the art of divination, we can learn to shift the course of our lives and to step around the pitfalls in our path. We can use the ogam as a tool for making wise decisions when many options are presented to us, or for seeking alternatives when the way seems dark and narrow.

It should be understood that divination of any sort rarely provides a definitive yes or no answer. The ogam offers symbols that must be interpreted in light of the given situation and with an understanding of the powers and energies involved. It will mirror your concerns and show you new approaches that you may not have considered. It will advise you on potential best or worst case scenarios, but no divination can give an absolute prediction of the future. We are each responsible for our own decisions. In the act of divination and making a decision, some doors are opened while others are closed. New possibilities coming to light may shift an entire range of potentials in ways previously unimagined.

The purpose of divination is not to get a yes or a no, but to open your mind to what is possible in any given situation. Learning techniques of divination teaches us to be flexible and to examine things in non-binary, non-dualistic ways. Rather than looking for that absolute yes or a no, it teaches us that it is possible to embrace many options and choose the best of them.

Divination is a way of guidance for adults who understand that everything is in flux and that certainty is difficult to come by. The binary of yes or no is often more suitable for children who have difficulty thinking in terms of many options. Embracing the power of "and" is important and necessary in life. "And" is a tiny word, but it moves us beyond binary into a multivalent world of possibilities. Remember that it is quite possible for the same outcome to be good for one person, bad for another, and entirely neutral for yet a third.

"Or" and "but" are two more tiny but powerful tools of divination. They are words of choice and flexibility, offering many approaches to any given situation. Your implied "yes" may be one option of many, to follow this path or that, or yet another stretching out before you. Your implied "no" may well have a "but" attached -- one door being closed while many others are opened. One choice may eventually need to be made, but "or" and "but" are words of power when you examine your path. "And", "but", and "or" are the reasons that divination is an art rather than a science. They demand subtlety, maturity, and wisdom from the practitioner. They require balance, insight, and sensitivity to the flow of life and circumstance. They teach us that even if all options in a situation are bad ones, some may be less harmful or destructive than others; if all are good, some may be more joyous or harmonious than others. In neutrality, they teach us how to make the most of our choices.

It is also important to recognize that no divination technique is infallible. It's possible to misinterpret the *feda* that fall. There are times when it's inappropriate to ask a question, and the *feda* simply won't give you an answer that you understand. Practice can help you recognize these situations and you will gradually learn which topics are more difficult for you to find answers to. As with ritual and magic, some people will specialize in one thing rather than another. You might be very good at questions dealing with rituals, but not with relationships. There's nothing wrong with this; work with your strengths, develop skills in your weaker areas, and recognize that you probably won't be an expert in everything.

Human beings also have a way of reading their desires into divination, and that desire can distort the truth of a situation as well. When doing divination, always ask yourself if you're reading what's there, or if you're just telling yourself what you want -- or are afraid -- to hear. Reading for others is actually often much easier than reading for yourself for that simple reason. This doesn't mean you should never read for yourself, but it does put you on notice that you need to be very careful when you do, and to understand your motives for asking any given question. Clarify what you hope for and what you are afraid of; the answer often lies somewhere outside of that binary.

Understanding your desires and fears will help you find the answers you seek and help you avoid interpreting a *fid* in the "best" (or "worst") possible way just because it's what you expect. Cultivating a certain emotional detachment from the question is a good technique when practicing divination. The more emotionally charged the situation or question is for you, the more difficult it may be to obtain a clear-eyed view of the interpretation. Cultivating detachment is another reason that meditation and ritual purification are useful before doing divination.

Words themselves are extremely important, not just in *Filidecht* or as keywords when first learning the ogam, but as the background for any act of divination. A query should be phrased as precisely as possible. Spirits, deity, and the mind all work more in symbol and image than in spoken language. It's very important to concretely and clearly imagine your question. The mind plays games with words, and may fall into punning or other wordplay, so it's wise to understand this as you phrase your questions and examine your answers. The way a question is asked can be framed to expect a certain outcome or to trap someone -- the clichéd question "have you stopped beating your wife?" is a good example of this. Be careful with the phrasing of your questions.

Answers may have mythic resonances as well, reaching deeply into patterns and images found in Celtic tales. This is why it's important to read the tales and work to understand their symbols and contexts. What the ogam presents to you may be deeply personal, having one meaning for you while presenting an entirely different meaning to another person. For someone whose patron is Manannán, the crane of Coll may be an important symbol of wisdom and mystery, while for others it may more traditionally presage misfortune and sorrow. Working with ogam and developing your own deity, herbal, or animal ogams is one good way of personalizing the system and making it relevant to your life and situation. To me, the gull symbolizes Manannán, while to a friend of mine the gull is Fand, his wife, instead. The difference here is very important and meaningful for both of us. You might create your own ogam *dindsenechas* --

your personal ogam-linked map of your life's territory with each letter representing a place, a river, a city, or a mountain. These personal interpretations and associations can lend great depth to your divination, ritual and magical work, contextualizing them in the place where you live.

You'll want to start out slowly, using the ogam keywords and each *fid*'s core traditional meanings as a basis for your work. As you develop familiarity with the keywords, the letter meanings, and the associated concepts, your web of personal, individualized meanings will develop and expand. It's like learning the alphabet before you compose metrical poetry, or learning individual strikes and blocks before you put them together into the dance of formal karate *kata*. Once the basics are understood, the deeper aspects of the work become much easier, and the process will eventually become second nature to you. Once you've learned to ride a bicycle, you no longer have to think consciously about keeping your balance or how to steer around a corner because it simply flows from your body. Divination is like that.

Keep in mind that some people have more natural talent with divination than others. This talent is like any other -- playing the piano, baking a pie, riding a bicycle. Anyone can do divination to some degree, though learning the techniques and learning to listen to personal intuition may take longer for some than others. Find the level of divinatory work that's comfortable for you, and press the boundaries now and then. You may surprise yourself.

I've been working with ogam for twenty years as I write this book, and I'm constantly finding new subtleties in the system. The writing itself has brought me new insights and methods of working, and each time I use the ogam in ritual I discover new ways of understanding its energies. Life experience broadens the field in which ogam can be used and understood. Don't let initial difficulties discourage you, and try to wean yourself from looking at the book's definitions as quickly as you can. Memorization isn't enough in itself, but is a powerful tool for triggering intuition while you're working on fluency with this new language of the soul.

The easiest way to approach divination with ogam is through drawing a single *fid*. After you have focused and feel comfortable, formulate your question carefully, close your eyes, and draw one *fid* from your set. This can be interpreted in light of the question or issue at hand and further development of the information can be brought forth by asking the questions associated with the *fid* and meditating on the keyword and the symbolism inherent in the ogam *fid* found within the lore.

Look for potential puns or other "sideways" or quirky associations with the *fid*'s keyword or images to your question. Examine the word ogams to see if they might relate to the situation in any way, or remind you of someone or something associated with your question. If you associate the *fid* with a place or a deity, ask yourself if that has any connection to the matter at hand. If you are working with the traditional bird or your self-created animal ogams, does the creature represent anyone to you, or is it strongly associated with particular abilities and qualities? If so, how do those qualities relate to the matter of your inquiry?

Listen to your emotions and the voice of spirit as well. Do you feel a strong emotion when you first read the *fid*? What emotion is it, and how is it related to the question, or to a potential answer? First impressions are often quite telling, even if they don't necessarily make logical sense at first. Do images form unbidden in your mind as you meditate on the *fid* and the question? They may be hints from Otherworldly allies about potential avenues to explore.

If you are feeling uncertain about a situation but don't know where to start asking questions, try drawing a *fid* with the intention of helping to frame the question. You may find that the *fid* drawn will lead you to a good place from which to start your inquiry.

Laying Out the Feda

In most divinatory systems, a three-lot draw is common. This can represent any triad you wish, whether the matrix of past-present-future; the three internal cauldrons of warming (body), motion (emotion), and wisdom (spirit/thought); or the spirits we interact with as land spirits-ancestors-deities. They might represent the three currents of the chthonic or physical, the oceanic or transformative, and the celestial or ordered energies. What each of these three *feda* represents will change depending on your needs and circumstances. Perhaps the triad of land-sea-sky might be revealing if you are inquiring about which types of spirits to look to for help or support. Read land as the land spirits, sea as representing the ancestors, and sky as the realm of deity.

Here's an example of a three-*fid* layout. The question is "What will the state of my health be over the next month?" The three *feda* represent the physical, emotional and spiritual realms. As ogam is traditionally inscribed from the bottom of the stone up, the *feda* are laid out and interpreted with the bottom *fid* first and the top *fid* last.

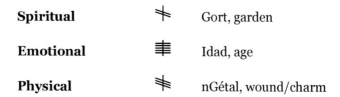

Spiritual		Gort, garden
Emotional		Idad, age
Physical		nGétal, wound/charm

Physically, nGétal suggests that I will be dealing with health issues as a major focus over the coming month. My health has always tended to vary wildly with the seasons and the local weather. As I write this, it is late October, with its attendant constantly shifting weather patterns. These usually lead to more frequent migraines and sinus or ear trouble for me at this time of year.

Paying attention to my body's messages and needs and taking extra care of myself are necessary during the coming month so that I remain in good health. I need to listen to my body to avoid potential problems like catching cold or injuring myself by pressing my limits too hard. As you can see, nGétal's appearance in this reading is neither good nor bad in itself; it serves to advise caution and good self-care.

Emotionally, Idad suggests that I'll have reasonable stability in my moods despite the likely fluctuations in my physical health. There will probably be an enduring feeling to the emotions I experience during this month, whether they are upbeat or depressed. Rituals and traditions surrounding Samhain will bring me into emotional contact with the spirits of the ancestors during this time. It will be a season for contemplating my own age and mortality, and meditating on the immortal soul that transcends the boundaries of death.

Idad also serves as a reminder that the pain in my physical body is transitory and that attention to creating and sustaining a positive mood can help me deal with the inevitable weather-triggered shifts in my body's condition. This *fid* asks what emotional patterns from the past affect me in the present, and what I should do to make improvements for the future.

Spiritually, Gort is a sheltered preserve for the growth that patience and steady work bring as I move through the Samhain season. Persisting in the spiritual work of writing my book and the ritual work of making offerings to the ancestors at this time are important ways to nurture what grows in my soul. Samhain is the beginning of the new year, and what is planted now, with focus and intent, will grow in the year to come as a seed buried in the soil will germinate in its proper time. I need to ask myself what needs weeding from the garden of my spirit -- what is blocking my growth and good health in a spiritual sense and needs to be removed?

Gort suggests that keeping myself within a spiritually nurturing place will have a positive impact on my physical condition. Doing difficult internal work at this time may lead me to ways of improving my health over the course of the month, as what is done in the spiritual realms is often reflected in the physical body for good or ill.

Some other questions I need to ask myself at this time include "where am I wounded physically and what will need healing within my body this month?" -- "how do tradition and my past affect me emotionally at this time of year?" -- "how do I cultivate my highest self through the Samhain season?" Meditation on these questions will lead to further insights on what needs work in my life at the moment.

Sample Three Fid Reading

Ann[112] is a woman in her fifties, with adult children at home in a time of economic difficulty, one of them facing disability. She was working three jobs at the time, trying to support everyone, in addition to attempting to move from her nearly finished Masters degree into a Ph.D. program near her home. She had tried once before, without success.

We did this reading online, and so I'll be using that format to show how a reading works and how *feda* are interpreted in reference to particular situations. In this sample three *feda* reading, you'll also see how pulling an additional *fid* can elaborate on an answer and give additional guidance if more clarity is needed.

---

[112] In the sample readings and rituals, the names of each person have been changed to protect their privacy. Permission was received from each person to use their reading or ritual for this book.

Erynn: What would you like a reading on?
Ann: Whether I'll get into the Ph.D. program this time around. I'm trying to get an advanced degree but my advisor is upset at me for not finishing my work. And family circumstances have given me far more to do than most students have to deal with.
Erynn: Okay. I want you to focus while I rattle the feda and tell me when to pull the three feda, one at a time.
Ann: now
Erynn: next
Ann: now
Erynn: next
Ann: now
Erynn: okay
Erynn: First is Lus, the flame or the herb. This refers to the fires of creativity, and it's a good ogam for intellectual endeavors and indicates a good deal of energy for a project. ᚈ
Ann: (nod)
Erynn: It's part of the paradigm of inspiration in that you're enflamed with these creative ideas and you have a good deal of energy for carrying them out. They spark things in you that are purifying and healing and helpful in your life.

Erynn: The second is Ruis, which means redness. This one can be about both passion and about anger. ᚎ
Erynn: What you're looking at again is an expression of that energy of the flame. If you have to push, you may get angry at delays and such, but with enough passion, you can pull things your way.
Ann: That's useful.

Erynn: The third is Edad, which is the vehicle of the journey. ᚕ
Erynn: Where Onn would be a physical or spiritual journey, this fid is the tool or vehicle used for it. What will help carry you toward that goal? Which tool do you need to use to bring this to fruition? Your passion can drive it, but what are you using to convince the committee or the person you're applying to? How can you make the journey from grad student to Ph.D. candidate? Your creativity, channeled through your passion can show you how to approach the challenge.

Erynn: Let's draw another to address those questions.
Ann: Okay. I've run out of fire and run out of confidence.
Erynn: Concentrate again and tell me when

Ann: now
Erynn: This one is Muin, which means esteem, love, the voice, and sometimes also trickery and wiles. ☩
Be the coyote. Carry yourself with pride and esteem for yourself. Go to your loved ones for support. Trick the administration into getting into the program if you must, because you have the capacity to do the work; or trick yourself into having the energy. Give yourself the chance by believing in yourself. Speak on your own behalf -- don't be afraid to voice your opinions and don't be afraid to ask for help.
Ann: (nod) I'm having a lot of trouble between being mentally tired, the money issues, the daughter issues, and the working three jobs.
Erynn: Right, understood. If the family has any way of helping you out, get that help from them. Have them take some of the things from your shoulders that are burdening you, for Muin is also the ox's back. It carries heavy burdens. In the same way, it implies strength of will.
Ann: I feel like an ox or an overworked horse a lot of the time.
Erynn: Yes. I would say that there are probably things they can be doing that they're not yet. They may not at all be intending to deceive you, but it's possible that there's some coasting going on. Make sure of clear communications and accountability. Do you have any questions about this?
Ann: No. That was helpful. I'm blaming myself for being lazy and chaotic but I'm not motivated enough to change.
Erynn: You're not lazy, you know. You're doing the work of a few too many people right now.
Ann: It seems like I did more in the past.
Erynn: You weren't so swamped with trying to take care of extra family members then, were you?
Ann: Well, yes, I was. I remember a time when my husband worked evenings, I had the kids, worked full time, and drew my comic strip in the evenings.
* *Erynn nods*
Erynn: Drawing takes time, but probably not as much emotional energy as fighting with the academic system.
Ann: I'm doing a little drawing lately, and that makes me happier.
Erynn: Good! That may help your energy level, and is a good use of your creative fire.
Ann: It makes me feel better.

Erynn: This is good. I think, generally speaking, you need to find your passion again, and you need to have the kids taking up as much slack as they're able.

Ann's situation at the time of this reading was complicated by the status of her adult daughter, who was living at home with her and dealing with disability, as well as her husband's poor health. Her other adult children were living in financial distress at the time. Ann was accepted into a Ph.D. program, though later than she expected, and is doing well with it. She is also no longer working at three jobs.

Rather than having to struggle to get into the program she originally applied to at the time of this reading, a program was offered to her shortly afterward by a nearby university because they were impressed with her Masters level work. She finds the work challenging and exciting, and has been giving papers at academic conferences in her field as she works through her program.

For Ann, the coyote as trickster is a strong symbol of herself and her approach to the world. This spirit gives her strength and inspiration in working through the problems that she faces. Its appearance as Muin in this reading was helpful to her for finding ways to approach her problems. She also recognized that her art was part of what helped her find her passion and reenergized her when she needed a break from the more difficult issues she was facing.

Cauldron and Tree Layout

One layout I use frequently elaborates on this three *feda* pattern, adding two or more others to refine what is being said by the initial three *feda*, depending on what the reading requires. I refer to it as the Cauldron and Tree. I lay three *feda* out horizontally in a column from the bottom up, representing the Three Cauldrons that the early Irish *Filid* said were in every person.

The Cauldron of Warming, at the bottom, represents what's happening physically or with your health. This is the physical world basis from which you act, or what is happening in the environment around you.

The Cauldron of Motion represents the emotions and what is in flux in the situation. This *fid* represents what is changing and shifting, whether coming into being or flowing away with the ebbing tide. It can describe how you feel about the situation and its potentials and developments, or suggest an emotional attitude through which to approach the question.

The Cauldron of Wisdom represents the spiritual and intellectual aspect of the problem and a potential outcome. It describes the way you deal with things using your mind and your inspiration and how you puzzle your way through a situation. It can indicate fruitful avenues of thought for pursuing your goals and may represent your highest ideals surrounding the issue.

Alongside these three, I draw a fourth and lay it vertically. This *fid* represents the World Tree. It is what connects the Three Cauldrons. It shows the way these three *feda* weave together, what influences all of them, and how they're influencing each other. It can illuminate the first three *feda*, elaborating on their interrelationships and the common threads between them.

Finally, I draw a fifth *fid* and lay it horizontally across from the Cauldron of Wisdom. This represents the likely outcome, based on a continuation of the path currently being taken. It shows the direction in which you are traveling if all factors in the situation remain the same. When you're first working with this layout, this is where your reading will end. Meditation on the *feda* and their relationships can help your understanding if the meaning is not clear at first.

An example of the Cauldron and Tree layout is offered here to show you how the process works. The analysis of the reading shows how meanings are drawn from the feda cast, and how the layers of meaning within each *fid* are woven together to arrive at an answer.

Sample Cauldron and Tree Reading

For this reading, I decided to ask about the trip I'll be making this summer with an old friend to go to Burning Man. I've never been there, so aside from accounts by friends, I have no real idea what to expect. We plan on being there early to help with the setup and work as volunteers during the festival. I wanted to know what issues I should be concerned with, and how the experience would go for me. The *feda* drawn were:

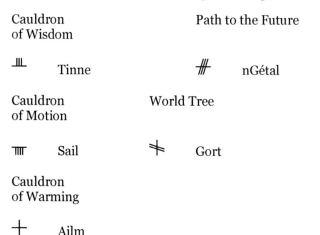

Cauldron of Wisdom		Path to the Future	
ᚈ	Tinne	ᚍ	nGétal
Cauldron of Motion		World Tree	
ᚄ	Sail	ᚌ	Gort
Cauldron of Warming			
ᚐ	Ailm		

Ailm as the cry of birth and death in the Cauldron of Warming suggests that the experience will be a very new and exciting experience for me. New ideas and the incubation of new creative projects are possible in a physical environment filled by performances, artists, and spiritual seekers of all kinds. Its keyword of Inception suggests newness all around.

Sail in the Cauldron of Motion, with its keyword of Flow, advises me to go with the flow of the situation. Emotionally, it's going to be easier to just take things as they come than attempt to schedule things tightly. In the context of camping in the desert, the willow tree is also a reminder to get enough water, as dehydration is a very real danger.

Tinne in the Cauldron of Wisdom echoes the creative spark of Ailm, and emphasises the thought that new ideas and projects are possible coming out of this event. New skills might be learned for later application when I get home. Tinne's keyword of Mastery may present an opportunity to master arts I've dabbled in before, or to show mastery of some skill or knowledge that I already possess. Its meaning of the ingot or iron bar also suggests that I manage my money around this situation wisely so as not to deplete my resources during the trip.

Gort, the garden, is the world tree that links the cauldrons together. It advises maintaining a calm, meditative space for shelter within the larger swirl of the festival's energies. Down time and rest will be important. Its keyword of Growth suggests setting down some roots as the community at Burning Man takes shape, and sheltering myself within that community, nourishing myself with the connections made.

The likely outcome of this reading is nGétal, the wound or charm. While this is a healing *fid* for me under most circumstances and its keyword is Healing, the hit I get from it in this reading is that if I don't conserve my energies as Gort suggests, I may end up exhausted -- "wounded" by overdoing the experience. My health tends to be precarious when I'm travelling, and there will be a lengthy road trip involved, as well as some hours of volunteer work in dry desert heat that I'm not used to. Health concerns will be central to the trip, but so long as I'm careful and watch myself, things should go well.

As you can see from this reading, interpretation and listening to intuition are both a part of working outward from the core traditional meanings of each *fid*. Deciding which of a variety of interpretations apply in a given situation takes practice, but it will come and it gets easier the more readings you do.

Divination being what it is, outcomes are subject to change given our actions in light of the information revealed in the reading. Divination doesn't predict the future so much as it shows potential paths and the flow of fate in the channels we've wrought through our actions. Given time, effort, and information, most outcomes can be shifted to something more desirable or a good outcome can be pursued more actively. In the case of this particular reading, whether or not I pay enough attention to my health by resting and getting enough water will determine whether the outcome's *fid* of nGétal carries a wound or a healing.

After you've had practice with the Cauldron and Tree, further *feda* may be drawn if questions remain at the end of the reading. These may add to or elaborate on other potential paths suggested by the reading. *Feda* could be drawn to represent the result of any course of action that is changed in accordance with the advice the reading gives. Other questions can be asked at this time to give more depth to the reading or to help clarify and illuminate the meaning of any of the *feda* on the table whose meaning may not be entirely clear in context.

It should be noted that this isn't an excuse to keep drawing *feda* until you get an "answer" you like. Doing this is only falling prey to the wishful or fearful thinking described earlier in this chapter. This sort of abuse of your divinatory tools invites confusion and will often result in an inability to get any kind of answer at all. Likewise, don't ask the same question over and over again in hopes that the answer will eventually suit you. These "answers" are only self-delusion.

Casting Cloths

For random casting readings, some people find casting cloths with patterns or designs on them useful for delineating what area of life a particular *fid* affects. Ideally, a casting cloth should reflect how you perceive life and the world around you. Because the ways of conceptualizing these things are so individual, many people end up making their own. Others find basic fourfold, fivefold, or threefold divisions very useful and may purchase a cloth with patterns on them that can be visually divided that way. Celtic Crosses and triskeles are fairly easy to find on altar cloths or decorative scarves. Creating a fourfold division can be as simple as folding a cloth in quarters and ensuring that there is a visible crease that divides the cloth into four equal parts.

A scarf with an equal-armed Celtic Cross on it could be used as a basis for either a fourfold or fivefold division based on the directional associations from the tale *The Settling of the Manor of Tara*, depending on whether the cross was extending from an inner circle or not. A fourfold division could also represent the year as symbolized by the four main insular Celtic holy days of Samhain, Imbolc, Bealtinne, and Lughnasadh and could be used to help determine the timing for a question. It could divide the query into things that effect mind, body, emotions, and spirit.

A cloth with a triskele design could be used as a base to read within any threefold paradigm. It might represent the three faces of a particular trifold Goddess, like Brighid who manifests as the Smith, the Healer, and the Poet. It could be read as the three internal cauldrons, or influences in the past, present, and future. Some people divide the worlds into an underworld of ancestor spirits, a middle world of human reality, and an upper world of deity, and these can be represented on the triskele as well.

A ninefold division drawn onto a cloth might represent such areas as ancestors, deities, land spirits, past, present, future, and the three internal cauldrons. There may be a number of messages coming from those powers and places regarding a question, represented by the fall of the *feda* on the cloth.

If there are particular spirits or deities that you work with who represent significant things or areas of life to you, you can include images of them or symbols related to them on a cloth you make for yourself. These fields can help you determine where a particular message is coming from if a *fid* lands on or near that figure's image or symbol. A cloth's fields and divisions are limited only by your imagination and how simple or complex your divinatory worldview is. Techniques used to design them could include fabric paint, screen printing, embroidery, iron-on designs you've made with your computer printer, or even just designs drawn on the sidewalk with chalk, or on the bare earth with a stick.

When designs are used, the boundaries between the areas expressed on them become important. Readings shift sharply based on whether a *fid* falls within a field, lies across a boundary, or even tumbles off the cloth entirely. A *fid* that bounces away may either be extremely emphasized -- did it end up in someone's hand or lap? -- or it could indicate that the *fid's* meaning is something that will most definitely not be encountered as a situation or issue within the context of the question. Intuition, context, and listening are very important when determining which of these it is.

A *fid* that crosses the boundaries between two or more areas on a pattern may indicate that both or all of those issues are involved, or it may be making a bridge between those areas. Ask yourself how the traditional meaning and keyword of that *fid* express through the concepts associated with those fields, and how it might bring them together. If the boundaries bridged are between "seasonal" areas on a design, it most likely implies that the task or issue will be a focus during several seasons, or that it may take more time than you expected.

Simple Random Casting Method

Even if blank casting cloths are used, they can indicate what lies nearer to or further from a situation, and what outside influences may be impinging on the issue. I use a blank cloth in my own work so that I can focus primarily on the relationships between the *feda* in the thrown pattern as they apply to the question at hand.

When deciding what's important in a random casting, I look for groups of *feda* and for outliers, determining which cluster of *feda* appears to be the focus of a throw. There may be lines of *feda* falling between different groups that appear to be bridging paths. When the *feda* form patterns, are they moving in smooth arcs or jagged lines? Are they all pointing the same way, or are they scattered and chaotic? Which *feda* cross or cover other *feda*?

Sometimes distinct separate groups of *feda* fall on different parts of the blank cloth, implying several forces at work in a situation. With a small number of *feda* being thrown for a basic random toss -- no more than nine -- the patterns will be relatively easy to pick out, and important groups will be obvious. I generally read from the center of the largest group of *feda* outward. My experience suggests that the largest group of *feda* in a reading is the immediate situation, and that the further a *fid* or smaller group falls from that main grouping, the further away or less important that influence will be.

If a *fid* lies outside the boundary of the others in a toss but still feels like it has a strong resonance within the context of the reading, it could be a person or influence from outside the situation that will have a profound effect on the result. There may be hidden forces at work, or someone behind the scenes pulling strings to effect the situation. Unexpected influences may appear and change things in ways indicated by the outlying *fid*'s meaning.

Left and right may be important in a reading. Traditionally, things that come from the left are unlucky while those that come from the right bring better tidings. You may find that this holds true when observing the patterns of random castings. Above all, listen to your own intuitions about which *feda* are important in a toss. Where is your eye drawn? What stands out to you? What are your feelings about the way the *feda* fall together and interact? What are the relationships between them? How do the meanings weave together to tell a story about the question or situation?

A *fid* that crosses several others in a toss is going to influence the meaning of each of the underlying *feda*. Depending on the size of the *feda* you use, you may see half a dozen *feda* or more beneath a single twig, or one disc may fall directly on top of another, hiding it from view. Observe which *feda* touch others, and how they touch. Are they next to each other or partially atop one another? Do they form a chain across the reading field? Where does the flow of the reading appear to be going?

Sample Random Casting Reading

For this reading, Eve randomly chose nine *feda* from the bag to help find her answer. After choosing the *feda* with her eyes closed, she tossed them onto the reading surface. While I don't use a casting cloth with a pattern on it, some people do. I find that a lack of background divisions helps me focus more on the patterns of the *feda* themselves. Eve asked if she was on the right path spiritually, as she has been reading outside of the tradition of her birth and was wondering what was right for her and if she should change religions.

Here we see that the nine drawn *feda* fell into two distinct groupings with one outlying *fid*. The central focus of the reading is the larger central grouping. It consists of the *fid* h-Úath as the anchoring bar across the top. Descending from that *fid* are Gort on the left and Ceirt on the right. Crossing over h-Úath and under Ceirt is Dair. Touching Gort and crossing over Ceirt is Ruis.

At the center of this reading is a strong conflict between anger, frustration, and a feeling of safety. H-Úath and Ceirt crossing each other is always an indication of a deep-seated conflict and great frustration. There are aspects of her current spiritual path that she intensely dislikes and that leave her feeling extremely angry, expressed by the appearance of Ruis.

Despite this, with Dair and Gort mixed into this complex, she finds a great deal of strength and growth in her tradition. Some aspects of her current spiritual life give her a safe place to live and grow, despite her frustrations with the perceived negative aspects of that path.

The second group of *feda*, to the lower left of the casting, consists of Edad flowing from top to bottom. Beneath it lie Lus at the top and Idad at the bottom, touching each other. This suggests that while she feels inspiration in her readings about the new spiritual path that she's interested in, she fears that the vision she has of it may be false or illusory. She is looking for something lasting, as Idad brings a sense of permanence and stability and a link with the ancestors. While she is very interested in a new path, she likes knowing what she's getting into and is uncertain where the truth lies in the complexity of her own thoughts on spirituality and deity.

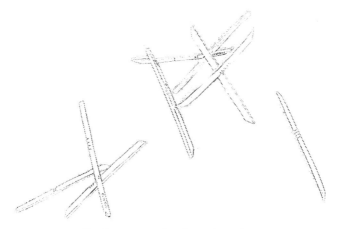

Random toss casting for Eve's reading

Sail lies at the right of the reading, alone. Sail, the willow, counsels going with the flow, and also waiting for an appropriate time. It also advises that she needs to clear out some of her issues with her current spiritual path that make her angry and frustrated and that disappoint her. Until she deals with what she finds unsatisfying about her current path, she won't be ready to move on to another. The possibility always exists that walking a new path will not solve spiritual problems that arise from within, particularly when part of the issue is about confronting the root of her anger and deciding exactly what she is so uncomfortable with in her current path.

When the time comes, she will be able to make a decision naturally, but her first task is to sort out where she needs to be and what nourishes her and allows her to grow and feel safe and strong spiritually.

On the Taking of Omens

There are many ways to use the ogam. Not all of them are dependent upon having a set of ogam *feda* with you when you're looking for answers. In fact, most of the recorded methods of insular Celtic divination had to do with looking for one's answers through vision-seeking ritual, by taking omens from the songs and activities of birds or other animals, or by the symbolic nature of the first thing seen when looking out with intent over one's threshold in the morning.

It should be noted that finding an omen is not the same as consulting an oracle. Omens are relatively rare spontaneous events that have significance and meaning. Reading, drawing, or casting the ogam in a formalized setting is a consultation of the ogam as an oracle.

Every day, we interact with the world around us. When we go out to work, or to walk the dog, or look out the window from the office, we're taking in the influences of what is out in the world. If we live in rural areas, much of our lives are immersed in the outdoors. All around us are potential signs and omens, if we open ourselves in a ritual way to looking for them.

Not everything we see, naturally, is going to be an omen. Even in the most spirit-driven life, sometimes things just happen and usually a flat tire really is just a flat tire and not an indication of great spiritual significance. Accepting that some things are omens and some are not is how a mature spiritual mind works.

Omens appear at significant moments that are startling or fraught with meaning, not unlike what the psychologist Carl Jung referred to as synchronicity -- acausal connections between an event and a question or situation in a person's life. Divination can be seen as a form of synchronicity, matching the random draw or toss of ogam *feda* to the moment a question is asked with the subsequent pattern offering a meaningful response from the universe. Others see divination as a connection with the spirit world and a way to actively seek answers from deities or spirits who watch over us and work with us toward various purposes.

Ultimately, what matters is not the source of the information received in divination, but the attitude with which answers are sought. Casual repetition of questions is likely to garner less and less relevant responses until nothing but nonsense is received. Respectful and ritualized framing of questions is more likely to bring our minds into a space where an answer can be meaningfully received and interpreted.

These answers can be found in many shapes, and the ogam can be useful in interpreting images in dreams or the physical manifestation of answers to petitions and questions.

Much of my personal spiritual work takes me outdoors. I go on regular trips to the coast or out camping in order to seek spiritual renewal, and part of what I do while I'm on these retreats is to look for answers through dreaming and ritual as I'm working on my path. When I'm at the coast, I go on beach walks as part of my meditational practice. I also make offerings of food and other things to Manannán at the water.

At one point when I was out for several days doing deep ritual work, I was doing some very intensive workings with gull spirits and with Manannán mac Lír. For me, Manannán and gulls are closely linked. As I finished my offering, I walked along the beach and found a stone that was marked with lines in a pattern that showed the letter Fern whose bird is the gull. Near that stone was a grey stone with a large white inclusion that looked like the outline of a heart, and Fern is also the guardian of the heart. I took these as a direct indication that my work was on the right track and that the offerings I made at that time were both appropriate and accepted. Note that though gulls are plentiful at the coast, it was not their ordinary appearance that was the omen, but the appearance of the *fid* linked with them.

Later that weekend, while I was working on interpreting some dream images, I came across Onn cut into a stump, and Muin and Ailm marked in white inclusions in a dark stone. Onn was a reference to the journey I was on that weekend, while Ailm and Muin offered counsel that a new beginning was at hand and that there would be hard work ahead, though the work was infused with positive emotion and pride. It was also a warning to avoid self-deception in matters of spirit.

If you look, you may find ogam *feda* anywhere. Graffiti on walls might be reinterpreted with hidden messages. Fallen twigs may lie in meaningful patterns. The veins in glass or stone may offer advice. Clouds and shadows may write shifting words in ogam for you to interpret.

Part of the key to using ogam for omens is to spend time with your mind on the question or the situation for which you need advice. Ritual before going out is a good idea, even if it's just a short prayer to your tutelary deities with an offering of water or incense on your altar. When looking for an omen or a sign, watch everything around you, from the flight of birds to the shapes of twigs in your path. Any of these things may be bringing you a message.

When you look, what catches your eye? What draws you? Are you getting a particular sense to walk somewhere different or unusual? Following these impulses can be useful and may lead to the revelation of something that relates to your situation. Perhaps something in your environment is an unusual color that attracts your attention -- is that color associated with one of the ogams? If it is, perhaps this is part of your answer. With the lists of trees and birds associated with the ogams, it adds more potential layers of meaning and possible interpretation to your omen seeking.

Symbols and images from dreams are also potential ways of seeking guidance from the ogam. This practice is particularly useful as you continue working with ogam and develop your personal correspondences, the way the early *Filid* were taught to create their own. In the *Auraicept na n-Éces* dozens of alphabetical lists are presented in different kinds of ogams as aids to memory, but they can be used as models for us in building our own ogam lists.

The original sources give us colors and birds, fortresses and crafts, and a host of other lists. We can create our own personal lists of deities, animals, local trees, birds, or plants that are significant enough to our personal sacred places and spiritual practices to be interpreted through the lens of Celtic practice. Working with ogam and images in the traditional tales can also be a fruitful way to approach the interpretation of dreams and omens through the use of the ogam alphabet.

It should be noted that the traditional ogam lists are primarily intended for mnemonic purposes -- they are for the most part simply alphabetical lists to aid memory for the composition of poetry. Given this, we need to understand that the attributes of any given traditional ogam list may not have relevance to you in terms of symbolic or magical purpose. In making your own correspondences, however, you can select for things that do mesh with the divinatory or magical meanings of each *fid*. If you create an animal ogam or deity ogam, you can do it based on which animals or deities resonate with the energy of each ogam *fid* so that your own magical, healing, or divinatory work is aided by the conceptual links that speak to you.

Given this, a South African animal ogam will be vastly different than a US Pacific Northwest animal ogam. The associations will be localized, just as the early Irish relied on local birds, trees, rivers, and fortresses for their own ogam lists. So long as we don't claim our personal ogam listings and inspirations as authentically "Celtic," we can still use the ogam system in this way and view our local environment and spirits through a Celtic lens.

This evolution of the system is as valid as any other, and it's important to realize that had Celtic Paganism continued uninterrupted by Christianity, it would look very different today than it did in the Iron Age. Our personal work and inspiration, checked against history and scholarship, is part of the work of weaving the tapestry of modern Celtic Reconstructionist spirituality. Together, our search for meaningful ways of bringing the old ways forward and working with the fragments of eroded and shattered pre-Christian traditions can create new spiritual paths that embrace the spirit of those Celtic traditions for a post-Christian world.

Erynn Rowan Laurie

CHAPTER 5
Three Cauldrons Meditations and the Dragon of Breath

Meditation and the Three Internal Cauldrons

In working with the ogam, you'll find that certain types of meditation will help with your understanding of the *feda* and your practices of ritual and magic. *Filidecht* demands a good grasp of meditative and transformative techniques along with a deep understanding of the ogam and its symbolism. One of the tools provided by traditional *Filidecht* is an internal energy system comprised of three cauldrons. These cauldrons are found in the body at the levels of the pelvic girdle, the chest cavity surrounding the heart, and within the head. They contain and process energy for various purposes and they correspond roughly to the physical, emotional and mental/spiritual realms in terms of your health and for receiving inspiration.

These cauldrons are spoken of in terms of filling, turning, brewing, and boiling, describing the desired actions and the results of work with them. These internal cauldrons are a very useful tool for understanding the ogam *feda* and for processing their energies within your body during meditation or study. Each *fid* can be internalized in the cauldrons at all three levels during the meditative process, and you can observe your energies and your physical body for their effects both during and after the meditative process.

The first cauldron, *Coire Goiriath*, is the Cauldron of Warming or Incubation. It's found in the pelvic girdle and is generally perceived as being upright in all people. It equates in part to one's physical health, and if this cauldron is not upright, it can signify illness or other physical problems. It's the source of bodily energy and the wisdom of the body found through movement and physical effort. Its task is to provide the body's heat and energy, and to incubate one's good health and foster new life.

Coire Érmai, the Cauldron of Motion, is the center cauldron. It is found in the chest cavity, encompassing the heart. In most people, it is found on its side at birth, and it is turned and made upright through the experience of intense emotions. The *Cauldron of Poesy* text says that it is turned "through joy and sorrow," and gives several categories of these emotions, including spiritual or religious joy, and the joy of sexual experience. In many ways the turning of this cauldron can be seen as the process of emotional maturation. This emphasis on the intense experience of emotion separates *Filidecht* from the many Eastern methods of meditation that seek separation from emotion and removal of the self from the wheel of incarnation. The *Fili* does not seek to escape emotion, attachment, and reincarnation, but embraces them as a great source of wisdom and profound knowledge that enables individuals and societies to mature and move with power in the world.

The third cauldron is *Coire Sofhis*, the Cauldron of Wisdom, found in the head. The text tells us that it is born upside-down, or "on its lips" in most people. Deep esoteric study and spiritual experience found through building on work with the emotions turn this cauldron. The ultimate result of its cultivation is wisdom, poetry, and prophecy, and only the most gifted of the *Filid* are said to be able to turn it fully upright. It is partly from the student's innate talent, partly from hard work, and partly as a gift of the Gods that this cauldron is activated.

In the Irish tradition, it's said that being descended from a line of *Filid* will help in the cultivation and turning of this cauldron, and that for one who was not born in such a line, attainment is more difficult. In modern times and particularly in western society, this idea is much less in favor because of the idealization of individuality and individual agency. I share the traditional opinion that having an ancestral connection of this sort can help, but it isn't absolutely necessary. Even the original texts admit that it is one's gifts more than one's ancestry that determines poetic ability. The difference really depends on how easy it is to cultivate, and being raised in a family where the poetic arts were openly practiced over generations would naturally give some advantage through early exposure.

It should be noted that in the *Cauldron of Poesy* poem, the reference says:

> *Ceist, cis lir foldai fil forsin*
> *mbrón imid-suí?*
> *Ní ansae; a cethair: éolchaire,*
> *cumae & brón éoit & ailithre ar*

dia & is medón ata-tairberat
inna cethair-se cíasu anechtair
fo-fertar.

Question: How many divisions
of sorrow turn the cauldrons of
sages?

Not hard, four: longing and
grief, the sorrows of jealousy,
and the discipline of pilgrimage
to holy places. These four are
endured internally, turning the
cauldrons, although the cause is
from outside.

From this passage, we can state confidently that all of the
cauldrons may be in motion, not just the Cauldron of Motion
itself. Each cauldron turns as a result of working with the
emotions -- both joy and sorrow -- and it is necessary to turn
each of them during the process of seeking *imbas*.

Ogam is one path among many that can lead to turning the
cauldrons and brewing the mead of wisdom within them. The
feda encompass a wide range of the experiences of life, spiritual
realities, and emotion within their ordered scores. Each *fid* can
be meditated upon and worked with in each cauldron, leading to
a deeper understanding of the ogam as a whole, and of the
cauldrons. It also helps the development of the physical and
spiritual self through the keen observation of breath and image
within the cauldrons themselves. Work like this is
transformative, changing your life in ways you won't expect.

It should be understood when embarking upon the path of
Filidecht that it *will* change you. Everything you do reverberates
through your life, sending ripples out from the center of your
being, reaching into the mists between the worlds. With enough
focus and practice, you will find that the entire way you relate to
the world, to your friends and family, to your society, and to
yourself will change. Some people find themselves experiencing
such a profound shift in consciousness that they can no longer
work at the same job or be in the relationships that have

sustained them in their lives. Others may find themselves questioning the nature of their being, their gender and sexuality, and the meaning of their previous spiritual paradigms. To work with the inner cauldrons and court their mysticism is to invite a sea of change whose magnitude cannot be predicted. The ogam *feda* are guides on this path through the mists.

Many societies have meditation techniques based around control of the breath and observation of breathing. There are hints in the Irish material that this was so for the *Filid* as well. One exercise is described as "stone on the belly" and refers to a meditation involving lying on one's back with a moderately sized stone on the belly under the diaphragm to strengthen the breath for the purpose of chanting and singing. The *Auraicept na n-Éces* or Scholar's Primer contains a cryptic phrase that tells us "five words are the breath of a poet"[113] and so the regulation and counting of breath was also likely to have been important to the practice of *Filidecht*.

Breath serves as a conduit through the body for energy, and in my own personal work I've developed breath techniques to help me with meditations on the cauldrons. These techniques enable me to more clearly visualize and focus on the cauldrons, to turn them and activate their contents, and to move energy between them for different purposes, such as healing, divination, or journeywork. With this breath work, there are also interesting possibilities of posture and gesture for the cultivation and direction of energy. Combined with later Gaelic poetic techniques such as partial sensory deprivation by isolation in a darkened room with a stone on one's belly and plaid over one's head, as reported in the Highlands of Scotland in the late seventeenth century,[114] intensive work can be done toward the rediscovery

---

[113] Calder, 1995, 71. The passage in this instance is describing the length of a poetic line as five words and equating them with the length of a poet's breath. On 57 we find another reference to breathing regulation. "Proper to bard poetry, i.e., its measure to suit the ear and proper adjustment of breathing." It should be noted here that bardic poetry and the poetry of the *Filid* were of two different classes, with the bards being regarded as untrained and the *Filid* being professional poets with a lengthy course of training behind them.

[114] Martin Martin's *A Description of the Western Isles of Scotland*, dated to around 1695, offers this passage: "I must not omit to relate their way of study, which is very singular: they shut their doors and windows for a day's time, and lie on their backs, with a stone upon their belly, and plaids about their heads, and their eyes being covered, they pump their brains for rhetorical encomium or panegyric; and indeed they furnish such a style from this dark cell, as is understood by very few; and if they purchase a couple of horses as the reward of their meditation, they think they have done a great matter." The entirety of the

and creation of appropriate meditation techniques for practitioners of CR.

Some of the work I've done is, admittedly, influenced by what I understand of yogic techniques and other forms of meditation, but the context is firmly within my work with the *Cauldron of Poesy* text that dates from approximately the seventh century in Ireland. With the original techniques of the *Filid* lost to history, there is a definite need to develop and test new techniques and methodologies that are appropriate and enable us to connect to the deities and spirits within Gaelic-based cosmologies and ontologies. Ideally, these methods of working will enable modern *Filid* to deepen their understanding of the ogam and the process of trance, ritual, and journeywork in a CR context.

In working with the cauldrons, there are several things to consider. The first is that not everyone will achieve the same results because not everyone's cauldrons are in the same starting positions and not everyone has the same innate level of talent. It is implied that only a few will be able to achieve the activation of all three cauldrons. Also, once a cauldron is turned, there is no reason to believe that it will stay permanently fixed in one position. The cauldrons are always in motion, their processes dynamic. Entering a new emotional state may turn a cauldron upright, or it may tip it back onto its side or its lips. In this chapter, I offer several breathing exercises, beginning with Sparking the Cauldrons to open and energize the cauldrons within. The breathing meditations for the three cauldrons presented here are not traditional. We have no way of knowing the exact methods that the early *Filid* used for meditating with the cauldrons, but there are oblique references to breath control techniques, referenced above.

Sparking the Cauldrons

This meditation is similar to a meditation I was taught for activating the three bowls of fire within the human body.[115] The gestures are my own, based on the position of each cauldron as it is situated within each person at birth, as described in the

---

text is in the public domain and can be found online at http://www.appins.org/martin.htm

[115] It was taught to me by my ex-husband, a martial artist, who told me the technique was from Tibet, though I can't be certain of its exact origins. I've modified it a bit for work with the three cauldrons.

medieval Irish *Cauldron of Poesy* text. This meditation is not intended to turn the cauldrons, but just to start the energy flow within them, regardless of their current positions.

You should stand for this meditation, keeping your body in alignment with your spine straight, feet solidly planted with your weight balanced between them, and your chin tilted just slightly downward in a relaxed position. The body should be at ease, not held stiffly. Make sure there's a little flex in your knees; locking your knees during this kind of breath meditation can lead to lightheadedness or even passing out.

Breathing will be in through the nose and out through the mouth, slow, deep, and steady with a slow three count for both inhalation and exhalation. The idea is to energize, not hyperventilate, so work with slow, deep breaths, rather than shallow, quick ones. Don't rush the process. You'll take nine full breaths in each cauldron before proceeding to the next. It will take some focus to maintain both the visualizations and the count, so you may wish to tick off each breath with the movement of a fingertip until you've counted nine.

Eyes should be closed to help facilitate the inward focus of the energy work. It minimizes distractions, allowing you to give your full attention to the meditative process and the internal cauldron work as you energize yourself.

The basic hand gesture for this meditation is with the hands flat, fingers together, forming a triangle with your thumbs, and index fingers. The gesture of the hands remains the same, though for each cauldron the position of the hands shifts, signifying the root position of that cauldron.

Hold your hands over your abdomen, index fingers down with your palms facing you so that the triangle you're making is point down. This symbolizes the upright Cauldron of Warming in the abdomen. As you hold your hands over your abdomen, visualize an upright cauldron settled in your pelvic girdle. With your first long, slow breath, inhale to the count of three and visualize a spark igniting within the cauldron inside your body. Exhale to the count of three. With each inhalation, visualize the spark growing brighter, allowing it to rest and warm you with each exhalation. Feel the cauldron spin within you like a whirlpool of energy. As you come to the ninth breath, feel the flame ablaze within the cauldron and see its light suffusing your body, illuminating all around you. As you exhale the ninth breath, feel the spark leap up into the second cauldron, within your ribcage, enclosing your heart.

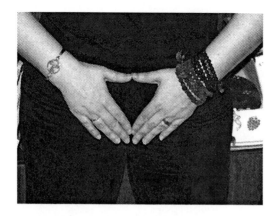

Sparking the Cauldron of Warming
(photo by Phillip Bernhardt-House, rendered by J. Buterman)

Raise your hands to heart level, with the index fingers pointing out, away from you, and your palms down. This represents the Cauldron of Motion on its side at your birth.

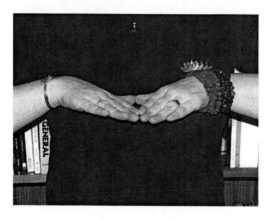

Sparking the Cauldron of Motion
(photo by Phillip Bernhardt-House, rendered by J. Buterman)

Once again, go through the series of nine breaths, inhaling slowly to the count of three as the flame brightens and the cauldron turns. Exhale as the flame warms you. With the ninth breath, feel the fire in the Cauldron of Motion blaze within your body, energizing you as you burn from within. See the flame leaping

185

upward to the third cauldron, sparking the fire of *imbas* within your head.

Raise your hands to your forehead with your index fingers pointed upward, palms out. This represents the Cauldron of Wisdom, born within us on its rim. This series of nine breaths sparks and lights the third cauldron, turning it until your entire body is filled with fire and energy, connecting the cauldrons within you by a fluid, flaming pillar of power and preparing you to work with them later in rituals.

Sparking the Cauldron of Wisdom
(photo by Phillip Bernhardt-House, rendered by J. Buterman)

You are likely to find that this meditation, properly done, leaves you feeling very warm physically. Your hands may tingle or you may feel like your whole body is shimmering with energy. It's possible that you will feel slightly buzzed and lightheaded, and that's okay so long as it's from the movement of energy and not hyperventilation. Feel your body, the energy flowing through the three whirling cauldrons within, and your connection to the world that your body manifests.

Looking Within the Cauldrons

Looking within the cauldrons can be done with or without first doing the Sparking the Cauldrons exercise. It is helpful to do this work both ways to examine how the cauldrons feel before and after being opened and energized, and you'll find that some meditational and magical applications of will work better in one mode or the other. Looking within is best done in a seated position, as you will be spending some time in the meditation examining the contents of a cauldron and meditating upon the images those contents evoke.

You can sit cross-legged or with your feet flat on the ground in a chair, whichever is more comfortable for you. I find that sitting with my legs crossed can be comfortable, provided my body is properly aligned and my bottom and back are properly supported. Mats and *zafu* cushions like those used for sitting *zazen* can be very useful for this work, as they help keep the spine straight and allow more circulation in your legs than sitting with legs crossed on the floor.

The cross-legged posture is seen in both continental and insular Celtic iconography over a fair stretch of time, for example in the famous antlered figure on the 1st century CE Gundestrup Cauldron, found in Denmark. In France, we find a masculine torc-wearing bronze figure with cloven hooves from Bouray dated to about the 1st century CE[116] and an earlier stone figure of a deity or hero from the Roquepertuse sanctuary dated to the 3rd century BCE.[117] In Ireland, we find an enamel-inlaid figure from a bucket handle that is seated cross-legged with its hands on its feet.[118] It's not unreasonable to think the posture might have had some kind of significance beyond merely being a common way to sit.

The breathing pattern for this exercise is slow and simple. It produces a much calmer, internalized, and meditative feeling than the Sparking the Cauldrons exercise does. Its intention is to provide a steady background for focus while altering your consciousness slightly.

The pattern is to inhale slowly for a three-count, hold for a three-count, exhale for a three-count and hold for a five-count. It should be focused on the particular cauldron that is the subject of the meditation rather than being moved upward through the series. The intention of the exercise is to hold attention within one cauldron, opening oneself to feel or otherwise sense what lies within. This may be an emotion, an image, a sound, or some other thing.

The examination of the contents of a cauldron can give you an idea of where you're at physically, emotionally, or mentally/spiritually. With practice, you may find yourself in

---

[116] Megaw, 1989, 156
[117] Brigitte Lescure article in *The Celts*, 1991, 362
[118] MacCana, 1986, 171

dialogue with figures found inside the cauldrons, or gaining information from the images there. As you learn what the cauldrons contain at a baseline, you can work with them opened and energized through the Sparking the Cauldrons exercise and see how they differ under those conditions.

Incubating the Feda

Once these basic exercises are comfortable and you're able to do them easily, you can begin to deliberately introduce different energies to your work by visualizing individual ogam *feda* in each cauldron in succession. At first, observation of energy and emotion are the goal. Each *fid* will vibrate a different type of energy in accordance with its meaning and purpose, and the subtleties of each should be studied to see how they differ when they are found in each of the three cauldrons. Beith will feel different in *Coire Goiriath* than it does in *Coire Sofhis*, and the way it moves and manifests will be different in *Coire Érmae* than in the others. Each cauldron will have its own effect on the energies of each *fid*, and learning to understand and recognize the manifestations of these energies will help you in your later ogam work. It is particularly important in working with the three currents of each *fid* discussed in chapter 8.

Each meditative session should focus on a single *fid* within one cauldron. This will give you time to focus exclusively on the combination of energies, emotions, images, and sensations without interruption. Taking notes on your work is extremely helpful for purposes of comparison as you progress through the series of ogam *feda* in each cauldron. Due to the nature of each *fid*, some will be more pleasant than others, but in order to fully understand and embrace the intensities and energies of each *fid*, the entire series should be done in order.

Remember that a palette of emotions and sensations, including joy and sorrow, pleasure, and pain, are necessary to turn the cauldrons within. It is the range of experience expressed through the ogam sequence that helps provide understanding and the ability to work successfully with the *feda* as spiritual, magical, and divinatory tools. Avoiding the more difficult or unpleasant *feda* and focusing only on the more pleasant ones will leave gaps in your knowledge, and the wisdom you derive from your work will be incomplete and imperfect. This avoidance is the spiritual equivalent of attempting to do healing work on an infected wound without first opening and cleaning it. We must embrace the dark and the challenging as well as the bright and the easy if we are to gain strength and understanding.

It's also important to remember that each *fid* has chthonic, oceanic, and celestial manifestations. NGétal is a *fid* of healing in its celestial aspect, but its chthonic side is wounding and slaying. Its oceanic manifestation is the transformation of flesh through the healing process. Each of these will have a different emotional resonance within your body and psyche. As with the initial study exercises, grounding and cleansing unwanted energies is important after doing cauldron work. The challenge of deep emotional work with the cauldrons and the *feda* is to gain dynamic balance through the motion of the cauldrons. It's a part of finding your spiritual center of gravity from which all movement flows.

Working with your emotions in each cauldron as you experience them, or after a very intense emotional experience, can be very helpful to your growth as a *Fili*. Bringing them into each cauldron and examining them can help you process them, and is a particularly powerful form of spiritual transformation magic. When dealing with the pain and sorrow of life, meditation on those emotions through the cauldrons can help you work through the hardships and achieve a greater emotional maturity. It can be a very helpful adjunct to therapy if you are seeing a counselor, as well.

Each *fid* will have a range of emotional resonances within your body, your mind, and your spirit. Working with your emotions within the cauldrons will help you develop distinctions between them in all their subtleties. It provides a broad palette from which to draw for your divinatory and healing work, as well. It increases your understanding of others by allowing a glimpse of what they might feel when they are under the influence of particular *feda* that appear in divination.

The energies and emotions of a *fid* can also be projected from within each cauldron as part of your work. In attempting to get pregnant, for instance, a woman might cultivate the *fid* Gort within *Coire Goiriath* in the abdomen and project that energy into her womb to encourage the development of a fertile and protected place for a child to grow. Focusing on Fern within *Coire Érmai* during a particularly difficult emotional situation can help you to maintain enough distance to protect yourself more effectively without either shutting down or losing your temper. Working with Tinne within *Coire Sofhis* can help spark inspiration for a creative project. Likewise, visualizing and projecting ogam energies into the cauldrons of those seeking help or healing from you may assist them in achieving their own goals.

Stone on the Belly

Another breathing exercise found in the traditional sources from Scotland, as noted above, is called the Stone on the Belly. This appears to have been a technique designed to strengthen the diaphragm for recitation, chanting of poetry, and singing. It may also have served as a physical sensory focus for the mind while poetry was being composed.

Diaphragm breathing is used today to help asthmatics and those with lung damage to increase lung function and capacity, and by singers who wish to strengthen their breathing for greater volume and projection. It can be used by *Filid* to aid and regulate energy flow in the body and for chanting and vibrating the ogam names for magical and ritual work.

Most people breathe largely with the upper part of their lungs, in their chest. This leads to shallow breathing and the pooling of stale air in the bottom of the lungs. Breathing with the diaphragm helps the lungs expand fully, reaching down into the bottom of the lungs to clear out carbon dioxide and oxygenate the blood properly. The diaphragm is a strong, curved muscle at the bottom of your ribs that regulates the pressure in your chest cavity, making your lungs expand and contract, moving the air you breathe.

You can get a feel for you how breathe and how much of your lung capacity you're actually using by lying down on your back with one hand on your chest and the other on your belly. Breathe normally. If the hand on your chest is the one that moves most, you're breathing primarily with your chest muscles. If both hands rise equally, you breathe about equally with chest and diaphragm. If the hand on your belly raises the most, you're breathing mostly with your diaphragm.

The Stone on the Belly uses a stone about the size of your fist laid on the belly just below the diaphragm at the bottom of your ribs. Lay a hand on your chest for comparison with the stone's movement. The object of the exercise is to focus your breathing so that you raise the stone without raising the hand on your chest. It's good to do a slow, deep inhalation through the nose to fill the lungs to capacity, and a short, sharp exhalation through the mouth that empties the lungs as completely as possible. It will take a little practice at first to avoid hyperventilation and to get a feel for the physical exercise aspect of it.

The stone will most likely wobble a bit when you do the sharp exhalation. If the stone is at least somewhat flat on the bottom, it should remain stable and stay on your body. A rounder stone will probably try to roll off, so when you're looking for a good stone for the exercise, look for one with at least one more or less flat surface.

The Stone on the Belly technique is definitely physical work, and you'll feel it within a few breaths when you're just starting out. Like any exercise, your muscles will get sore at first, but with practice you'll develop strength and endurance and the soreness will diminish until you can do it without pain.

Work on this, building up to five minutes a day for a week to two weeks, depending on your progress. When you feel confident in your stamina and ability, increase the time gradually and in small increments until you can do about fifteen minutes of this work without a break. You want to breathe at a normal speed; the object is increasing lung capacity and energy flow, not inciting dizziness and hyperventilation.

When you are used to doing this work, you can direct the energy of your breath more fully into each cauldron for meditation, or through your body for self-healing. It can be moved from your own body to another's for doing healing work on those who ask for it, and the breath can carry the energy of healing *feda* with it as you sing or chant their names and visualize them flowing out of the appropriate cauldron.

As your diaphragm strengthens, you can use heavier stones to increase the power and capacity of your breathing. Use good sense and moderation in determining what is heavy enough and how far to go. As you work with this exercise you'll find that you can sing or chant longer phrases and hold a tone longer with each breath. The longer and more faithfully you practice your technique the easier it will become to project sound further and with a stronger vibratory effect.

Control is an essential aspect of energy movement in ritual and magic. Focus of attention and being in the moment are critical in omen seeking just as attention and balance are necessary in the practice of martial arts. These methods of breath work are very useful for centering yourself in your body and achieving controlled trance states as you do more advanced ritual and divination. The focus you develop and your ability to maintain particular states for an extended period of time will serve you well in Otherworldly encounters and allow you to draw on energy through different breath focusing methods when needed. In the Otherworlds, your ability to focus and maintain your attention is one of your greatest strengths.

CHAPTER 6
Using Ogam in Ritual

Rather than offer a series of rituals for each ogam letter, or offering cookbook style rituals for readers to follow without thought, I felt it was most appropriate to describe and analyze rituals that use the ogam *feda* as components. A great deal can be learned by seeing the tools in use and then discussing the ways in which they were used. In each ritual presented in this chapter, the reasons behind the use of each *fid* and how they were used is given so that you can see the principles at work. It's my hope that by this method, you will learn how to analyze your own rituals and understand how to use ogam within their frameworks.

Because ritual in *Filidecht* is so personalized and context-driven, it's not possible for me to create rituals that everyone can use. I don't expect people to do the rituals presented here as I did them. Individual circumstances call for a sensitive appreciation of how each *fid* might be approached and its energies integrated into the overall structure of your own ritual life. The rituals here serve only as examples and as guides along your path. Observation of the contexts, reading and understanding the traditional lore and folkways, and meditation on your own ritual needs is the best way to learn how to use the ogam for your own purposes.

Aisling For Manannán

The night is wide around me and the fire writhes and climbs before me in the dark. I have spent the last three days in preparation for this night. I carried everything in, several miles up a deserted coastline, hiking around points of land only passable during low tide.

I have purified myself and presented myself to the sea, meditating, singing, chanting, intoning the names of ogam *feda* and drawing them in liquid fire before me to prepare myself for a ritual of *aisling* -- of seeking visions and dreams. I will sit, tending the fire, through the darkness of night then bathe in the sea at dawn.

Each ogam *fid* used in these preparations was chosen with care long before my journey started. Ogam *feda* were drawn on stone earlier in the day to aid my journey, chosen in the moment, intended to reflect the flow of magic and purpose behind my work. With each *fid*, new energies were introduced, new meanings projected, new goals stated. Here, before the fire, they have come together in one great matrix. My purpose is transformation and the seeking of wisdom.

It sounds dramatic, but it isn't really. The ritual was composed slowly, in pieces, over time. I found a companion to go with me, as it isn't always safe for a woman to go alone into the wilderness. We were not always alone -- other hikers passed by during the times of low tide, but when it rose, we were cut off from the world. Carrying a pack was hard for me, but not as much as I worried it might be. The isolation and the birds and the sea were worth the effort, and the results achieved from the ritual itself were more than worth the time and preparation required for the task.

I received no grand visions, but I found myself transformed. In acts of ritual and the worship of deity, small steps over time add up to grander things. In the act of tending a fire from dusk to dawn, it was the preparation that made all the difference in my perceptions and the effects I achieved. Insights arrive as much by giving them fertile ground to grow as by the lightning strike of *imbas*. Gort and Coll are companions. Lus and Onn intersect in their motion.

Selecting ogam *feda* for ritual is part intuition and part web of meaning. Each ritual is its own entity; each deity or spirit will resonate with different ogam *feda*. Part of the secret of choosing *feda* for your work and worship is found in your personal development of meanings and associations. While the information in this book can offer you a traditional baseline of meanings and kennings and introduce you to my personal associations, ultimately it will be your own work that leads you to connect different *feda* to your deities, to local herbs, to spirits you work with, or any other web of connections you choose.

In the ritual laid out here, my aim was a connection with Manannán mac Lir through the agency of *aisling*, or dream/vision seeking. I meditated on what was necessary and the phases I wanted the ritual to go through for several months beforehand, knowing that preparation was critical for a wilderness ritual intended to last for several nights. Locations had to be considered, a companion chosen, and the ritual itself outlined and prepared. Issues of isolation, access to water, types and amounts of food, protection of food from animals, whether or not we had to carry water in, an equipment list, and other physical issues were very important considerations. It wasn't until most of these things were decided that the body of the ritual itself was written.

In the traditional Irish bird ogam, Fern is *faelinn*, the gull, a bird I associate strongly with Manannán, and so this *fid* was a powerful centering energy for the ritual. It is part of the definition of my relationship with this deity, and gulls have been a sacred presence in my life from my earliest memories. Fern carries meanings of the alder tree, a container for milk, and a shield. Its keyword is protection, and to me, Manannán is a protective deity, shielding the Isle of Man with his cloak of mists and guarding the approaches to the Otherworld as well.

A word-ogam for Fern is "guarding of the heart" and so its protection extends to the emotional as well as the physical realm, making it an ideal choice for the center of a ritual involving reaching out into the Otherworlds. Any expedition into the mists bears some risks, and having guides, guardians, and aides is imperative, whether they are physical, spiritual, or both.

In choosing my companion for the ritual, I wanted someone who was walking a similar path, and who was familiar with camping and backpacking. Fortunately, an old friend was willing. He sees himself as walking a warrior path in the CR community, and so to accompany me as a buffer between the sacred and the mundane world of passers-by was ideal for both of us. He didn't have to participate in the ritual, but he understood what I was trying to accomplish and why, and this is very important when you are opening yourself on such a deep level. While it's possible to work with those on other paths for such sensitive rituals, it can happen that their expectations for your work may influence what happens to some degree, or that they may unintentionally end up attempting to interpret your experience for you within the boundaries of their own tradition. The guardian for your heart in any vision-seeking ritual should be someone who will respect your ritual and your processes within it completely.

Within any given ritual the ogam *feda* can serve as metaphor as well as magical force. They can represent people as well as powers that take roles in your work and your worship. These are useful considerations when you're designing rituals to take you deeply into your practice of *Filidecht*.

The *aisling* I did was intended to help bring back information that might be useful in reconstructing the rituals of *imbas forosnai* and *tarbhfeis*, as well as the *tigh n-áluis* or traditional Irish sweathouse. Each of these is mentioned in the early Irish texts or the living lore, though the actual procedures have been lost to the past. In seeking information about these rituals, I also hoped to open myself to transformations on many levels, recreating myself as a better vessel for the restoration of a magically and spiritually based form of polytheistic *Filidecht* in the modern world. Toward this purpose, I spent time meditating on which *feda* I would use, and the form my *aisling* would take.

The process started with a feeling that I needed to spend time out on the coast, far from other people, and that I should be there for three nights. The tales speak of those who went out to sit on the *sídhe* mounds seeking poetry, madness, or death, and I felt that this ritual should be a part of that lineage of dangerous knowledge. Risk is a necessary part of the process of growth and development, and the life of the spirit requires challenge just as the life of the body does.

As the ritual outline developed, I knew that each day of the ritual should be dedicated to working with one of the three internal cauldrons, and with one of the three realms to give myself time to feel their energies working in me and flowing through me without the distractions of my everyday life. While I do cauldron meditations on a regular basis, it's good to get out into the wild world, away from people and the accompanying physical and psychic noise of urban life. Meditations that are done within the backdrop of daily life can be profound, but to do them surrounded only by nature and the sounds made by wind and wave give them a different quality and brings forth a different kind of energy.

The choices of *feda* made for each ritual will be different because the nature of each ritual is different. A ritual intended for praise and sacrifice to a deity is going to be very different in structure and energy from the ritual outlined here, for journey and vision seeking. This is, in part, why it's important for you to develop your own series of localized ogams and associations. Meditating with the ogam *feda* and developing associations for each one with a deity or with spirits you work with will be helpful to you in choosing *feda* for rituals or for contacting those deities or spirits. It's best to avoid assigning *feda* randomly; choosing a *fid* for the quality of each deity or spirit will help you connect with that entity in your work.

For this ritual, I chose *feda* in pairs to work with complementary energies, but it is entirely possible to work with them individually, or in triads or other combinations as well. Ogam glyphs can be created to combine the energies of more than one *fid* into ritual symbols personal to you that express the particular focus or vibration of a ritual or deity that can be called upon over and over, gaining resonance and power with each use.[119]

Over time and with practice, you'll find that you develop a vocabulary of *feda* that you use for particular types of ritual. You'll go back to certain *feda* again and again for the same purposes, and mix them in similar ways for similar goals. With work and use will also come new ways to look at the meaning of each *fid*, and expansions of your consciousness regarding their energies and powers. H-Úath, for instance, is a difficult and challenging *fid*, but along with its association with horrors, fear, danger, and nightmares comes the power to break through negative patterns, and the protection of the thorny thicket about your most sensitive places. Such things must always be approached with caution and great respect for their destructive ability, but destruction has its necessary place in the circle of life, death and rebirth.

Part of *Filidecht* is the ability to see the spaces between dualities, to appreciate things within triadic relationships. Each ogam *fid* will have its brightness, its dark side, and the shadow of those between places that allow access to the Otherworlds through the mist. Working with the *feda* in ritual will help teach you the different faces of each *fid*. The CR path works less in dualities and binaries than in triads, finding the still point between opposites, the dynamic balance of three legs in motion, and the neither-nor that expresses what can't be positively stated in words. This is why the times of dawn and dusk are so vitally important in ritual; they are neither one thing nor another -- not light nor dark, neither day nor night. The process could be seen as one of thesis, antithesis and synthesis, if you lean in that direction philosophically.

Ritual develops in a flow from preparation and purification through the invocation of spirits and energies, then into completion. The culmination of my *aisling* would be a nightlong vigil tending a fire, searching for answers. The *feda* chosen needed to reflect this intended flow and the shifts in energies and

---

[119] The creation of ogam glyphs will be discussed in detail in my upcoming book on ogam in healing and magic.

consciousness as the rite unfolded. The outline for the ritual ended up looking like this:

Ritual notes: Manannán *aisling* at the coast

Tuesday:
Prayers to Manannán at the water
Site glannad & setup tent
Build a fire for offerings & make some food
Offerings & dinner
Beith & Fern calls & meditations -- purification and protection, Gull
Meditation on *Coire Goiriath*

Wednesday:
Glannad & breakfast
Prayers to Manannán at the water, offering of food
Songs for journeying
Edad & Onn calls & meditations -- vehicle for the journey, process of journeying
Meditation on *Coire Érmai*
Lunch break
Gort & Coll calls & meditations -- space for growth, wisdom
Three Realms work
Fire for dinner and offerings
Dair & Nin calls & meditations -- strength, support
Prayers to Manannán at the water, offering of food for dreamwork

Thursday:
Glannad & breakfast
Prayers to Manannán at the water, offering of food
Songs for journeying
Lus & Tinne calls & meditations - inspiration, mastery
Meditation on *Coire Sofhis*
Lunch break
nGétal & Ruis calls & meditations - healing & passion
Inscribing ogams for the journey
Fire for dinner & offerings
Muin & Straif calls & meditations -- communication & transformation
Prayers to Manannán at the water, offering of food for the journey

Songs for journeying
Fire-tending vigil and journeying work for the night to seek aid
for the *tigh n-aluis* and *imbas forosnai* rituals

Friday:
Bathing in the sea at dawn
Prayers to Manannán and offerings of food
Thanks to Manannán and the spirits
Break camp and head home

Let's look at the progression of the *feda* in this ritual. With these examples, you can work through your own ritual processes and choose *feda* to guide and direct your personal work. In examining the ritual outline in concert with the keywords for each *fid* chosen, the logic and flow of the ritual energies become clear. We work our way from an initial purification to a prayer for transformation with each section of the three-night ritual.

Within the context of CR, a ritual period of three or nine nights is called a *noinead* in the Old Irish language. This is traditionally associated with the *imbas forosnai* ritual, where three or nine nights are spent in trancework, guarded and guided by four companions who chant truth-spells over the seer. This is part of the reason I chose to work the ritual over a three-night period.

Because the coast is several hours' drive from my home, I chose to do very little on the first day except setting up camp and working on purification and some initial meditations. The meditation on *Coire Goiriath*, the Cauldron of Warming, was useful for getting in touch with my physical body and the source of my strength after the long hike in carrying my pack. Beith and Fern were chosen for their associations with purification and protection, as well as Fern's association with the seagull in the Bird Ogam.

With any ritual, purification and protection are both necessary on some level. In coming before the Gods and spirits, it's best to cleanse oneself in both body and spirit. In part, this sets us apart from our mundane daily lives. When we do rituals, particularly rituals of vision seeking, we open ourselves to vast possibilities, and to many different spiritual entities and powers. Purifications reduce our chances of interaction with spirits drawn to chaotic energies, and protection and shielding is a part of our declaration of intent and separation from spirits and energies that might interfere with our work and our prayers.

Edad and Onn are next, declaring the purpose of the ritual -- in this case, an attempt at a spiritual journey. Edad, the *Amanita muscaria* in my system, is the vehicle for spiritual journeys. It is the coracle in which the *Fili* makes the *immram*, the horse ridden through the mists into the Otherworlds. Onn as both wheel and foundation is the journey itself and the process of our movement. In the use of Onn, a wish for a smooth journey is expressed, and our intent declared.

Gort and Coll are next in the process. Gort as the garden is a safe space for growth, and a removal of extraneous energies as weeds are pulled from the crops to keep them from choking out what is important. Coll's presence is a prayer for wisdom and in concert with Gort it is a plea for wisdom to grow in the fertile ground being prepared as a part of this ritual.

Dair, the strength of the oak, and Nin in its aspect of support and weaving a web of connections are vital to the process. Without strength and spiritual support, the journey may fail. Any wisdom found might come to nothing, or be lost before it can be retrieved and integrated into daily life after the return from the journey. Without strength and support, the journey itself might fail, or we might never return. These help to ward against the risks of madness and death that are a part of the warnings surrounding such rituals in search of poetry and *imbas* in the traditional lore.

Lus is the fire of inspiration, and Tinne is mastery, both of the smith's creative fire and of the material world. These are also important to the process of the recovery and understanding of what is found on Otherworld journeys and within visions. Inspiration is necessary for both finding and interpreting what is seen, and mastery allows us to safely and accurately work with and manipulate what is found. Mastery is a part of the deep integration of understanding, and the result of long work with what is discovered and meditated upon.

NGétal and Ruis, healing and passion, might seem unusual in the context of a ritual such as this, but part of seeking lost wisdom and ritual is the intent to heal a breach in the continuity of history and tradition. It is also a plea for our own personal healing through the working of these rituals and our contacts with the Otherworld and those deities and spirits that dwell there. Ruis as passion is a necessary part of our work, for without passion we might lose the thread of our work and fall into depression or apathy. Passion can be a healing in itself, as passionate engagement with life and the spirit are a part of what keeps us alive and our minds and hearts youthful. Spirit sought without passion is more pitiful than powerful.

Muin and Straif are the final *feda* in the series for this ritual. Muin is called upon as the path of the voice, for open communication between this world and the Otherworlds, and Straif, sulfur, is transformation. Straif's transformative power is important in rituals seeking Otherworld contact. Each time we go to the Otherworlds in hopes of bringing back wisdom, we return changed. Straif calls out for positive change and transformation, alchemical in its purpose and mysteries.

The final part of the ritual was a vigil at the fire. For the vigil, I made a talisman inscribed with ogam *feda*. The first step was finding a suitable stone or piece of driftwood to mark for the altar. On one of my walks along the beach, I found a stone that was shaped roughly like a foot. This felt very appropriate for the journey aspect of the vigil, as one way that Onn is interpreted is as the sole of the foot. I had asked that Manannán and the spirits show me the appropriate base for my ogam talisman, and this stone presented itself to my attention quite strongly as I walked, praying for guidance.

Back at the campsite, by the fire, I passed the stone through the smoke of juniper, cedar, and other plants to purify and prepare it for inscription. I cleansed it with water from the sea as well. I then meditated and chose five *feda*, symbolizing the five rings of protection, the *coic creasa*, drawn about the infant Cormac mac Airt in the tale *Scéla Éogain*, found in *Cath Maige Mucrama*.[120] In the tale, these rings were drawn about the infant to protect him from wounding, drowning, fire, enchantment, and wolves, which were symbolic of every danger. I interpret these as danger in battle, danger during travel, spiritual and magical dangers, and the dangers of the natural world.

They are not merely protections, however. These five *feda* also symbolized the *lorga fuach* or stave of words for the ritual -- the work of the *Fili* as magical and sacred poetry. They are protections, gateways, and the *Fili's* passage into Otherworld realms. These *feda* were as carefully chosen as the *feda* for each stage of the preparatory ritual and meditation.

I sat by the fire and inscribed them with a felt pen on the stone. Muin for communication and the clear path of the voice; Edad as the vehicle of the journey into the Otherworlds; Onn for the journey itself; Coll for the wisdom sought; and Straif for the

---

[120] Mairin O'Daly trans, Irish Texts Society, 1975

alchemical transformation that results from the journey and the process of ritual. As I inscribed each *fid*, I called its name, singing my intent to the world around me. I worked to feel the energy of each *fid* going into the stone and settling itself in the fabric of my reality.

After inscribing the five *feda*, I drew the outline of a footprint around them, setting in stone the idea of a successful journey. Upon finishing, I drew a *fid* from my bag as an oracle to see if the work with this talisman was complete. I drew the *fid* h-Úath, terror, which was a strong "no" and so I drew another to see what was lacking. This *fid* was Úr; soil, which is also flesh or the body. In this case, I interpreted the lack or the need as a flesh sacrifice, and so made an offering of dried salmon to Manannán in the sea. Walking back to camp, I found a seagull's feather and offered that to the fire as well, with prayers for blessings and success. After this, I drew a new *fid* to see if the work was properly accomplished. This *fid* was Gort, the garden and the protected space for growth. This is a very positive *fid*, so I was satisfied that the offerings had been accepted and I was now in an appropriate place to continue with the ritual after dinner.

After eating, I offered a piece of sea lion scapula that I'd found on the beach to the fire, asking the help of seal and sea lion in my work, and uniting fire and water, allowing fire to arise from a creature of water. This image mirrors that of *imbas*, inspiration that rises glowing from the well of wisdom. After the bone was consumed in the fire I drew Coll, the hazel, from my bag. This is the symbol of the perfection of fire arising from water and bringing wisdom forth into the world. With the final offerings of food at dusk, I sang songs for the journey and upon returning to the fire to begin the vigil, the final *fid* drawn was Edad, the vehicle for the journey and the coracle of the *immram*. It was a fine sign for the work before me.

As you can see, it isn't merely the inscription of ogams or the projection of their energies that is important to ritual, but listening to them through divination as well. Divination is a necessary check-in with the spirit worlds and your deities to make sure your work remains on a good path, and that your actions are proper and appropriate for the time, the place, and the energies you are working with. It should always be done after offerings or sacrifice of any sort to determine if the offering was sufficient. Without the practice of divination in ritual, our place and progress are more difficult to assess. I always try to listen carefully to the voice of spirit, both through feeling the emotional vibrations surrounding me and asking the spirits for their guidance, and through active divination with a physical tool like the ogam *feda*. I never simply assume that an offering was accepted or a ritual properly done. Clarity, when pursuing important rituals, is critical. Divination can also help clarify the results of ritual and vision seeking when the images and energies are obscured in some way. Interpretation of images and results can be much easier when a dialogue is set up between the *Fili* and the ogam *feda*.

The ritual outlined above used three methods of working with the ogam: intoning the ogam names and projecting their energies outward through visualization and energy projection; making ogam-based talismans; and divination with the ogam. There are a variety of other ways ogam can be used in ritual as well. These three methods are only the beginning. The word ogams and other traditional ogam sets can be used as parts of ritual poetry, intended to evoke particular energies or images into a ritual. *Feda* might be engraved onto stones or staves as a part of an altar or permanent ritual area, or to symbolize the world tree or other important cosmological concepts in personal and group ritual. Individuals might, through invocatory work, carry ogam energies for the duration of a ritual. The applications are limited only by your imagination and experience. Experimentation will undoubtedly yield many more ways to incorporate ogam into your ritual and spiritual life.

Erynn Rowan Laurie

Trevor's Ritual to Face Fear

In the example below, Trevor decided to do a ritual to confront his fears based on the *fid* h-Úath. He had practiced CR for a few years but returned to the Christianity of his youth based on fears that were a result of how he was taught that religion. After spending a year as a Christian, he realized that it wasn't the religion itself that had called him back, but the fear of hell and damnation that still lived in the back of his mind. As he developed that understanding, he reexamined his attraction to the Celtic deities and felt it would be appropriate to do a ritual to help exorcise his fears and see if Celtic Paganism was the path he was really meant to follow.

This is his story:

I started working in the backyard today. I paid special attention to the lowest part of our property where the cultivated land ends and the wild land begins. This is the place that I had really started working with last year, as I believe this to be the seat of the land spirits. I definitely get the feeling that the spirits of the cultivated land and the spirits in the wild part are different spirits.

I went back into the woods to do some work that I felt compelled to do by the land spirits. It turns out they had a lot planned for me! I wound up ripping out and cutting away roughly nine feet of old, rusted fencing and removing a piece of rebar as the property marker. There's a wooden marker there too and the spirits didn't seem to like the rebar being there. There were several brightly colored plastic markers tied to the branches of a small tree. That too had to go. There was also some assorted junk back there that I took out as well. I must've missed some of this last summer, probably because the foliage was denser then.

The effect was staggering, as removing all of that manmade junk from the wild part did a lot to purify the energy in that area, which can sometimes be kind of prickly. It felt good to get out there and do some physical and spiritual work. At one point while I was back there I was bending a large piece of privet out of my way and for some reason glanced down at it. The branches were spaced and facing in such a way as to reveal two ogam feda: Beith and Lus. Starting from the bottom was Beith, a little further up was Lus, and then Beith again. This really stuck me, as I wasn't actively looking for an omen. I was more focused on getting the work done before the bottom dropped out of the sky. The impression I got seemed appropriate and straightforward for where I am right now.

First there is the need for purification and clarity of purpose and intent, as well as dedication and discipline when it comes to confronting my fears and responding accurately and appropriately. With discipline, clear understanding and receptive, purified motive I can better seek out understanding and enlightenment concerning the origin of my fears and the best way to overcome them. Following that, there seems to be the need for more purification and clarity. This probably hints at the need to be doubly sure of where I stand or to further underscore the importance of purification, clarity, and caution. After the events of later this evening and the things revealed by that experience, I think I can see another reason why this is necessary.

The after effects were even more staggering, and very disconcerting. I came inside to get cleaned up while my wife made dinner. I told her that I was planning on doing some serious work tonight, such as confronting some of my fears. I really identify with the idea of using h-Úath to turn negativity against itself and to summon a pack of wolves in magical workings to route things that threaten me. I take this very seriously; it's not something I really want to risk playing around with and having it blow up in my face.

As I sat down to eat I was suddenly overwhelmed with a sense of uneasiness and anxiety. My hunger disappeared and I was barely able to eat my dinner. I felt an unidentifiable fear bubbling up within me. My wife noticed and I told her I thought that with the combination of reconnecting with the land and announcing that I was going to do some specific work with my fears, something inside of me started yanking on those fears. For a few moments I felt panicked, like I was making a mistake by coming back to my Celtic Pagan roots. It wasn't a feeling of "you chose -- poorly," rather it was a generalized feeling of terror and anxiety that didn't seemed to be attached to any one particular thought. All I could focus on were the feelings of fear and anxiety I was experiencing.

She encouraged me to do what I had intended and graciously agreed to let me use her wolf pelt. She chased the cats out of the office and laid it out in front of our main altar with care.

I took a shower by candlelight while playing some

*personally meaningful music and prepared myself for the work
I was going to do. My wife left to give me some privacy. I did
some more preparation, lit three candles for the three realms
and began.*

*I usually start off any workings with a breathing and
visualization technique intended to carry me over nine waves
into the Otherworld, this time while beating a steady beat on
my bodhran. I've found this an exercise in focus and
coordination, as keeping a steady beat while mentally focusing
on journeying over nine waves and counting one's breath all at
the same time can be a little difficult.*

*I kept playing the drum in a steady cadence, just banging
out a beat that got faster and faster in tempo. Inside my body I
felt my blood racing and this deep energy rise up and when I
finished playing I let out a deep, primal yell that reverberated
off the walls.*

*I tend to use different tools in my workings and one of
them is the Celtic style long sword. I lifted the sword up and
spoke aloud a prayer and my intentions. Almost immediately
fear, doubt and questions assailed me:*

"You're going to suffer in Hell for eternity!"
"You're making a huge mistake!"
"You're being duped by demons and the devil himself!"
*"What is your father going to think? He started going
back to church out of gratefulness when you returned to
Christianity!"*
"You're going to lose a childhood friend!"
*"You just want to do what you want and will find any
way to justify it!"*

*Each time something came up I considered it and firmly
rejected it from a place of confidence and courage. I identified
these thoughts as being rooted deep in my psyche and
acknowledged that while not all of Christianity is negative,
certain aspects and certain teachings (particularly among
particular sects) are very toxic and damaging for me.*

*I lay down and rested my head lightly on the wolf's head,
grasping the h-Úath fid in my right hand. I started drifting to a
place of liminal consciousness and finally felt a sense of peace
wash over me. I sat back up and directed some energy into
turning this negativity against itself to purge my fears and
these thoughts. I verbally called on a pack of wolves and got a*

mental image of wolves baying and howling while they chased away the purged fears.

After all this, I grasped a section of river birch I had come across as dead-fall some time ago and prayed to Brighid for a healing of the scars left by these fears.

I gave my thanks and extinguished the candles. I realized that at some point there are two key people I need to talk to about these issues in a non-confrontational manner.

The first person is my father. While he was understanding and even supportive of me as a Pagan, he was elated when I returned to Christianity and he started going back regularly to the Catholic church I was raised in, and started reading his Bible more. He said, "The Lord had answered my prayers, how could I not go back?" While I was grateful at the time, looking back on it, it has become a more loaded statement than he intended. I'm sure he will be disappointed, but he has to understand that his personal spiritual choices can't be based upon what path I may or may not walk.

The next person I need to talk to is my friend Jack. Jack and I grew up together. I got into fights with just about every kid near my age in my neighborhood. Jack is the exception; we never got in a fight. As we got into our teens we started becoming close and studied martial arts together. By the time I got to college, Jack and I were having deep conversations about Eastern philosophy, life, martial arts, what it meant to be a warrior and the like. Jack was my most intelligent childhood friend and the one person I could have really deep and meaningful conversations with.

Jack had just been accepted to medical school when he decided to give it all up and become a minister. When I became a Christian last winter after having spent some time as a Pagan he was, as one might expect, very helpful. Even though I kept his fundamentalist approach to Christianity at arm's length, we still had some pretty good discussions.

Jack is a good guy, but I know I can't continue to have a friendship with him and not say anything about my spirituality, especially since he's under the impression that I'm still a Christian. To do so would be to censor myself and hold back out of a sense of fear and shame. I won't do that.

I realize that many of these fears are personal, internal things that I have to face on my own and without any fanfare or grandiose gestures. However, there are certain relationships where I have to be honest and be my authentic self, now that I'm discovering who that really is. I have to assert myself in a polite but firm way and this has to come from a place of spiritual truth and knowledge. Otherwise there's that element of fear and being controlled by fear and letting it control my personal relationships.

Trevor feels that the ritual helped him get a handle on his fears and understand his relationship to both Christianity and the Celtic deities better. Despite the inherent hazards, working with h-Úath is giving him the strength to break through the fear that had been haunting him through his life, and to approach his father and his friend honestly. It has also helped him make useful positive decisions about the spiritual path he wishes to pursue. He no longer considers himself a Christian, and even during his time practicing that religion, he found the ogam a useful guide in times of uncertainty.

Ritual for Healing

This ritual is one I designed to do healing work for a relative who had an immense aneurysm, long enough to extend from just above his heart down into one leg. At some points the aneurysm was as much as 7cm wide. After getting permission to do ritual for my relative, I developed an outline that made use of several different healing ogam energies. Ogam and healing is an immense subject, and will be the topic of a book of its own, but the general principles of this ritual can be used in creating ogam-based healing rituals for your own purposes.

The *feda* chosen for this healing ritual were specific to its circumstances. I debated for quite some time about the inclusion of h-Úath, but it does help with the sharpness of surgery. In the ritual, its energies were specified and contained by the other *feda* surrounding and moderating it. Onn was chosen for its relationship with the legs and feet, since the aneurysm extends from the heart down into the leg. Nin was used for its connotations of weaving together, stitching the aneurysm closed and weaving the healing tightly. Dair was for strength and recovery. These four *feda* were engraved on a taper candle placed in the center of the altar space.

Surrounding the central candle were three tealights marked with the *fid* Fern. Its word ogam "guarding of the heart" expresses the power to protect the heart physically and also helps with healing that organ. The heart metaphorically can extend to

Altar set for healing ritual

the veins and arteries that are so intimately connected with it. These surrounding repeated *feda* guard the heart and damaged arteries against the sharpness of h-Úath's blade. Outside that circle were nine *feda* marked with Gort for rest and recuperation. The post-surgery hospital stay was anticipated to be about two weeks, with a three-month recovery following that.

Behind the candles was an icon that I created some years ago with the *fid* nGétal drawn on it as a focus for my healing work. I have used this consistently on my altar and it has taken on a deep connection with healing energy through this work.

The deities involved in the ritual were Dían Cécht, the main Irish healing deity, and his son Miach, the God of surgery.

The tools I used for this ritual were:

Taper candle
3 tealight candles
Candleholders
Knife for marking candles
9 feda marked with Gort
Juniper for glannad
Matches
nGétal icon
Offerings for deities
Images of deity and helping spirits
Healing items used in my work (crystals, etc)

Here is the outline for the healing ritual I did:

Offering to Outsider spirits
Glannad of self and materials with juniper
Center Point meditation
Sparking the Cauldrons
Making the Gort feda
Marking the taper
Marking the votives
Setting the altar
Asking the presence of ancestors and helping spirits
Asking the presence of Miach and Dian Cécht
Making offerings of food and drink
Lighting the candles and focusing intent
Offering the prayer for healing
Draw oracle for the ritual
Thanking the ancestors, spirits, and deities
Allowing the candles to burn down

I had spare wood ovals from some ogam sets I had worked on a few years ago, so I marked the nine Gort *feda* on those to use for the ritual. Paper, twigs, wax discs or any other material available could have been used. I chanted the name of the *fid* over them, pushing that power into them as I marked the bare materials.

I marked the taper from top to bottom with h-Úath, Onn, Nin, and Dair so that the energies would be released in that order. While ogam is traditionally inscribed from the bottom upwards, because candles burn down it made more sense to inscribe the first *fid* at the top so that the energies were released as I intended.

H-Úath came first in the order, symbolizing Miach's skills in surgery. Onn was next, as the surgery would affect the body from the heart to the legs. Nin followed, for the knitting of tissue and the effectiveness of the stitches. Dair was the final *fid*, to send endurance to survive the surgery and strength and stability for the recovery process.

The three tealights were each marked with Fern to guard the heart and heal it physically. They surrounded the central taper candle as a barrier against all negativity and misfortune. The Gort *feda* were placed around the outside of this arrangement so that all the healing energy was contained within their peaceful space to allow for proper rest and recuperation and to encourage the proper growth of new tissue in the arteries that were affected by the aneurysm.

Each *fid* that was made, either on wood or on the candles, was touched with the blade as I focused power into them to symbolically link them with the first *feda* made by Ogma, the creator of ogam, and to lend them some of his power.

When the altar was set, I asked the presence of the ancestors to help my relative and called upon some of the healing spirits that work closely with me, then asked Miach the surgeon and Dian Cécht the supreme physician of the Tuatha Dé Danann to come to my relative's aid and help him heal. When I felt their presence, I made offerings of food and drink to them and lit the candles.

As the candles were lit, I offered this prayer for healing that I adapted from a traditional prayer found in the *Carmina Gadelica*.

> *Living charm sent from Dian Cécht*
> *to Miach noble, beauteous,*
> *for wound, for breach,*
> *for failing strength,*
> *for heart, for swelling, for veins,*
> *for wounding, for tearing,*
> *for aneurysm, for bleeding,*
> *for pain, for weakness,*
> *for illness in your veins;*
> *Be it for good and for excellence*
> *if you have healing*
> *between the tips of your two ears,*
> *between the bases of your two soles,*
> *May disease ebb from you downwards*
> *as ebbs the ocean*
> *into the belly of the great whale*
> *and into the great grey depths*
> *'til these divide each other;*
> *As Dian Cécht and Miach healed the people*
> *it is in their nature to heal each of these distresses.*[121]

As I prayed for my relative, I focused that desire into the candles, intent upon sending that healing energy to him for the

---

[121] This charm is adapted from Carmichael, 1978, 313. Deity names have been changed, illnesses and symptoms were changed to reflect the situation, and an irrelevant bit of the charm has been omitted.

surgery and for his swift recovery. I also asked that the spirits and deities would be gentle with him and to send him their healing rather than revealing themselves to him. My relative is a very devout Christian and might perceive their presence as evil, but he was willing to accept prayers for his health regardless. I was careful to ask the permission of my mother before doing this ritual, as she was with him during the surgery. Even in doing healing work, it's best to get permission from the person you're working for, or from someone who can speak for them. There are those who may feel that accepting prayers or healing work from people outside their religious tradition is wrong in some way, and it is better to respect their beliefs and their feelings if that is their desire than to force your own work upon them.

After offering the prayer for healing, I sat with the candles for some time, focusing on sending the healing to my relative and offering my own love and support to the working as well. When I felt ready, I drew the oracle for the ritual and received the chthonic current of Gort. Given the context of the ritual and that Gort was repeatedly invoked for its protective and rejuvenating powers of fertility and healing space, I felt this was a very good oracle for my relative's healing.

I offered thanks to the ancestors, the deities and the spirits and allowed the candles to burn down so that their energy would be released. The taper candle stub was burned with the Gort *feda* in my fireplace along with the food offerings.

In checking with my mother after the surgery, my relative not only came through the surgery itself spectacularly well, but he went home from the hospital after only five days, rather than the two to three weeks initially projected. Rather than needing live-in assistance, within a day or two from his return from the hospital he was up and doing much of what was necessary to take care of himself in his own home. I would in no way claim that my ritual was responsible for his healing, for he had a good many people praying and working for him, but I do believe it contributed to his almost miraculously rapid recovery.

The use of ogam in ritual can take many forms. From basic ogam inscriptions to mark sacred objects to advanced works incorporating many *feda* for different uses and in different ways, the ogam is a flexible and powerful ritual tool. The few examples shared here offer guidelines and ideas for different ways to approach ogam use within different ritual types and settings.

With practice and experience, each student will come to their own conclusions about how ogam works in ritual for them and how best to use it for transformative and magical purposes.

Erynn Rowan Laurie

CHAPTER 7
Creating Your Feda

Choosing Your Tools

A set of ogam *feda* is a very personal tool. When used properly, it carries your energy and helps you to see into other worlds and possibilities as you walk the path of *Filidecht*. It becomes a focus for magical and spiritual work and for meditation. Even if you buy a commercial set of *feda*, you will want to imbue them with your energy to help you connect with their lessons and read them more easily and accurately. This chapter will offer several approaches to personalizing or creating your own set of *feda* to aid you in your work.

My strong recommendation is that each student of ogam creates their own set of ogam *feda* on wood or stone for their personal use. Other materials like bone or shell can be used as well if you resonate with them, though I would not recommend artificial materials like plastics. Artifacts of bone with ogam inscriptions on them have been found, as have amber beads inscribed with ogam, so these have historical precedent as items possessing magical and possibly divinatory powers and associations. The primary reason I don't recommend artificial materials is because they never feel quite right to me; plastics don't have the right energy, though some people might feel comfortable using glass or metal.

Stone, wood, bone, or shell have a variety of living energies within them that manufactured materials usually don't have unless they are somehow imbued with them through later ritual. I don't see a good reason to put that much effort into creating what already exists in other places. There is also the added advantage of being able to work with the spirits already associated with or dwelling within the materials you choose for the creation of your *feda*. That isn't possible if you're working with artificial materials.

Each *fid* you make should, at the very least, have the individual ogam letter and a mark to distinguish top from bottom. You can include the letter or the name of the *fid* as well if there is room. I find that including the letter can be useful, because sometimes I find myself visually scrambling right and left in my head, especially when I'm tired. When you're just starting out, it can be easy to forget whether the *aicme* to the right or the left comes first (it's the right). That's what determines whether you have the B or the H *aicme* -- mistaking one for the other can be problematic, to say the least.

You will probably want to work with cabochons, wood or antler discs, tumbled stones, or twigs that are *no smaller than three-quarters of an inch in length at minimum,* simply for the sake of readability and to make the task of marking them easier. With twigs, two to three inches is a better measure, depending on your tastes and how they feel in your hand. The twigs should not be so thick that you can't hold the entire set of twenty in your hand at one time, but they should be thick enough that you're able to mark on them easily, either on a flat, peeled place marked with a center line, or across an angled edge. Carving, wood-burning, or painting are all possibilities for marking the scores on your material.

There should always be an indication of which end of the *fid* is up, so that the B-*aicme* is not mistaken for the H-*aicme.* Usually just including the Roman letter or letters on the *fid* will be enough to cue you. I use a dot at the bottom of each of mine, and still have to keep reminding myself that it's right hand first, left hand after. With twigs, the top end could be colored or burnt to distinguish it from the bottom. You might only peel away bark on the end of the twig where you're carving or otherwise marking the *fid,* eliminating the need for further distinctions.

For advanced divinatory techniques, it will be necessary to create three sets of *feda* in different shapes or colors so that you can distinguish between the energies of each of the three currents of meaning. You may wish to create a single set of *feda* for basic workings and a threefold set for more complex issues, or you might start by creating the set for the oceanic current, which can serve as your single set because its liminal nature links all of the realms and currents and represents the mists that hide the mysteries of the Otherworlds. Once you feel able to advance to the next level, creation of the *feda* for the chthonic and celestial currents can follow.

The colors I chose to represent the three currents are green with red lettering for the chthonic, grey with green lettering for the oceanic, and blue with white lettering for the celestial. The symbolism behind these choices is dealt with in more depth in Chapter 8 on advanced divinatory techniques, though it will be touched upon here in the instructions for creating a triple set of *feda*.

Your choice of materials for your ogam sets may be symbolic as well. A set made of antler discs or bone beads will feel very different than a set made of stone, not just physically but energetically. Deer and other animals have mythic resonances and powers that you may wish to evoke; the stag is a frequent guide into the Otherworlds beyond the mist in Irish and Scottish lore. Carving your *feda* on antler or deer bone would bring this boundary-crossing influence into your divinatory tools. If you work closely with particular animal spirits, you might wish to engrave your *feda* on bone, horn, or teeth from that animal, provided it's both legal and practical to acquire the necessary parts. Working with particular stones that you associate with different deities might allow you easier contact with their energies in divination. If you do a lot of healing work, making and dedicating a set with a stone or wood you particularly associate with healing or with your patron deity of healing can be a very good idea. Within the CR community there's a shared gnosis that moss agate resonates well with Airmid, the Irish Goddess of herbal healing. A set made with that stone might carry her energy well for healing divination.

Twigs might be chosen for the lore associated with a particular tree -- oak or hazel twigs are most appropriate for general-purpose ogam sets due to their associations with truth or wisdom. Birch is highly symbolic of ogam work in all its varieties and as a connection with Ogma because it was the wood upon which the first ogam *feda* were carved. Yew is useful for work that involves contact with ancestor spirits. Given its traditional association with danger and the *geas* against bringing it indoors, hawthorn isn't a good choice for most people unless they are in tune with its potentially dangerous and disruptive energies and work with them on a regular basis. Even if that is the case, to work with a set of hawthorn-twig *feda* may be inviting trouble where none is wanted. I would certainly not read for other people with a set made from hawthorn even if I kept one for my personal use. The triple set of *feda* I usually use are made of paua shell cabochons, in part for its natural color variations and the fact that it can easily be found pre-dyed in a number of colors, but more because I work a great deal with Manannán mac Lir and shell is very much in tune with the sea energies he controls.

There are different levels of energy and time you can invest in the work. If you aren't particularly crafty, buying a set of *feda* may be the best answer for you, but you should still take the time to work with each individual *fid* to mark it with your own energy and charge it by chanting its name as you focus on its meanings.

Empowering the Feda

Not everyone will have the skills or desire to create their own set of *feda*. In this case the easiest thing to do is buy a commercial set. The physical marking is already done for you but they will, at best, be psychically and magically neutral. There are ogam card decks available, but all of them seem to work with the tree ogam metaphor and so are only marginally useful for the interpretive meanings and methods presented in this book. Still, if they are the only option available, you can use the same cleansing and empowering ritual on them that you would for any other type of ogam *feda*.

Even if you get a set of *feda* made by a Pagan artisan, the energies in them will not be your own. The maker's understanding of ogam may not be anything like yours. To have someone else put their personal magical energy and imagery into your set of *feda* can have you working at cross-purposes with your own tools. If you commission a set of ogam from an artisan you know, ask them not to imbue them with any extra magical energy as they work so that only your own energy and intent will be entering what should ideally be a blank slate.

Set aside an hour or two of undisturbed time to work with the new *feda* when you first bring them home. An altar can be set up very simply for this ritual. You'll need the following things:

A set of ogam *feda* or cards
Bag or box for the *feda*
Juniper (berries, branches, or oil)
Container for burning juniper or diffuser for juniper oil
Knife or sickle to charge the *feda*
Offerings for Ogma and the spirits

If you wish, you can cover your working surface with a cloth, but any clean, level surface that will hold your *feda* and the other items will do. If you're outdoors you can do this on the ground, under a tree, at the shore of the sea, or the bank of a creek. Any place that feels right for ritual will be a good place for this work. If you do decide to do your work outdoors, make sure the place is private and, if you're going to have any kind of open flame, be aware of any fire risks in the area and be sure to observe any laws regarding burn bans that might be in effect. Accidentally starting a forest fire isn't a good way to do ritual or to bring the attention of the spirits and deities to you and your work.

If you have a regular altar in your home where you make offerings and do other ritual, clear a space about a square foot or so in diameter so you can spread out your *feda* and work with them. If you have an image or object that you use to represent Ogma, place this in your working space as well.

You won't be using the knife or sickle to actually mark or carve the *feda*; it symbolizes the knife of Ogma, who made the first ogam. It will only be used to trace the lines of each *fid* lightly as you focus your energy into each one. If you don't have a knife or sickle for this work, a finger will do, but the symbolism of Ogma's knife is important in working with the ogam. Ritually and mythically speaking, the hand of Ogma is the father of ogam and the knife is its mother.

For your offerings, honey is an excellent choice. One of Ogma's epithets is *Milbél* -- "Honey Tongue" or "Honey Mouth" -- for the sweetness of his speech. In my experience, honey, mead, spring water, Irish or Scotch whiskey, hazel nuts, pork, apples, Atlantic salmon, or steel cut oats are all good offerings, though if you don't have any of these things, other food or drink will do. Try to have honey and water at a bare minimum, if you can't get anything else. Remember that Ogma is your honored guest, and that offering hospitality to guests is a very important part of Irish and Scottish culture, as well as of CR spiritual practice in general. Whatever you offer to Ogma be sure that it's the best you have and that it's cheerfully given. Grudgingly offered hospitality is not much better than open hostility, and that's not the kind of relationship you want to foster with your tools or with a deity.

It's a good idea once the altar is set, but before you purify yourself and the space, to make a small offering at a distance from your main ritual or work area to the spirits you don't work with, and to any entities that might otherwise interfere with your ritual. Ask them to accept your offering and not interfere with you. This act acknowledges them but it also gives them something else to focus their attention on while you work. Giving an offering to the Outsider spirits helps you maintain a respectful distance with them while not giving them any reason to be jealous of your work with more benevolent spirits. It isn't absolutely necessary, but it is respectful and cautious to do so.

Remember that our luck is at least partly a result of our interactions with the spirit world, and keeping the spirits well disposed to us is just a good idea.

It should also be noted here that Outsider spirits are not necessarily malevolent, nor are they always spirits that will interfere with your work. They may very simply be spirits or deities you're not working with who may otherwise be well disposed toward you. It's important to remember this when thinking of the Outsiders; at some point some of those spirits may become more important to you and start to work with you closely, meaning they will no longer be Outsiders at all. If you maintain cordial relations with the Outsider spirits, these transitions will be much easier and more natural, and there will be fewer potential misunderstandings if communications begin between you.

After the offering, cleanse your body and tools with juniper smoke. If you have problems with smoke, using an essential oil diffuser with juniper oil will produce a light, scented steam that you can use in the same way. You can make your own diffuser fairly easily by using a fireproof container, a tea light candle, and a second fireproof container that fits partially over the first. Fill the second container with hot water and a few drops of juniper oil and place it over the candle inside the first container. So long as oxygen is able to get to the candle inside the lower container, you'll be able to keep the water on top heated and the scent will diffuse into your space. I use a small cauldron for the lower container and a ceramic bowl for the upper container when I

Tools for glannad: Home made oil diffuser, shell with juniper, juniper berries, oils of juniper berry and juniper branches, birch oil.

work with this method. A small ceramic tea-warmer would also work perfectly if you have one.

In places where smoke or open flame are forbidden or not practical for safety or health reasons, the use of a fresh juniper branch is the best alternative. Brush your body and tools with it as though you were using a feather to catch and brush away any unwanted energies or spirits, then flick them away from yourself at the end of each stroke. *Glannad* should be done with intent; just going through the motions without focus and intent does little or nothing to the energies within and around you. Your intention should be to dissolve and drive away any negativity or any spirits or energies that will interfere with or cloud the work you are about to do.

When you are purified, center yourself in the three realms. This is easily done with a few gestures and a brief meditation and breathing exercise that I call The Center Point. I use it in many ritual contexts when I want to center and calm my energies or to remind myself of my small place in the cosmos. You can speak the lines aloud or simply focus on them internally to bring your mind and body into harmony with each other and your place in the world. If you wish, substitute your own words with the same intent.

Center Point Meditation

Stand quietly and relax with your hands resting at your sides. Clear your mind and concentrate on your breathing. Breathe in and cover your heart with your hands.

I am at the center of the world.

Exhale, move to one knee with your palms on the ground before you.

I stand upon the sacred land.

Inhale and rise to your feet, moving your hands behind at hip height, palms up, cupping.

Exhale and move your hands in an arc until they meet in front.

The nine waves of the sea surround me.

Inhale and bring your hands to your sides, spreading the fingers wide.

Exhale and raise your arms, bringing your hands together above your head, thumb & forefinger meeting to create a triangle. Peer through the triangle at the sky.

The sky spreads itself above me.

Inhale and lower your hands to your heart again.

I am at the center of the Three Realms.

Exhale and lower your hands to your sides

A lovely alternate meditation created by my friends Bob and Brenda Daverin adds the image of the world tree, called the *crann bethadh* (tree of life) or *bile* (great sacred tree), to the meditation. Bile is also the name of a deity who appears to be an ancestor of the Tuatha Dé Danann and may be related to that sacred tree. My own intuition sees him as a chthonic and celestial deity linked to the birch, the stag, and the sun at night, so in many ways he is a very appropriate deity to deal with in working with the ogam. I'm presenting it here with their permission and my great thanks. As with The Center Point meditation, you can speak the words aloud or recite them silently to yourself.

Honoring the Three Realms

Standing with feet balanced firmly on the ground, left hand resting at your side, gesture with your right hand to the earth.

With the sacred land always supporting me

Raise your hand in an arc to waist level, indicating the surrounding sea.

The eternal sea surrounding me

Continue to raise your hand until it is above your head, indicating the sky.

The endless sky above me

Lower your hand to your groin and draw a straight line up the center of your body, visualizing the tree that grows within, its roots in the earth and its crown in the sky.

The world tree, Bile, aids me
To connect the realms through my body

At your forehead, draw either one side of a triangle or one spiral of a triskele from the center of your forehead, moving clockwise from the lower left corner, with each quality evoked.

Bringing wisdom
Sight
And health.

When you have centered yourself and feel ready to begin, it's time to call on the spirits, ancestors, and deities. If you have spirits that aid you -- animals, plants, stones, ancestors, spirits of place, or others -- feel free to call on them for their assistance in giving life to your tools. They can be very powerful aids in your work with the ogam if you understand how to listen to their direction and watch for their hints. This will be discussed at greater length in the chapter on advanced divination techniques.

Ancestors may also be willing to help you in your work. These don't have to be strictly your personal ancestors of blood. They can be your spiritual ancestors as well -- those individuals who have inspired you or whom you have looked to as guides on your path. They might be teachers you have had or philosophers, artists, or thinkers who left writings or other work that helped you understand yourself and the world around you. They can be friends who have gone into the Otherworlds before you, whose kindness and advice you valued in life and whose presence you feel from time to time.

When you have gathered your spirits and any ancestors to you and are comfortable with continuing the ritual, make a small offering of food and drink to them. After this, ask for the presence of Ogma and say a few words dedicating the best of your offerings to him as your gift for his guidance and favor in your work with the ogam. If you have an image, raise the offerings up to it as his representative. If you do not, you may wish to sprinkle a little of each item you've offering onto the earth or into a bowl on the altar for him at this time. The rest will be offered at the end of the ritual.

The *feda* should now be sorted into order from beginning to end, laid in rows of each *aicme* from right to left, bottom to top. Ordering is an important part of this process, as it reflects the origins of ogam as it was first created. This is a symbolic act, taking you back to the very beginnings of ogam, and allows you to identify with Ogma as its creator. The first letter of an inscription is at the bottom of the line.

The bag or box you will be keeping your *feda* in should be cleansed and blessed, passing it through the juniper and asking the aid of Ogma and your spirits to make it a fitting vessel for your *feda*. If you will be using a cloth for casting your *feda* on, this can also be cleansed and blessed and placed into your bag or box for storage.

Take the first *fid* in your hand and pass it through the smoke or otherwise cleanse it. Visualize it strongly in your mind as you chant its name, asking Ogma to purify and bless it for you. When you feel it is sufficiently cleared, lay it on the altar and take up the knife. Trace the lines of the *fid* with the blade, chanting its name, and see the energy associated with that letter entering into the *fid*. Keep the keyword for the *fid* in mind as you ask Ogma to help you empower it for divination and magic. Trace the lines of the letter three times with the blade, symbolizing its presence in the three realms of land, sea, and sky.

Set down the blade and take the *fid* up between your palms and chant its name as you place your energy within it. See the energy as light that moves from you into the *fid*, anchored there by your will with the aid of Ogma and your spirits. You may feel the energy as heat or a tingling in your hands as you work. Breathe into the *fid*. Whisper the name and keyword of the *fid* into it as you hold it between your palms. Breathing life into the *fid* through the invocation of its name is important; remember that the words for breath (*anál*), soul (*anam*), and name (*ainm*) are closely related in Gaelic. This part of the working breathes a soul and a name into the *fid* so that it takes on a spark of life.

Pass the energized *fid* through the smoke again and thank Ogma and the spirits for their help and aid in your work.

Repeat this process with each of the twenty *feda*.

Offer the food and drink you've prepared to Ogma and to your spirits, thanking them for the help they have given you.

When you are done with the ritual work, draw one *fid* to determine if the ritual was successful. If you draw a *fid* that suggests there was a ritual error or problem, you will need to do further consultation by drawing other *feda* to find out what the problem was. You may find that you need better focus, or that you need to make further offerings. If the oracle for the ritual is bad, consider re-doing the ritual on another day, after spending time in meditation and possibly fasting to purify yourself and your tools. Wait at least one day at minimum between rituals. A three-day wait with purifications and offerings to Ogma is advisable if the oracle is very bad. This would usually only arise with a combination of h-Úath and Ceirt or something equally problematic as the *feda* drawn for your ritual oracle.

That said, so long as you have done your best, the oracle isn't likely to be so disastrous that you need to repeat the ritual. This happens rarely, but it's a possibility that you should be aware of. It's important to understand that not every ritual is going to be a perfect success. Ritual work is a process of learning, and mistakes are a part of the process.

When the oracle has been received, take the food and drink offerings outside and leave them under a tree, bury them somewhere, or give them to the water. If you have a fireplace or have a fire going outside, you can offer them to the fire to carry them into the spirit world. Giving the food and drink to fire or water are almost always the best ways to make your offerings to deity if you are able to do so. You shouldn't partake of the offerings yourself, as the *toradh* or energy and substance of them has been taken by the spirits and the deity. It isn't considered healthy for people or animals to eat such things.

In summary, the steps outlined for the empowering ritual are as follows:

Gather the necessary tools and items for the ritual
Arrange your altar or working space
Make an offering to the Outsiders away from your ritual area
Center yourself in the three realms
Purify yourself, your tools, and your space
Call upon any spirits you may wish to have aid you
Ask Ogma's presence and dedicate your offerings to him
Arrange the feda in order by their aicmi
Cleanse the bag or box that will contain your feda
Cleanse your casting cloth if you choose to use one
Take a fid and pass it through the smoke or otherwise purify it
Visualize the form of the letter in your mind while chanting its name

Press the energy into the fid as you keep its keyword in mind, still chanting its name

Trace the lines of the fid with the blade three times as you chant its name, anchoring it in the three realms

Take the fid between your hands and breathe its name and keyword into it with Ogma's aid, anchoring that energy into its form

Pass the finished fid through the smoke with your thanks to Ogma and the spirits

Repeat these steps with each fid

Make your offerings to Ogma and the spirits with your thanks

Draw a fid as an oracle for the ritual

If the omen is good, thank Ogma and the spirits for their aid

If the omen is poor, draw other feda for clarification and determine if any part of the ritual needs to be redone later or if more offerings are called for

Collect your ritual tools and return the altar or space to its previous condition

Dispose of the offerings in fire or water, or leave them outdoors for Ogma and the spirits

Short Ritual of Making

Even if you work with a commercial set of *feda* at first, as you develop in your ogam work you'll likely find yourself wanting to learn the skills necessary to make your own set eventually. The advantages of this work are enormous because you can put your own energy and dedication into the work, from choosing specific materials that resonate for you and your own deities and spirits, to the satisfaction and personal connection that comes with the creation of your own tools. Any tools you make, regardless of how plain or beautiful they are, will naturally work better for you than a commercial set. Your own understanding of the work becomes a part of their making and their use. Your personal and emotional investment is much larger, and the results will be at least equal to the effort you put into the work. It's my strong feeling that making your own *feda* is the best way to work with the ogam.

There are several options if you want to create your own *feda*. These may be as simple as using paint or markers on twigs, unfinished discs of wood, or slices of antler. It might be more complex, involving wood burning or engraving with a Dremel or other tool if you have such things available or can rent them for a few days. Your needs will be very similar to the previous ritual, but will include having the tools for actually marking your *feda* at hand, and your chosen materials to receive the marks.

If you are doing engraving, which will take more time and effort than painting or using a marking pen, you might choose to do one *aicme* per day for four days. This will allow you to put a good amount of focus and energy into each *fid*. Set aside an hour or two per day for this if you do choose to create a set of five *feda* per day. If you make all twenty on the same day, it could take three hours or more, depending on the method you're using for making them and how much time you spend in meditation with, and investing energy into, each *fid*. It would be advisable to use the bathroom before you begin so you aren't interrupted by the call of nature while you're working. Getting back into the flow will take time and effort, so it's best not to interrupt the process at all.

It will be useful to have a reference sheet to look at if you aren't deeply familiar with the ogam *feda* and their order. If you haven't worked with them on a regular basis and you're uncertain of the meanings as yet, it will help to have the keyword and basic meanings on this reference sheet so that as you create each *fid* you'll be able to focus on infusing it with the appropriate energy and meaning.

This ritual, like the previous one, can be done indoors or outside, but if you're using an engraver, a wood burner, or any other tool requiring electricity, you'll need to either be indoors or somewhere with an electrical outlet. You'll also want a few extra pieces of the material you're using to make your *feda*, in case you make a mistake. Working with small pieces if you haven't had practice can take a little time to get used to, and rushing the work can lead to ruining a piece and having to replace it. Having one or two extra in your stack just in case is a good idea and will help with your peace of mind, even if you don't end up needing them. Doing a few practice runs with material you won't be consecrating is also a good idea to assure yourself that you're up to the work.

Even if you will be engraving the *feda*, you'll probably still want to paint the engraved *fid* with a color that contrasts with the base material. Red is a good color for this unless you're using it for your base. It symbolizes blood and life, but it also has associations with the Otherworlds -- Otherworldly cattle or dogs are often white with red ears in the mythology, and the salmon of wisdom have red spots on them, one for each of the hazels of wisdom that they've consumed. Red is also the color of fire and of *imbas*, the poetic inspiration or "fire in the head" that the *Fili* seeks. A good acrylic artist's paint works on most surfaces and will dry quickly. Paint pens can be better for precise control of where the paint ends up than a brush. If the surface is glossy, you can easily wipe the excess paint away without staining the material itself. On very porous materials like antler or bone you'll need to be careful not to mark too much outside the engraved lines and to wipe the excess away quickly and thoroughly to avoid staining the rest of the antler slice. Sandpaper might be necessary if things get extremely messy.

Some materials may need to be sealed with a clear substance like nail polish or lacquer so the paint won't chip or wear away, especially if you are painting on a smooth, unengraved surface like polished or tumbled stone, glass, or shell. This will be less of an issue on rougher surfaces, like beach stones or twigs with the bark left on.

If you have good, steady hands and some experience with carving or sculpture, you may wish to try carving your *feda* onto twigs with a knife or a carving or engraving tool. My hands shake so this is not a method I'm able to use, but it would be the ideal method in a symbolic sense. It was the one used by Ogma when he originally created the ogam on a birch twig. With this method, you can ritually identify with Ogma in a very powerful way, but be sure your knife is as sharp as possible and keep a sharpening stone close at hand, for dull knives slip easily and you are much more likely to cut yourself with a dull knife because of this. Wearing work gloves to protect your hands would be a very wise precaution if you use this method of engraving.

This ritual proceeds like the ritual above, except that in this case you'll be physically making each *fid* yourself. The *glannad*, calling upon deity and spirits, the offerings, and chanting the energy into each *fid* all take place just as before. As you mark each *fid*, you will be anchoring your intent and its keyword into the physical object as you chant its name. As you breathe into it, you ensoul it with a spark of the divine. Ask Ogma for his aid and to guide and steady your hand as you do this vital work of creation. The focus required to properly paint or engrave each letter is part of how the energy is imbued into your chosen material.

Don't rush while you're doing your work. The idea isn't to get the set done as quickly as possible, but to spend deep and involved time meditating with each *fid* on its meaning and energies, asking Ogma and your spirits for their guidance and help as you do the work of creation. Taking your time will also mean you do more careful and more artistic work on your tools and that slips of the hand or other mistakes will be less likely. Beauty in craftsmanship is definitely an ideal to strive for, and the nicer your tools look and feel in your hand when you're done, the happier you will be when you work with them in years to come.

Remember that you're making tools with the intent that they last a lifetime. Do justice to that ideal with your attitude and your concentrated attention. Spending three or four hours working on this ritual now will pay off handsomely in years to come, both in the utility of the tool and your pride in a job well done. If you feel called to do so, you may wish to ask the blessing of Brighid on your work in this ritual as well, for she is a Goddess of smithcraft and guides the hands of skilled workers in their tasks. Her patronage of poetry means that she also has a link with ogam through its use as a source of poetic knowledge and a tool of prophecy, which are functions of the *Fili*.

Even with this knowledge, please understand that your work doesn't have to be "perfect"; it merely has to be the best you can do. No human, no deity and no spirit can ask more of you than your honest best effort. It's far better to have a set of *feda* you've made for yourself that don't look like they were machine-carved with absolutely precise and even lines, but which contains your own effort, sweat, and energy in them, than a commercial set that looks perfect but has no real emotional link or magical investment in it. The true value of any spiritual or magical tool is in the time and effort you invest in making and working with it, not how pretty it looks when it's done. If you feel during the course of the ritual that you've ruined one *fid*, remember that this is why you have a few extra blank bases. Go ahead and let it go without regret. You can dispose of the damaged *fid* after your ritual is ended by burning or burying it with a small offering to release the energies back to Ogma and the Otherworlds.

Here is the outline for the ritual of making:

Gather the necessary tools and items for the ritual
Arrange your altar or working space

Make an offering to the Outsiders away from your ritual area

Center yourself in the three realms

Purify yourself, your tools, and your space

Call upon any spirits you may wish to have aid you

Ask Ogma's presence and dedicate your offerings to him

Arrange your blanks for the feda on the altar where you can reach them easily

*Cleanse the bag or box that will contain your feda - **first day only***

*Cleanse your casting cloth if you choose to use one - **first day only***

Take your paintbrush, engraver, or other marking tool and purify it in the smoke

Take a blank and pass it through the smoke or otherwise purify it

Visualize the form of the letter in your mind, marking it clearly on your chosen surface while chanting its name

Press the energy into the fid as you keep its keyword in mind, still chanting its name

If you are engraving the fid and wish to add color, paint it now, chanting its name as you focus your energy on it

Clean away any extra traces of paint with a soft cloth

Trace the lines of the fid with the blade three times as you chant its name, anchoring it in the three realms

Take the fid between your hands and breathe its name and keyword into it with Ogma's aid, anchoring that energy into its form

When the paint has had a few minutes to dry, coat with clear lacquer if necessary and allow that coat to dry enough to touch without smearing

Pass the finished fid through the smoke with your thanks to Ogma and the spirits

Repeat these steps with each fid -- if you are going to do one aicme a day for four days, set the finished feda aside in their container at this time, separate from the unfinished materials

On the last day of the ritual, ask Ogma's blessing on the entire set of feda and fix a final charge of energy into the set as a whole

Make your offerings to Ogma and the spirits with your thanks

Draw a fid as an oracle for the ritual

If the oracle is good, thank Ogma and the spirits for their aid
If the oracle is poor, draw other feda for clarification and determine if any part of the ritual needs to be redone later or if more offerings are called for
Collect your ritual tools and return the altar or space to its previous condition
Dispose of the offerings in fire or water, or leave them outdoors for Ogma and the spirits

If you are doing the ritual over a period of four days and you've dedicated altar and work space in your home, you can leave your altar and materials set up until the ritual of making is finished -- repeat the ritual each day with the new *aicme* until you have completed all twenty *feda*

Obviously, if you are making your first set of *feda* a few per day, you won't have a full set with which to draw an oracle. In this case, you may wish to use another divinatory system, like the tarot, for taking the oracles for each day's ritual, or a commercial set of *feda* if you were working with one before you decided to make your own. Any system you're familiar with will do. The final day of the ritual, you can draw the ritual's ending oracle from your completed set of *feda*.

It's important to remember that each day of the ritual calls for new offerings. Consider each day of the ritual a separate rite and set your mind and your altar accordingly. Be generous with your offerings to the spirits and the deity just as you would want someone to be generous to you if you were helping them. The offerings for the Outsider spirits should also be renewed every day. Every effort you make adds to the energy and effectiveness of your ritual work and builds your relationship with both your *feda* and with Ogma and your spirits.

Twenty-Day Ritual of Making

A single or triple set of *feda* can be made over a twenty-day series of rituals following this same basic outline as well, creating one *fid*, or three of the same *fid*, each day. It also involves an additional set of meditations, described below. A triple set of *feda* is a little more involved ritually and takes more materials, but is very useful for working with the divinatory currents individually. The triple set involves making one of each *fid* for the chthonic, the oceanic, and the celestial currents, each in different shapes or colors so that you can distinguish them in readings and for magical workings. This means that there are separate meditations that go with each current for each *fid*.

If you're going to do this though, you'll need to set aside twenty consecutive days for the project without skipping any day. You should do the ritual in the same place and at the same time each day if at all possible. Don't interrupt the cycle unless it is absolutely unavoidable. Part of the effectiveness of such a lengthy cycle of rituals is the magical and spiritual momentum and connection built up during this kind of intensive working. Some people are naturally not going to have a schedule that will allow for this, and that's all right. Using the four-day ritual cycle to make five *feda* per day is quite acceptable and the set will not be in any way inferior for your work.

I would recommend doing the full twenty days if you're going to make and consecrate a triple set of *feda*. The focus required is very intense and being able to focus thoroughly on each of the currents takes time. I found that my ritual averaged forty-five minutes to an hour per night when I was making my triple set. I was exhausted afterwards from the amount of effort involved, but I was working with partial possession during that time. That aspect of the ritual will be described in the next section, and I don't recommend doing the partial possession version of the cycle unless you have several years of experience doing spirit work and possession trance of different kinds. It's definitely an advanced technique, and can be dangerous for beginners, particularly if it's attempted while you're alone and without guidance or supervision.

A commitment to twenty days of ritual is a significant one, so be certain it's what you want to do. Not only is it a lot of time to devote to ritual work on a single project, it's also a strong signal to yourself, to Ogma, and to your other spirits that you are serious about your study of the ogam and your work with this tool. Ending the cycle before you're finished or breaking it without good reason will weaken that intent and send the wrong signals to the powers you work with. It will also drop the magical and spiritual momentum you've built over the consecutive days of working with the same energies each day, and rebuilding that force will take time and great effort.

In my experience, Ogma prefers a clear routine and serious dedication from the *Fili* or the ogam student for this twenty-day rite. While I was able to shift the time of the ritual a little when I had to be away from the house later into the night during the ritual cycle, he was adamant about my beginning by the chosen time when I was at home. Starting fifteen or twenty minutes late was not an option and he made his displeasure quite plain on the one occasion when it did happen. Arriving later than my designated ritual start time after attending a class outside the house, I would literally drop everything, use the bathroom, and go into ritual immediately as soon I got home.

Ignoring the routine you've set up for this ritual cycle without a very good reason could very well be taken as an insult and will require a good deal of work to repair your relationship with Ogma afterwards. The Celtic deities may insist that we stand on our own feet and not grovel before them, but they don't take slights very well either. Keeping your word and following through with oaths you've made to them and rituals you've begun is extremely important. If you don't feel you can commit to the full twenty-day cycle, don't start it; go with the shorter four-day cycle instead.

Another thing that I noted in my own twenty-day ritual cycle was that Ogma insisted the kitchen be clean while the ritual was going on, with all dishes either in the dish washer if they were dirty, or clean and put away, unless they were in use. No food or drink could be out except what was being offered in the ritual. I considered this a *geas* or ritual injunction for the duration of the ritual cycle. Keeping your home and kitchen clean is a good idea as daily ritual anyway, but there is folkloric and magical precedent for not leaving dirty dishes or vessels out, particularly during ritual or at significant times of the year.

In the tale called *Echtra Nerai*, the Adventure of Nera, the hero goes out on Samhain eve on a dare to wind a withy around the ankle of a corpse hanging in a tree. It demands to be taken on Nera's back so it can get a drink, as he was thirsty when he was hanged. Nera does so, carrying him to three houses.

Around the first house there was a ring of fire, and the corpse explained that there was nothing to drink there, for the fire was properly covered. The second house was surrounded by a great moat of water, and the corpse said that this was because no vessel was left with water in it at night. In the third house, there are dirty water vessels lying around and the corpse takes a drink of water from one the vessels, spitting the last sip of it into the faces of the people asleep inside. The inhabitants die from this attack.[122] The lesson in this is that even tiny, seemingly

---

[122] Rees & Rees, 1990, 298

unimportant details may make an immense difference. It doesn't hurt to keep your home in order, and it may help a great deal with some forms of ritual.

The basic outline for each day's ritual is very similar to the two formats above, with a few additions. These differences are bolded in the text below. Explanations and instructions follow the outline.

Gather the necessary tools and items for the ritual
Arrange your altar or working space
Make an offering to the Outsiders away from your ritual area
Center yourself in the three realms
Purify yourself, your tools, and your space
Sparking the Cauldrons meditation to connect with the cauldron energies
Call upon any spirits you may wish to have aid you
Ask Ogma's presence and dedicate your offerings to him
Arrange your blanks for the feda on the altar where you can reach them easily
*Cleanse the bag or box that will contain your feda - **first day only***
*Cleanse your casting cloth if you choose to use one - **first day only***
Take your paintbrush, engraver, or other marking tool and purify it in the smoke
Take a blank and pass it through the smoke or otherwise purify it

First Current - Chthonic
Meditate on the fid in the Cauldron of Warming and the chthonic current's colors
Create the fid and imbue it with the chthonic current's energies
Press the energy into the fid as you keep its meanings for this current in mind, still chanting its name
If you are engraving the fid and wish to add color, paint it now, chanting its name as you focus your energy on it
Clean away any extra traces of paint with a soft cloth
Trace the lines of the fid with the blade three times as you chant its name, anchoring it in the three realms

Take the fid between your hands and breathe its name into it with Ogma's aid, anchoring that energy into its form

When the paint has had a few minutes to dry, coat with clear lacquer if necessary and allow that coat to dry enough to touch without smearing

Pass the finished fid through the smoke with your thanks to Ogma and the spirits

Second Current - Oceanic
Meditate on the fid in the Cauldron of Motion and the oceanic current's colors
Create the fid and imbue it with the oceanic current's energies

Press the energy into the fid as you keep its meanings for this current in mind, still chanting its name

If you are engraving the fid and wish to add color, paint it now, chanting its name as you focus your energy on it

Clean away any extra traces of paint with a soft cloth

Trace the lines of the fid with the blade three times as you chant its name, anchoring it in the three realms

Take the fid between your hands and breathe its name into it with Ogma's aid, anchoring that energy into its form

When the paint has had a few minutes to dry, coat with clear lacquer if necessary and allow that coat to dry enough to touch without smearing

Pass the finished fid through the smoke with your thanks to Ogma and the spirits

Third Current - Celestial
Meditate on the fid in the Cauldron of Wisdom and the celestial current's colors
Create the fid and imbue it with the celestial current's energies

Press the energy into the fid as you keep its meanings for this current in mind, still chanting its name

If you are engraving the fid and wish to add color, paint it now, chanting its name as you focus your energy on it

Clean away any extra traces of paint with a soft cloth

Trace the lines of the fid with the blade three times as you chant its name, anchoring it in the three realms

Take the fid between your hands and breathe its name into it with Ogma's aid, anchoring that energy into its form

When the paint has had a few minutes to dry, coat with clear lacquer if necessary and allow that coat to dry enough to touch without smearing

Pass the finished fid through the smoke with your thanks to Ogma and the spirits

Set the finished feda aside in their container at this time, separate from the unfinished materials

On the last day of the ritual, ask Ogma's blessing on the entire set of feda and fix a final charge of energy into the set as a whole

Make your offerings to Ogma and the spirits with your thanks

Draw a fid as an oracle for the ritual

If the oracle is good, thank Ogma and the spirits for their aid

If the oracle is poor, draw other feda for clarification and determine if any part of the ritual needs to be redone later or if more offerings are called for

Meditation to ground the process and the energies

Record impressions and the results of meditations

Collect your ritual tools and return the altar or space to its previous condition. If you are able, you may wish to leave your tools and altar set for the next day's ritual.

Dispose of the offerings in fire or water, or leave them outdoors for Ogma and the spirits

One of the important things that separate this ritual cycle from the ones already outlined is that you will be making three sets of *feda* rather than just one. The ritual can certainly be used to make a single set, but the instructions will cover the triple set. Adjust the ritual instructions accordingly if you'll only be doing one.

Each of the three individual sets resonates with the currents that run through one of the three internal cauldrons and the three realms. It will be necessary to do meditations intended to open you to the energies of each of these cauldrons so you can empower each *fid* within them. The first part of this process is a breathing meditation intended to open and energize each cauldron.

It's important to remember that the three cauldrons and the three realms aren't exact equivalents philosophically or spiritually. You can run the same types of energy through them, but in each case they are their own particular things. The three realms are the immediate physical realities of our lives; you can't call and banish the three realms like you would call and banish a Wiccan circle. When land, sea and sky are not in their place, the world is ending. Attempting to make them go away is unwise.

Energy runs through the realms and beings dwell in them, but they are in no way an equivalent of the classical Greek or Neopagan "elements." At best, it can be said that each of the cauldrons resonates a bit better to one of the realms than the others, but all three cauldrons can be worked with in each of the three realms, and the realms themselves can be experienced and meditated upon within each of the three cauldrons.

The cauldrons themselves are described as *Coire Goiriath* -- the Cauldron of Warming, *Coire Érmai* -- the Cauldron of Motion, and *Coire Sofhis* -- the Cauldron of Wisdom. They appear to be found in the abdomen, the chest, and in the head. Traditionally, the Cauldron of Warming is said to be born upright and to govern a person's health, particularly in their youth. The Cauldron of Motion is born on its side and turns upright with the processing of intense emotions like joy and sorrow. The Cauldron of Wisdom is found in the head and is born upside-down or "on its lips" and can only be turned upright by work with the other cauldrons and by inspiration from the deities.

The cauldrons are important to the work of this ritual and to *Filidecht* generally because of the way they link us to inspiration as well as to our physical and internal energies. Without the activation of the Cauldron of Wisdom, divination is more of a rote affair, concerned with memorization of symbols and meaning. When the Cauldron of Wisdom is activated and your *imbas* begins to flow, connections and links are formed and inspiration becomes a more integral part of your divinatory, spiritual, and magical work. It's easier to perceive the patterns that underlie the world and its weaving. Breath and bodily energy combine and spark to produce magic.

Using the Sparking the Cauldrons meditation from chapter 5, focus your breath and body and draw energy into each cauldron. When you have gone through the meditation, open your eyes and focus on the altar for the work before you.

At this point you'll proceed with the ritual as outlined above, asking the presence of deity and spirits, dedicating your offerings, purifying your tools, and the blanks for the *feda* as you prepare to create one *fid* as manifested in each of the three currents.

Because you're the only one who knows exactly which spirits and deities you work with aside from the work with Ogma and perhaps Brighid that goes into this version of the ritual of making, it's important that you use your own words to call upon their aid. Part of the art that goes into working with the ogam is accessing the creativity we each have within us, and beyond a few basic meditations, rote memorization of ritual scripts has never seemed to me to have much benefit. Your own words within the framework of ritual are best for your own work.

For each day of the ritual of making, you'll be doing the same series of cauldron meditations with a different letter, starting with Beith and working through to Idad. The ritual framework for each day is the same, only the visualizations are different, and they are based on the keywords and the meanings and concepts associated with each *fid*. If you've advanced enough in your ogam studies to want to do a twenty-day cycle of rituals to make your own triple set of *feda*, their meanings and keywords should already be a strong and steady part of your ogam practice and there's no need for me to set up a specific guided visualization for each *fid* in this ritual. The patterns of each cauldron meditation repeat; only the visualization work changes.

Part of the purpose of this ritual is incorporating your own personal gnosis and your work with each *fid* into the making of it. If you have been studying and reading the ogam and doing your own research on the *feda* and their lore, you have been developing your own set of extended images and associations elaborating on the information presented in the chapter on basic ogam meanings. Just as with the personal deity and spirit invocations, a rote script for a guided meditation here would only restrict your ability to draw your own web out of the threads of poetry that connect the ogam *feda* to your local environment and your spiritual reality.

Take the first blank *fid* in your hand and pass it through the smoke or otherwise cleanse it. Visualize it taking the smoke within it and clearing out all impurities and unwanted energies as you chant its name, asking Ogma to purify and bless it for you.

Feel it spark and blaze with the power of his touch. When you feel it is sufficiently cleansed, move on to the cauldron meditation.

Cauldron of Warming Meditation

Hold the blank *fid* over your abdomen, between your palms, chanting its name continually through the meditation. Breathe deeply into the cauldron and visualize its contents as deep green energy: strong, fertile, and earthy. This green is the power of the land and what lies beneath it. It contains all that is stable and strong, all that is solid and fixed. This is the current of the body and the physical world. It contains the power of the land spirits that guide and aid you.

Link your energy with the chthonic current and draw upon its strength. Feel its power flow into the cauldron of warming, filling and charging it so that it can flow into the *fid* you are making. Place the blank *fid* within the cauldron, seeing its substance as a deep green field ready to be infused with the energy you are calling upon.

With each breath, intone the name of the *fid* and focus on the *fid*'s keyword and the meanings of its chthonic current. As you breathe and call out the name of the *fid*, push the energy of those meanings and the images that arise as you meditate upon them into the *fid*. Hold your focus as steadily as you can, moving your mind back to your purpose if it wanders. Feel the *fid* taking in the energy of the chthonic current, soaking it up as the earth soaks up rain.

Take your time working with the *fid*, concentrating on each image as it arises, and mentally tracing the connections it brings. Anchor those energies within the physical material of the blank *fid*. Feel it surging and glowing with that energy between your palms, and when the energy is at its height, visualize the shape of the *fid* itself in brilliant, glowing red upon the field of green, burning itself into the surface of the *fid*. Red is the blood and the physical body of the *fid*'s manifestation. It's what is sacrificed for the sake of the deities and spirits. Green field and red blood together become the chthonic current of this *fid* expressed in the physical realm.

Continue chanting as you fix the *fid*'s image powerfully within the physical object. Trace the shape of the *fid* a total of three times in blazing red, seeing it with as much clarity as you can develop. Take all the time you need to do this.

When you have traced the shape of the *fid* three times, anchor it within the physical object with a brilliant red bolt of power.

Place the blank *fid* on your altar's work surface.

Take up the tool you'll be marking the *fid* with and pass it through the smoke to purify it. Call upon Ogma to guide your hand, and to make this tool his knife, the mother and father of ogam. Intoning the name of the *fid*, carefully carve or mark the blank with the shape of the *fid*, infusing it with the *fid*'s chthonic energy until you are satisfied with its appearance and the energetic feel of it. Mark the top or bottom, as you have previously chosen, so that you can distinguish which *aicme* the *fid* is from. If you are also adding the letter or name to the surface of the *fid*, do that at this time, still intoning its name.

When the carving is done, carefully paint the engraved letter, chanting the *fid*'s name as you do so. Focus on the meanings and keyword and pushing the chthonic current's power into the *fid*. Wipe away any excess paint, making sure that the *fid* itself is left clear and easily read on the surface.

Taking your knife or sickle, pass it through the smoke to purify it. This is the knife of Ogma, doing the final work of carving the *fid* into the three realms. Touch its tip to the *fid* and chant its name three times as you finish fixing the energy of the *fid* into the object. Set it aside until the end of the ritual.

Take the second blank *fid* in your hand and pass it through the smoke or otherwise cleanse it. Visualize it taking the smoke within it and clearing out all impurities and unwanted energies as you chant its name, asking Ogma to purify and bless it for you. Feel it spark and blaze with the power of his touch. When you feel it is sufficiently cleansed, move on to the cauldron meditation.

Cauldron of Motion Meditation

Hold the blank *fid* over your heart, between your palms, chanting its name continually through the meditation. Breathe deeply into the cauldron and visualize its contents as misty grey energy: unstable, flexible, and chaotic. This energy is about depth, tidal and mysterious. It's the mist that moves between the worlds and the passages between all things. It's the energy of flow, unpredictability, and creative, originating chaos.

Link your energy with the oceanic current and draw upon its swirling tides, feeling its power flowing into the cauldron of motion, filling and charging it so that it can flow into the *fid* you are making. Place the blank *fid* within the cauldron, seeing its substance as a shifting grey mist ready to be infused with the energy you are calling upon.

With each breath, intone the name of the *fid* and focus on the *fid*'s keyword and the meanings of its oceanic current. As you breathe and call out the name of the *fid*, push the energy of those meanings and the images that arise into the *fid*. Hold your focus as steadily as you can, moving your mind back to your purpose if it wanders. Feel the *fid* taking in the energy of the oceanic current, enveloping it as mist takes in and conceals everything in its reach.

Take your time working with the *fid*, concentrating on each image as it arises, and tracing the connections it brings. Anchor those energies within the physical material of the blank *fid*. Feel it surging and glowing with that energy between your palms, and when the energy at its height, visualize the shape of the *fid* itself in intense, glowing green upon the shifting curtain of grey, washing itself into the surface of the *fid*. Green is the mystical and mysterious internal power of the dark waves of the sea and the emotional force of the *fid*'s manifestation. It is what moves and swirls, unstable and shifting within the *fid*. Grey mists and green depths together become the oceanic current of this *fid* expressed in the physical realm.

Continue chanting as you fix the *fid*'s image powerfully within the physical object. Trace the shape of the *fid* a total of three times in deep green, seeing it with as much clarity as you can develop. Take all the time you need to do this.

When you have traced the shape of the *fid* three times, anchor it within the physical object with a brilliant green bolt of power.

Place the blank *fid* on your altar's work surface.

Take up the tool you'll be marking the *fid* with and pass it through the smoke to purify it. Call upon Ogma to guide your hand, and to make this tool his knife, the mother and father of ogam. Intoning the name of the *fid*, carefully carve or mark the blank with the shape of the *fid*, infusing it with the *fid*'s oceanic energy until you are satisfied with its appearance and the energetic feel of it. Mark the top or bottom, as you have previously chosen, so that you can distinguish which *aicme* the *fid* is from. If you are also adding the letter or name to the surface of the *fid*, do that at this time, still intoning its name.

When the carving is done, carefully paint the engraved letter, chanting its name as you do so. Focus on the meanings and keyword and pushing the oceanic current's power into the *fid*. Wipe away any excess paint, making sure that the *fid* itself is left clear and easily read on the surface.

Taking your knife or sickle, pass it through the smoke to purify it. This is the knife of Ogma, doing the final work of carving the *fid* into the three realms. Touch its tip to the *fid* and chant its name of three times as you finish fixing the energy of the *fid* into the object. Set it aside until the end of the ritual.

Take the third blank *fid* in your hand and pass it through the smoke or otherwise cleanse it. Visualize it taking the smoke within it and clearing out all impurities and unwanted energies as you chant its name, asking Ogma to purify and bless it for you. Feel it spark and blaze with the power of his touch. When you feel it is sufficiently cleansed, move on to the cauldron meditation.

Cauldron of Wisdom Meditation

Hold the blank *fid* over your forehead, between your palms, chanting its name continually through the meditation. Breathe deeply into the cauldron and visualize its contents as deep blue energy: calm, eternal, orderly, and spiritual. This energy is about the spark of divinity, of thoughts in motion, and the focus of *imbas*. It is the blue of the night sky, sparked with circling stars and the depths of space beyond. It is the energy of the sacred, of time's boundaries, and what transcends time, and of the power of the mind to perceive mysteries.

Link your energy with the celestial current and draw upon its spinning stars, feeling its power flowing into the cauldron of wisdom, filling and charging it so that it can flow into the *fid* you are making. Place the blank *fid* within the cauldron, seeing its substance as the dark blue sky of night ready to be infused with the energy you are calling upon.

With each breath, intone the name of the *fid* and focus on the *fid*'s keyword and the meanings of its celestial current. As you breathe and call out the name of the *fid*, push the energy of those meanings and the images that arise into the *fid*. Hold your focus as steadily as you can, moving your mind back to your purpose if it wanders. Feel the *fid* taking in the energy of the celestial current, accepting it as the sky accepts the rising smoke of fires and incense.

Take your time working with the *fid*, concentrating on each image as it arises, and tracing the connections it brings. Anchor those energies within the physical material of the blank *fid*. Feel it surging and glowing with that energy between your palms, and when the energy at its height, visualize the shape of the *fid* itself in bright, shining white upon the deep sky of blue, blazing itself into the surface of the *fid*. White is the sharp truth and the intellectual and spiritual force of the *fid*'s manifestation. It is what marks the boundaries of known and unknown, pursuing wisdom and discerning details within the *fid*. Blue space and white stars together become the celestial current of this *fid* expressed in the physical realm.

Continue chanting as you fix the *fid*'s image powerfully within the physical object. Trace the shape of the *fid* a total of three times in shining white, seeing it with as much clarity as you can develop. Take all the time you need to do this.

When you have traced the shape of the *fid* three times, anchor it within the physical object with a shining white bolt of power.

Place the blank *fid* on your altar's work surface.

Take up the tool you'll be marking the *fid* with and pass it through the smoke to purify it. Call upon Ogma to guide your hand, and to make this tool his knife, the mother and father of ogam. Intoning the name of the *fid*, carefully carve or mark the blank with the shape of the *fid*, infusing it with the *fid*'s celestial energy until you are satisfied with its appearance and the energetic feel of it. Mark the top or bottom, as you have previously chosen, so that you can distinguish which *aicme* the *fid* is from. If you are also adding the letter or name to the surface of the *fid*, do that at this time, still intoning its name.

When the carving is done, carefully paint the engraved letter, chanting the *fid*'s name as you do so. Focus on the meanings and keyword and pushing the celestial current's power into the *fid*. Wipe away any excess paint, making sure that the *fid* itself is left clear and easily read on the surface.

Taking your knife or sickle, pass it through the smoke to purify it. This is the knife of Ogma, doing the final work of carving the *fid* into the three realms. Touch its tip to the *fid* and chant its name three times as you finish fixing the energy of the *fid* into the object. Set it aside until the end of the ritual.

After you have empowered, carved and painted the *fid* in each cauldron, place them in the center of the working space. Cover them with your hands and as you sing the name of the *fid*, project its keyword and energy into all three of the *feda* one more time. Set them aside in a container until all twenty days of the ritual are finished.

At this point, give your offerings to Ogma and to the other spirits, with thanks for their aid and blessings. Draw an oracle to determine if the offerings were acceptable and the ritual completed properly. If the indication is unfavorable, you may need to do more divination to discover what the issue is. It's possible you may need to make more offerings, or to do some step in the ritual over again. Meditation may also be necessary here, particularly if there has been some ritual error that makes it necessary to redo part of the ritual.

If the oracle is good, center yourself in the three realms again. Allow the blazing energy of the lighted cauldrons within your body to fade into the earth. Visualize it draining from you. If it helps, you may wish to lie on the ground, face down, with your hands spread, palms open and on the earth to help release what is left over from the ritual.

Realign yourself in this time and place. Have food and something to drink as you make notes regarding the day's work and your interpretation of the divinations associated with the ritual. Record your impressions of the energy, notes on new images arising during the meditations in the cauldrons and upon the *fid*. If you received any information from your spirits or deities, write that down as well for further contemplation. A ritual notebook can become an excellent resource as you deepen your work with the ogam, both magical and divinatory.

If you are unable to leave your altar out for the full twenty days, put away the ritual items and clear your space, purifying it with juniper.

On the final day of the ritual, after the last *fid* is made, bring all the *feda* together on the altar in the container you've been storing them in. Take up the blade that is Ogma's knife and trace each *fid* over the container and the assembled *feda*, chanting its name. Visualize its meanings and feel its energies passing through your body into the *feda* in this final consecration. Ask

Ogma's blessings upon the *feda*, so they will be powerful tools for your use.

Place the knife back on the altar and take the *feda* up between your hands. Raise them up as an offering and thank Ogma and the spirits for their aid and blessing on your work. Place the finished *feda* into their final container.

The final day of the ritual cycle should have a larger, finer offering than the daily offerings. This represents gratitude for the lengthy work that has been accomplished. After the offering is made, draw the oracle from the new set of *feda* and interpret it. If the oracle is favorable, do a final centering in the realms and ground out the excess energies as usual. Eat and drink something and record your notes on the ritual. In addition to the notes on the final night's work, think on the entire ritual cycle as a whole, and note your impressions about how the energy has ebbed and flowed, what seemed to work best for you, where problem areas came up, and what you did to resolve the problems.

Put away all the tools and materials used for the ritual and do a final purification with juniper.

Possession Ritual of Making

The final version of this ritual builds upon everything covered in this chapter so far. The difference here is that the ritual works with partial possession techniques, asking Ogma to share your body and use your eyes, your arms and your hands to create the ogam *feda*, as he created the first *feda* in the time of myth. In taking on Ogma's presence for this ritual, you will effectively be putting yourself into his place in the very first time of making and enacting the original act of the creation of ogam. Being in this place sets you adrift in time in a sense. Your hands are Ogma's hands. Your eyes are his eyes. It is not you doing the creation, but the steady hand of Ogma in the moment of origin. The boundaries will blur between you and deity, between then and now.

This is a very powerful method of working, but it isn't a ritual for beginners at all. Unless you have some experience with possession work, don't attempt this version. People who have worked with possession before should find the techniques I present here fairly familiar and reasonably easy to work with. Those who have experience horsing the Loa or the Orixa in Afro-Diasporic traditions like Umbanda, Santeria, or Voudon will have no trouble with this method at all. Some Neopagan traditions do overshadowing (a milder form of full possession) in rituals like Drawing Down the Moon or the Sun, while people who are familiar with some shamanic styles of working may have experience with possession or partial possession by helping spirits. All of these experiences are similar to what this ritual is intended to produce, to one degree or another.

Partial possession work is not channeling. You are not being a conduit for the voice of a spirit. There are no questions involved about who you're inviting to share your body or why. You aren't giving over full control of your body and voice, just selected parts of it. You're not imparting any secrets of the universe through this technique; you're working on a physical task with an intended result.

The invocations you do should be specifically intended to call upon Ogma and only Ogma, using his epithets and calling upon his skills and attributes. There will be discussion and negotiation with the deity regarding exactly how much control he will have over your body for the ritual in question (just the eyes, arms and hands) and what he will be doing with them (making the *feda*). With partial possession, you will retain most of your control over your body within the parameters negotiated with the deity, and you will remember everything that goes on while you are in the partially possessed state.

If you want to do this ritual cycle and you don't have a lot of experience with partial possession work, arrange to have someone with you who has had more experience to act as support so that if you run into any trouble, you'll have someone there who can help with grounding you and bringing you fully back to your body. Chances are you won't need their assistance, but if you do, you'll be grateful for their presence. Emergencies are rare, but they can arise, particularly for people whose grip on consensus reality is tenuous.

Possession work takes training and practice because without them sometimes people don't come back or they carry the spirit or deity with them outside of ritual to the extent that it makes daily living difficult or impossible. People in this state may exhibit behaviors that can be interpreted as dangerous emotional or psychiatric problems and getting them back into a "normal" state can be a long and arduous process. Please be cautious and don't be one of the folks who get stuck between worlds.

With this form of ritual, the quality and quantity of the offerings made are particularly important. They should be the best you can get every day. They should be plentiful to the extent you can afford them. Listen to your impressions and dreams during this time to help guide you in refining what goes on the altar for offerings. When I went through this process, Ogma asked me to make the final day's offering one of pork, which I never eat and don't buy, so I had to make a special purchase of it to fulfill the conditions he set for working with me in this way. You are going to be asking a great boon of Ogma, and it is fitting that your gifts to him match the gift he is giving you.

Possession work will take more out of you physically and energetically than the other forms of ritual presented so far. It's best to do this kind of work in the evening or at night, and not to have anything expected of you afterwards. You should arrange to do the rituals in a place where you won't have to travel afterwards unless someone else is driving you. Expect to be both tired and wired when you come out of possession trance at the end of the day's work.

Paying attention to post-ritual food and grounding are going to be essential to your ability to carry on with the work for the full twenty days. You are likely to feel somewhat spacey as you regain full ownership of your body, so having a list of things to do as you come out of the partial possession state and come down from the energy that's flowing through you may be necessary so that you don't leave anything out. Protein and hot tea helps me a great deal when I'm coming down. One person I know uses very strong cinnamon candies to make sure she is entirely back in her body. Some people use salt to reconnect to their bodies -- she doesn't do this because one of her primary deities is Manannán mac Lir, a sea God, and salt will actually send her into a strong trance state. Pay attention to your body and the relationships you have with your deities and spirits. They can make a great deal of difference in the form your work takes within a ritual like this.

Set the altar for Ogma
Make an offering to the Outsiders away from your ritual area
Glannad of the self
Glannad of tools and materials
Centering in the three realms
Invocation of Manannán as Gatekeeper and raising the mists
Enter into the mists

Cauldron breathing meditation to connect with the cauldron energies

Ask the presence, blessings, protection, and guidance of the spirits and ancestors
Ask the presence of Brighid
Ask the presence of Ogma
Make offerings to the deities, ancestors and spirits
Take on the presence of Ogma as the Creator of the Ogam

First Current - Chthonic
Meditate on the fid in the Cauldron of Warming and the chthonic current's colors
Create the fid and imbue it with the chthonic current's energies
Press the energy into the fid as you keep its meanings for this current in mind, still chanting its name
If you are engraving the fid and wish to add color, paint it now, chanting its name as you focus your energy on it
Clean away any extra traces of paint with a soft cloth
Trace the lines of the fid with the blade three times as you chant its name, anchoring it in the three realms
Take the fid between your hands and breathe its name into it with Ogma's aid, anchoring that energy into its form
When the paint has had a few minutes to dry, coat with clear lacquer if necessary and allow that coat to dry enough to touch without smearing
Pass the finished fid through the smoke with your thanks to Ogma and the spirits

Second Current - Oceanic
Meditate on the fid in the Cauldron of Motion and the oceanic current's colors
Create the fid and imbue it with the oceanic current's energies
Press the energy into the fid as you keep its meanings for this current in mind, still chanting its name
If you are engraving the fid and wish to add color, paint it now, chanting its name as you focus your energy on it
Clean away any extra traces of paint with a soft cloth
Trace the lines of the fid with the blade three times as you chant its name, anchoring it in the three realms

Take the fid between your hands and breathe its name into it with Ogma's aid, anchoring that energy into its form

When the paint has had a few minutes to dry, coat with clear lacquer if necessary and allow that coat to dry enough to touch without smearing

Pass the finished fid through the smoke with your thanks to Ogma and the spirits

Third Current - Celestial

Meditate on the fid in the Cauldron of Wisdom and the celestial current's colors

Create the fid and imbue it with the celestial current's energies

Press the energy into the fid as you keep its meanings for this current in mind, still chanting its name

If you are engraving the fid and wish to add color, paint it now, chanting its name as you focus your energy on it

Clean away any extra traces of paint with a soft cloth

Trace the lines of the fid with the blade three times as you chant its name, anchoring it in the three realms

Take the fid between your hands and breathe its name into it with Ogma's aid, anchoring that energy into its form

When the paint has had a few minutes to dry, coat with clear lacquer if necessary and allow that coat to dry enough to touch without smearing

Pass the finished fid through the smoke with your thanks to Ogma and the spirits

Thanks to Ogma and leave the possession trance
Thanks to Ogma and Brighid
Thanks to the ancestors and land spirits
Release of the mists
Thanks to Manannán
Offerings of incense, food and drink
Meditation to ground the process and the energies
Record impressions and the results of meditations

This ritual required one extra component to help trigger the partial possession. I used sweet birch oil, which smells very much like wintergreen, as incense specifically for Ogma. I used it in an oil diffuser so that the sharp scent of birch was all around me as I

Erynn Rowan Laurie

carried Ogma's presence. This was an extremely important physical cue for the possession experience. I used birch because it was the tree upon which the first *feda* were carved. I also had paperbark birch bark on the altar, as bark was all I had. Ogma would have preferred a branch or a wand of birch, but I didn't have one available. White and paperbark birch are not native to my area and I would have had to get a branch from someone's ornamental trees rather than being able to go out into the forest and harvest a branch from the wild. The birch bark or branch acts as a sort of conduit and anchor for Ogma in the ritual.

As you go into ritual, set the altar with your tools and images. Place the offerings before the images or deity symbols and make offerings to the Outsider spirits. Cleanse yourself and your tools. This *glannad* should be particularly intense, for one of your tasks is to make your body a suitable vessel for the touch of deity so that Ogma can express himself through you. Take particular care with the *glannad* for this type of ritual. Center yourself in the three realms as you would for any of the other rituals outlined above.

One of the processes that is different in this ritual is the invocation of Manannán mac Lir and the calling of the mists. In the other ritual formats for this work, calling the mists and the Gatekeeper aren't necessary. You're remaining in the world even though you're in a ritual state. For the partial possession, you'll need to enter the mists to make contact with deity easier and the transitions a little softer. Think of it as meeting the deity halfway, for the mists are what separate our world from the Otherworlds. They're not somewhere far away -- they are right next to us, just a twist outside of our ordinary perception. The mist is the gateway we and the deities pass through as we make the shift from Here to There and vice versa.

Manannán's presence as a guide is asked so that we don't get lost between. He controls the mist, for it is the cloak he wears, and he guards and grants access to the Otherworldly realms. Prayers and offerings should be made to him individually in thanks for his aid and protection. It should be noted that he is a bit of a trickster with a healthy sense of humor. This may or may not come into play when you work with him here, but many CRs also see him as a guide of souls and a psychopomp; one who brings the dead into the Otherworld realms. As such, he's the one who makes sure that you get safely from one place to another -- or not. Honor him with the greatest respect and understand that he can be very concerned with protocol and following the rules of a situation. His "tricks" don't generally cause permanent harm, and they may end up making you have to laugh at yourself for being a fool, but they'll certainly drive the lesson home if he wants to teach you one.

One of the epithets I use for Manannán in my work with him is Lord of Mists, *Tiarna nan Cheo*. Guide, Gatekeeper, and Steersman are other epithets I use when calling upon him. He is a shapeshifter and may appear to you in many different forms. His presence, to me, always feels protective and wise though there is humor there beneath the surface.

The mist comes with him, but it's important to reach out to it and draw it up through and around your body with your energy. I reach out with my hands to do this as I ask him to bring the mists, pulling it up from the earth to surround me and encompass me. Its presence is cool and soft, obscuring the physical world to my inner eye. Feel the mist rise up within and around you gradually, filling your body and your ritual space and shifting the energies there. As the mist rises, the gates between worlds begin to open, allowing an outpouring of Otherworldly energies that mix like eddies and shifting tides with the energies of the physical world. I tend to feel these energies as temperature shifts and tingles in and around my body. Ask Manannán to lay his Cloak of Mists upon you and feel it envelop your shoulders and fold about your body, shifting and protecting you. Paying attention to your own reactions is important in judging when the mist has come and you are in a sufficiently liminal space for the rest of the ritual work to begin.

Within the mists, do the Sparking the Cauldrons meditation, energizing those energy centers within your body. You may note a difference in quality to the meditation when done within the mists as opposed to doing it in the ordinary physical realm. For me, the meditation is easier and sparks more energy in this liminal space between the worlds.

When the cauldrons are sparked and blazing, ask the presence of the ancestors and the spirits you work with, requesting their guidance and protection. Ask for their aid and their strength as you do the work, and to actively lend you their energy and support. Make a small offering to them for their help. Their protection will surround you while you are partly out of your body, keeping you safe and whole and diverting the attention of any uninvited spirits who might take an interest in the work while part of your attention is elsewhere.

Next, call upon the aid and presence of Brighid, who is the maker of tools and poetry. Generous offerings and prayers should be offered to her for her guidance and protection, asking her to shield you with her mantle. If you feel a need, you might wish to recite a version of the Descent of Brighid as a protective prayer. This is a version adapted from the *Carmina Gadelica*, a collection of Scottish Gaelic prayers and invocations extant in the Highlands and Islands at the end of the 19th and beginning of the 20th century. As I pray to her, I offer water to the four cardinal directions by flicking a few drops from my fingers, and to the above and below, then anoint my heart with the circled equal armed cross as a sign of her presence. I don't turn to each of the directions for this, I simply flick the water before me, behind me over my shoulder, to the right and the left, then toward the sky and the earth, ending with the circled cross on my breast.

Every day and every night
That I say the descent of Brighid,
Daughter of Daghda
Mother of the Three Gods,
Anamchara,
Guide in darkness,
Ever-flaming star,
I shall not be killed, I shall not be harried,
I shall not be put in cell, I shall not be wounded,
Neither shall She leave me in forgetfulness.

No fire, no sun, no moon shall burn me,
No lake, no water, nor sea shall drown me,
No arrow of fairy nor dart of spirit shall wound me,
And I under the mantle of Holy Brighid.[123]

Brighid to enfold me
Brighid to surround me
Brighid to comfort me

Brighid is my light and my everlasting life,
Body to body, form to form, breath to breath,
Throughout all time and eternity.

---

[123] Carmichael, 1976, 157-163

When Brighid's presence and protection is with you, ask Ogma's presence in preparation to inviting him into your body. The use of his name and his epithets is a very important part of the identification of the deity you're calling upon. Precise and exacting identification is a large part of keeping yourself safe when you're only partly in your body. You maintain the largest part of the control of your body, but knowing exactly whom you're dealing with adds to your margin of safety and your knowledge of what to expect. His traditional titles include *Milbél* (Honey-mouth) and *Grianainech* (Sun-face). I also call him Lord of Words and Eloquent One. Gaulish images of Ogmios are equated with an elder Herakles -- we don't know for sure if Ogmios and Ogma are the same figure, but my personal feeling is that they are. His image was that of an older man with many followers linked to him by silver chains from his tongue to their ears, signifying the strength of his words.

Ogma is not a trickster like Manannán. He is a warrior and one of the great champions of the Tuatha Dé Danann, and a deity of eloquence and skill. He's an honorable deity, and one who respects strength and courage. He is unlikely to attempt to push things beyond his negotiated boundaries with you, simply as a matter of honor, unless his generosity is in some way abused or hospitality is refused to him. Acting with honor toward him will go a long way for your safety and sanity in this work. When you negotiate with him, do so honestly and openly, and keep your word to him in both letter and spirit. When particular things are offered to him, make sure that those things are given to him in full measure.

He can be a bit picky about things. When I gave Ogma offerings of salmon he accepted them, but I definitely got a sense that he considered Pacific salmon a somewhat inferior offering to Atlantic salmon. Since I had only offered to give "salmon" to him without specifying an origin, I told him that he'd have to settle, because that was what I had, living as I do on the Pacific coast, and he hadn't asked for Atlantic salmon. If you're familiar with the use of a pendulum, this can be a useful tool in doing your negotiations and getting fairly clear answers. With this in mind, listen carefully when asking what he wants in return for his service. Don't be afraid to say no if you have to; sometimes he may want something you just aren't able to provide for whatever reason. The relationship between you is not strictly one-way.

When carrying Ogma, even in partial possession, one thing you may encounter is a request to consume the offerings you've made to him through your body. Generally speaking, eating an offering given to the Gods or the spirits is not done in Celtic tradition. When I was confronted by this situation, I felt that I had been given a choice between violating tradition (eating the offerings) and violating my hospitality to Ogma (not eating the offerings). In the end, I chose to let Ogma eat the offerings with my body, feeling that it was better to offer proper hospitality to a deity who had done me a great service than to stand on protocol and possibly insult the deity. There was a good deal of debate within the CR community about this decision, and some people still consider my action somewhat heretical. It isn't guaranteed that you will come up against this situation when you do the ritual, but if you do it's best to examine your own feelings, do divination concerning the issue, and decide how to handle it for yourself.

After the negotiations are done, make the initial offerings to Ogma and the others, dedicating the largest and finest portions to him.

Taking a deity into your body can be a touchy process. With partial possession, the trick is to balance your control and the deity's. After the invocations, spend time in meditation and divination working out the details of the possession work. This may take a good deal of time during the first night of the ritual, so allow extra time for the work. The ritual is intended for making a set (or a triple set) of *feda*, so all that the deity should require is your arms, hands, and eyes. Outline the offerings you will give in return for the work and his presence. Make sure they're plentiful and that you have extra just in case things get difficult.

When I did this ritual, Ogma seemed very eager to work with me and had no issues with the restrictions I placed on the partial possession. Taking him within grew easier with each day. His release of me was never a struggle, but the possession work did take a lot out of me each day, and I was ravenously hungry after ritual. Though Ogma consumed the offerings of food and whiskey through me each night, it was as though I didn't eat anything at all, and I never felt the effects of the whiskey. This is apparently quite common in Afro-Diasporic traditions. I needed to eat for myself after the ritual was over and it sometimes took half an hour or more to finally feel like I was entirely in possession of my own body and back in the physical world. This isn't a problem, so long as you've scheduled the rituals so that you don't have to do anything afterwards.

Because the deity is already present by the invocation, no extra invocatory work needs to be done after the negotiation, but you do need to invite him in. I was very specific in my invitation, using this format each day, though the words might vary slightly:

> *Ogma Milbél, Ogma Grianainech; come into my body. Make my arms your arms. Make my hands your hands. Make my eyes your eyes. May my blade be your blade. See through my eyes. Create with my hands. Carve these feda with my blade as you carved the first feda. Give them the power and presence of the first feda.*

With the scent of birch oil heavy in the air, repeat these words or others to this effect over and over as you draw Ogma's presence into you. His energy will come into you as you breathe in and settle deeper within as you exhale. As Ogma settles into your body, you may feel it sway and tremble. Your temperature may shift, sometimes drastically, and your hands or feet may tingle strongly. For me, this was one of the primary signals of his possession, along with a slight lightness in my head. Your vision may shift somewhat as well, becoming slightly sharper. When you feel his presence settle into you strongly, begin the meditations on each current's *fid*.

As you make and mark each *fid* by engraving and painting, repeat the request for your blade to be Ogma's blade and ask that his hand be the hand that makes the *fid* as the first *feda* were cut by the Mother and Father of Ogam. Ask for his power and presence to go into the *feda* as they are created, that they will be a tool to discern the will and the voice of deity and spirits in your work. Ask that they be made powerful with magic for healing and shifting the world by your will. Chant the name of the *fid* as you work after you have made these requests.

When all three currents for the night's *fid* are created, gather them together on the altar and trace the shape of the *fid* over them with the blade three times, asking Ogma to mark them with his power in all the realms and all the worlds. Chant the name of the *fid* as Ogma sends his power into the newly made *feda*. Touch the *feda* with the blade and anchor the power within them. When they are empowered in this way, set them aside in a container until the end of the ritual cycle.

On the final night of the ritual, place all the *feda* on the altar and inscribe the entire series, chanting their names and asking Ogma to anchor their energies into these physical forms.

Shedding the partial possession takes the same acute attention to detail that taking on the possession does. It may well take more time than the possessory process itself. You need to reverse the process verbally just as you do energetically when regaining your body.

> *Ogma Milbél, Ogma Grianainech, I give*
> *you my thanks; return my body to me.*
> *Make these arms my arms again and*
> *return them to me. Make these hands my*
> *hands again and return them to me.*
> *Make these eyes my eyes again and*
> *return them to me.*

Thank Ogma for his gift of presence and the manifestation of his art as you feel his presence recede from you. Breathe him out as you breathed him in. You will probably feel some lingering effect as tingles or as temperature or energy shifts as his presence departs until you've grounded and eaten after ritual. When you feel you have possession of your own body again, give Ogma thanks for his work with you.

Offer thanks to Brighid for her presence, her protection, and her creative fire.

Give your thanks to the spirits and ancestors who have worked with you and protected you in your work.

Ask Manannán to take his Cloak of Mists from your shoulders and as you feel it being lifted, release the mists and feel them fade back into the earth from your body and your ritual space. Feel yourself returning to ordinary reality, becoming more and more grounded as the process continues. Give thanks to Manannán for opening the gates between worlds for you.

Make offerings to all the spirits and deities, either to the fire or to water, or set them aside until they can be offered in that way. Do divination to discern the success of the ritual, and if there are signs of problems determine what they are and how to rectify the situation.

If all is well, put away your tools and materials and do a final purification with juniper. Ground yourself thoroughly. You may want or need to lie on the ground to help this process. Have something to eat and drink to help with the grounding. Record your impressions of the night's ritual and the results of your meditations.

Erynn Rowan Laurie

CHAPTER 8
Advanced Divination Techniques

The Art of Designing Layouts

As you progress in your work with ogam divination, eventually you'll come to a place where simple layouts won't cover the territory you need to examine. When that happens, understanding the principles behind designing layouts becomes important. No layout structure, no matter how "traditional" it is among practitioners of divination, is inherently any better than another. The common "Celtic cross" layout so familiar to Tarot readers is just one way of approaching that divinatory material. It covers very general ground and does a good job at offering a standard template for approaching a number of different situations. But even though it's familiar and flexible, it can only go so far.

The beauty of understanding how to create your own layouts for particular situations is that you can allow for each variable in a given reading, designating one or more positions to symbolize aspects of the problem at hand. Readings can be designed with a position symbolizing each person involved in a situation, or a group of positions indicating the various aspects of a particular approach.

With twenty *feda* to work with in a standard set of ogams, you won't want to design too many positions for a reading. Broadening it to a triple set of sixty to deal with the three currents provides more options and a finer filter for information. This gives the system more flexibility and depth and means you can design more complex layouts for your readings if need be.

When designing a layout, you need to ask yourself or your client a lot of questions to determine how many *feda* will be needed and what each one will represent. Because a reading is a way of attempting to understand the flow of the universe, time, and fate, each *fid* drawn will represent some aspect of that flow and pattern. Ask yourself what you want or need to get out of the reading, what it's necessary to know about a situation, and what influences are affecting your life as the situation unfolds.[124]

You may find yourself reading for someone who doesn't want to tell you her question. Doing a reading without knowing the question is like asking a doctor to make a diagnosis without hearing any of the symptoms -- it can be done, but it makes things unnecessarily difficult for both parties. Openness and trust is part of the process of doing divination, and as such, confidentiality is important. Keeping the private lives of others private is a necessary part of reading for others in an ethical way, and to violate that privacy is also a violation of your hospitality to them when they come to you looking for help and advice. Keeping your own counsel and respecting the trust others place in your skills and discretion is an important part of working as a seer in your community. There are a few exceptions to this rule, including such things as reporting incidents of child abuse that might be confided to you -- laws regarding this kind of reporting vary from state to state. It's wise to check the local codes and know where you stand legally as a spiritual counsellor if you're working with clients on a regular basis.

The questions most people ask fall into several large categories. Questions about relatives and relationships are very common, as are questions about jobs and money. Health is also a very important issue in many people's lives. Spirituality is often a question asked, but I find that it's less common than issues regarding love, family, money, and health. Another very common question is how the coming year will work out and what issues will need to be addressed during each season or month.

Sometimes people want to know if there are messages for them from loved ones who have died, or from their deities or spirits. These are trickier readings, but can be done if the identity and nature of the spirits in question are worked out clearly before the reading begins so there will be no confusion about whom or what is being contacted. The contacted spirits may not always want to talk, however, so it's not always advisable to do this kind of work for someone else. I've found that sometimes dead people don't necessarily appreciate being asked questions, and that often another person's deities or spirits want them to listen, but don't want to go through an intermediary. There could

---

[124] Some excellent advice for designing Tarot layouts is found in *Choice Centered Tarot* by Gail Fairfield. Although the Tarot system is different than working with ogam, the same principles apply to layout design, and Gail's approach is very accessible.

be a number of reasons for this, ranging from the dead person not approving of the living talking to dead things, to a deity having already delivered a message that hasn't been listened to. Generally speaking, when things like this happen you'll either get a negative response or nonsense that you can't make heads or tails of, and you may just have to give that particular reading a pass. I have, on rare occasions, refunded a client's money when the readings just wouldn't happen and I was unable to get a clear answer for their questions. It does happen, even to professional readers, so don't be discouraged if sometimes it happens to you.

As you contemplate designing the layout, list the questions surrounding the issue. Chances are they will fall into several general themes that can be translated into positions within the pattern of *feda* laid on the table. *Feda* can be drawn to represent individuals, influences, choices, places, potential outcomes, or time markers. There may be any number of potential questions involved in a reading or series of readings.

What aids or opposes you in the situation? What are the roots of the situation and how did it arise? What are your assumptions and beliefs about it? What are the hidden aspects of an event or situation? Why is a given person reacting in a particular way? What problems or potentials should be watched for and what precautions taken? What are your hopes and fears regarding the issue? Where will different options carry you if you choose to follow up on them? What benefit do you derive from the situation as it is? Will you benefit or be harmed by pursuing a particular option? What are the motives and desires of those involved? Should you advance, wait, or retreat, and what will happen if you do? How can you make the best of what's happening or turn the situation to your advantage? Who or what is influencing the situation from the outside? What is the best way to avoid an unwanted or difficult outcome?

When working on formulating questions and establishing the flow of a layout, sometimes it happens that just getting to the bottom of the issue with enough clarity to name it provides an answer without even having to do a reading. A good assessment of the situation and making the questions clear can sometimes reveal an answer that had been there all along, hidden under confusion and conflicting desires. Though it has nothing to do with ogam, sometimes when a person comes to me asking which of two options they should choose, I'll ask them to flip a coin and decide which choice is heads and which is tails -- what often happens is that before the coin falls, they already know which answer they're hoping for. In situations like that, asking for a reading is really just a way of trying to confirm a gut feeling, and there's nothing wrong with that at all. Once that decision is made, a reading can still be done to examine the potential results and the factors influencing the choice.

As you work through the questions surrounding any layout and consolidate them, consider how the intention of each question or group of questions links to the others. Part of the work of designing a clear and cogent format for a reading is in understanding the web of meaning you're attempting to discern. How do clusters of ideas fall together? How do concepts lead from one point to another? How are different ideas or individuals linked? These concepts can be expressed spatially with the layout when you decide where you're going to lay each *fid* and which positions to read first. When a reading is well designed, the flow will be apparent from the first *fid* to the last.

Think visually when you're designing a layout. Ask yourself if the nature of the questions surrounding the issue is linear or not; do the questions spiral out from a central issue or surround a person's situation like a ring? Are there clusters of *feda* connected like veins in a leaf? The visual impact of a layout has a big influence on how each position might be read, and should be taken into consideration when you're doing your initial design. Working out positions so that they flow smoothly makes for an easier reading process than having to jump from place to place without an apparent pattern.

A reading may seem linear at first, but there could be a place in the reading where a choice must be made -- the design of the layout might need to take that metaphorical fork in the road into consideration and lead off in two directions with "answer" *feda* connected to each *fid* in the fork.

Understanding the flow of energy and meaning in creating a layout takes practice, like everything else about doing divination. It may help to think of a layout as a storyboard, taking a snapshot of action or intent at different points during the unfolding of the answer to the query. Each *fid* on the table expresses a factor or a focus of the situation and suggests a direction in which energy or attention is flowing, or ways in which they may be blocked.

It can be important to determine who is involved in a situation and structure positions to understand how each individual will be affected. If the reading concerns the health, finances, or relationships in a family, it may be necessary to create a position, or more than one, for each member of that family involved -- parents, children, grandparents, or others in an extended family may all be influenced. Roommates or other friends or partners might need to be represented, depending on the issue at hand. For situations at work, particular co-workers and the project itself might be represented. Multiple *feda* might be needed for each person to assess their physical, emotional, and mental or spiritual response to the situation they all face.

You might consider laying out a connecting *fid* between each person to help understand how that individual relationship expresses itself in the matrix that is developing. If three people are involved in a situation, you might lay *feda* out in a triangle to represent each of them as individuals. Place a *fid* between each person to understand how each of the relationships operates. Place another in the center to express how they interact as a triad.

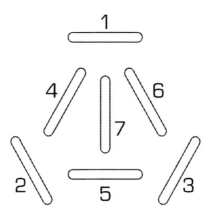

Expressing relationships in a layout
Illustration by Bob Daverin

The illustration above shows a pattern between three people where *feda* 1, 2 and 3 represent the individuals, 4, 5 and 6 represent the nature of the interactions between each individual, and *fid* 7 represents the overall relationship between them as a group.

In a relationship or situation involving more than three people, some *feda* will need to be moved so that you cay lay out others to express the nature of the interactions between those *feda* not next to each other in the original pattern.

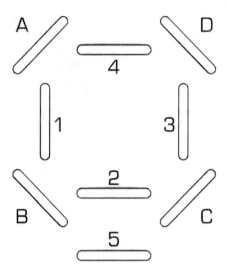

Larger relationship dynamics, first stage
Illustration by Bob Daverin

Here we have a pattern between four people, marked A, B, C and D. The interactions between the individuals are marked 1, 2, 3 and 4, but as you can see, this leaves out the interactions between A and C and between D and B. *Fid* 5 is the expression of the synergy of the relationship between all four of them.

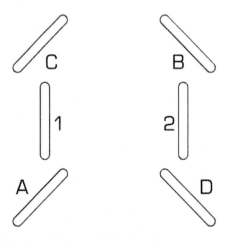

Larger relationship dynamics, second stage
Illustration by Bob Daverin

Because we want to examine all the interactions between each person, two of the *feda* will need to be moved. C and B are swapped to places above A and D and new *feda* marked 1 and 2 are laid out to examine those interactions, as in the illustration for the second stage of the reading.

The number of individuals can be expanded as needed for the dynamics in a family, a household, a committee, or any other kind of group. With groups larger than five, using the triple set of *feda* usually works better, allowing for a wider and more accurate variety of responses. The interactive web suggested here also shows that a layout need not be static to be effective. If moving the *feda* around to examine relationships and energies between individual segments of a reading is necessary then go ahead and do that. Your intuition in these situations is a good guide.

If you had a question about changes in your living situation, you could lay out a *fid* for yourself, one for your home, and one for your landlord if you're renting, because each of these factors will need to be taken into account. In a situation like this, anyone else living in the house with you, related or not, would also need to be accounted for, because their reactions to the situation can impact the results and influence your own reaction to events. More than one *fid* might be necessary for some of these positions, because not only financial but also emotional or other dimensions may need examination. If your employment influences the changes in your situation, adding a *fid* for that would be logical as well -- the money you need to initiate or deal with the changes is going to be important to how you work with what the reading tells you. Whether or not you will be financially stable enough for a move or a renovation will depend on what's going on with your source of income.

For people looking at the potential for several choices -- for instance deciding which schools to apply to for a degree -- laying a *fid* for each of the options makes sense. You might consider laying out two for each so that you can see the gifts and challenges of each option.

Keep in mind when doing a reading with a layout that if you want to examine the meaning of a particular *fid* in greater detail, its okay to pick up the already used *feda*, mix them again, and pull new ones to elaborate on the circumstances arising from that *fid*. When using the basic 20 *fid* set, this allows for recurrences of *feda* that have already appeared. These recurrences, when they happen, are an important emphasis on or reinforcement of a concept.

Sample Layout Design Reading

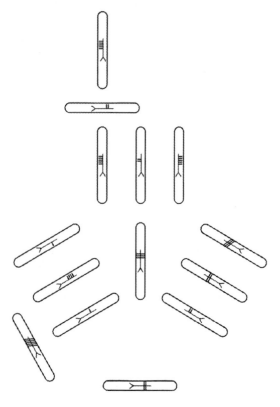

Layout expressing issues surrounding building a home
Illustration by Bob Daverin

A few years ago, I was called in to consult with a couple who were in the process of designing and trying to build a new home on some land where they were living. They were running into repeated problems and complications, and I was asked to come out to do divination for them, and possibly to negotiate with the land spirits if necessary.

We talked for about an hour about the different issues involved in the situation and what needed to be looked at in terms of where problems might lie and whether they would be able to build on the land or not. Eventually we decided that there were three general categories of potential influence: land issues, spirit issues, and human issues. This gave us a triangular concept for the layout, and each side of the triangle was divided into three different *feda* to express different potentials or areas of influence.

At the top of the triangle was the realm of spirit. The couple are both very involved in their spiritual lives and understood that the deities and spirits would be important to the situation. Three *feda* were positioned across the top for the gods, the ancestors, and the land and house spirits.

The physical realm, on the left side of the reading, was divided into the three realms; land at the lower point, sea in the center, and sky at the upper left point, dealing with issues in the ground, issues of water and plumbing, and issues of power and energy.

To the right, three more *feda* were designated to represent the past at the bottom of the triangle, motion and transition in the present, and at the top of that leg of the triangle was the future.

At the center of the layout was a position for the mist or the gateway between all these concepts, expressing the solution or resolution of the situation and its likely outcome.

The *feda* were mixed and laid out from the bottom point of the triangle clockwise, from land on one end to past on the other, with the center *fid* being placed last.

When the *feda* were laid out, it was very clear that there were serious problems with the situation. Both h-Úath and Ceirt were part of the reading, and these are usually warning signs for trouble. Land was where h-Úath fell. Sea received Coll and Sky got Beith, so neither of those aspects seemed to be a particular problem. In the realm of Spirit, Ceirt fell into the slot for the Gods, while Dair and Nin were received for the ancestors and the land and house spirits.

In the human realm, Lus was received for past, Onn for the present and what was in transition, and nGétal for the future. In the center of the reading was Úr.

H-Úath indicated that the land itself was going to be the big issue. They had been having trouble with getting good results for perc tests for a septic system because of how the land was laid out. Much of it was on a very steep slope, and there would be water table issues as well. The paperwork involved was proving to be a nightmare, in true h-Úath fashion. While I would generally have considered water table issues to be a Sea involvement, what we're really talking about is underground water, buried in the land. Siting the septic system proved an insurmountable obstacle to the new construction.

We drew a *fid* to clarify h-Úath, which turned out to be Ruis. As frequently happens with this *fid*, the situation led to a great deal of anger and frustration for the couple. Adding to the issues was Ceirt in the position of deity. While the land spirits and the ancestors had no problem with the plans for the new house, it was apparent the Gods wanted them somewhere else. When the *feda* were returned to the bag and two *feda* were drawn to try to get a clearer picture of the situation, Dair and Ceirt were drawn. This indicated a very strong resistance and reiterated the frustrations and roadblocks being set up.

In looking at the human side, Lus indicated some wonderful, creative ideas being brought forward in the plans for the new house. The shape and nature of the land were taken into account and worked with to produce a design that used the steep slopes and the surrounding woods to very good effect.

Onn in the present indicated that things were most definitely in transition and that movement was necessary. How necessary didn't become apparent until later. NGétal was the future *fid*, and we all hoped that it meant the situation could be resolved positively for the building of the house.

The gateway *fid*, however, was Úr. This *fid* signifies a death or an ending. Considering the persistent difficulties indicated in the other areas, we took a somewhat too optimistic view in hoping that it spelled an end to the troubles. Drawing a final *fid* produced Onn again. We interpreted this as movement after dealing with obstacles, thinking it might be an ability to move forward with the new construction.

It turned out that the combination of Úr and Onn actually meant an end to their residence at the old site and moving to a new location a few miles away, reflecting Onn's meaning of a physical journey. The process was laden with frustration and disappointment for them, but their new home is beautiful and spacious, and they settled in nicely with nearly all the amenities they wanted to build into their custom home. The energies in the new place are much more conducive to their work and their lives.

Casting Twenty Feda

In the chapter on basic divination, random castings for nine *feda* were discussed. Moving from this small number to the use of the whole set of *feda* can be a challenge, but the general principles are the same regardless of the size of the reading. Patterns and groups of *feda* falling together will often be larger, introducing more variables into each area of the reading. You will still often encounter single *feda* falling alone on the casting space, and small groups of *feda* forming relationships.

Part of the secret of larger castings is to look first for the overall structure of the cast. As with smaller castings, look for distinct groupings, for patterns formed by the fall of the *feda*, or for bridges or walls made between groups by *feda* falling between them. Observe where the top of each *fid* falls, as this can indicate the direction that *fid*'s energy is moving in relation to the reading as a whole.

Sometimes a group of *feda* will all fall facing the same direction, pointing toward a particular *fid* or other group of *feda*, pushing the issues of the cluster in that direction. This often suggests that what is being pointed out is of great importance to the situation addressed by the group facing it. These energies will often either blend or be at odds. Part of the work then involves understanding how the clusters interact and how or whether they can be brought into harmony.

Occasionally a random cast will fall with no apparent center or focal cluster of *feda*. Energies in this case are often just as scattered as the reading itself. Finding ways to connect the various diverse energies and purposes may be necessary in both the reading and the querent's life. Intuition and follow up castings can help with this work.

When casting with *feda* that may fall face down -- cabochons or discs, for instance -- you will be faced with choosing whether to see those face down *feda* as irrelevant to the reading or as hidden influences. Both approaches are valid and useful, and I have used both, depending on circumstance. You may wish to wait until you're done reading the face up *feda* before deciding, as sometimes issues can arise within the face up *feda* that might be clarified by what is face down nearby.

If you feel strongly that the face down *feda* are irrelevant, it might make the rest of the reading easier if you clear them away from the reading surface. This can be particularly helpful if you are just starting to work with the full set for random castings, allowing you to see the patterns on the table more clearly and to understand the relationships between *feda* and clusters without the clutter of face down pieces disrupting your focus.

It will also occasionally happen that the majority of the *feda* will fall face down, with only a few *feda* showing. When this happens, it's usually a very strong message about the situation, showing a narrow focus and some fairly imperative instructions. I did a reading where only three *feda* fell face up out of a random handful from my sixty-*fid* set. The main issue stated for my client was to guard his health during a journey he would be making the next week. He requested that I read the face down *feda* as well, and they strongly reinforced the initial message from the three previously revealed *feda*. While we got a little more detail from the reading, the message was identical, with all three currents of nGétal appearing.

It's important to remember to listen to your intuition and to any spirits that aid you as you do work of this type. Sometimes a *fid* will speak to you very strongly with a message that seems peripheral to its usual meaning, but may still connect to the core traditional meanings in some sideways or punning manner. Pay attention to those moments, and to your emotional reactions to the *feda* in the places that they fall. They can be important information, and may end up adding to your web of meanings for that *fid*. The further you advance in your ogam work, the more important it is to be open to those messages and this is much of what makes divination an art as opposed to an exact science of memorized tables of correspondence or fixed meanings.

When working with the full ogam set, you may find that working with a casting cloth eases your way from smaller random casts, helping you sort and define your parameters for each reading. This can be a very fruitful approach with larger readings, especially if you have been working with a cloth in your smaller castings. The set background really helps some people to understand the patterns and flow of a large reading more easily and thoroughly, and that understanding is what is important about the work, not the specific tool set in use.

Working with the full twenty *feda* is essentially the same as working with nine *feda*. The principles all still apply; they're just expanded to encompass a larger field of meaning. Each aspect of the ogam is present in every life. The art of interpreting a full ogam reading is in understanding how each *fid* relates to the others and how the full range of that experience applies to the situation at hand.

Because so many factors are involved in a twenty-*fid* reading, some will naturally be more emphasized or more important than others. Some will be buried under a pile of other *feda*, some will be off to the side all alone and isolated, and some will be focal points because they lie between two groups and provide a solution to conflicting energies. There will be times when you feel that a *fid* is not particularly relevant to a reading or the situation addressed in it, and it's all right to gloss over or ignore that *fid* if this is the case. Although every *fid* may be read when it is face up, the relative importance of each one varies with where and how it falls.

Using a Pendulum

One useful tool for working with a full ogam random casting is a pendulum. A pendulum can be made of anything at all, and consists of a chain or string and a small weight at the end of the string. Some people swear by particular crystals or stones, some use glass, and some use wooden pendulums with small vials of essential oils in their bodies. What you use is up to you -- it isn't the physical components of the pendulum that are particularly important, it's what you do with it that helps refine a reading.

Pendulums work by reading the tiny, usually unnoticeable muscle motions in your hand and arm as you hold them by the end of their chain, letting the weight dangle freely beneath. These muscle movements are controlled by your subconscious, which is usually in deeper contact with the psychological and spiritual realms than the conscious mind. By working with a pendulum, you can open yourself to intuitions that might not come fully to your conscious mind.

Pendulums are capable of a range of movements: circling clockwise or counterclockwise, swinging right and left, swinging at angles, swinging up and down, trembling, or even bouncing. Each person who uses a pendulum will eventually develop a small vocabulary of what these motions tend to mean. For me, an up and down swing is usually an affirmative while a side to side swing is negative. Circling clockwise or counterclockwise may indicate the direction or type of energy in motion, and whether it is helpful and benign or disruptive and blocking in a situation. You can designate beforehand what a yes or no will be, or ask the pendulum to demonstrate a yes and a no to you before you begin.

Like any other tool, the pendulum should be cleansed before using it in a reading, to remove any previous influences on it. It can be purified and blessed just like the *feda* were, and passed through smoke or sprinkled with water before using it in each reading. Regular work with your pendulum, like your work with the ogam, will connect it with your energies and each time you use the tool it will take on more of that charge. All that's necessary to use it is simply to hold it by the chain, clearing your mind. Focus on the *fid* and what you want to know about it, and let the pendulum move as it will.

Using a pendulum in an ogam reading can help you determine whether an outlying *fid* is relevant to a reading or not, how its energies interact with the main body of the reading, or whether you're interpreting its meanings properly for the situation at hand. The pendulum can be used to consult your own subconscious understanding or to get a clearer message from spirit or deity regarding the item it is held over. I carry one in the bag that stores my *feda*, just in case I need it. I don't use it in every reading, but when I have questions about an aspect of a reading that isn't coming clear, it is often very useful.

Sample Full Ogam Casting

In this reading, the full set of twenty *feda* is used. The form of the *feda*, long slips of wood, does not allow for any *fid* to fall face down, so all twenty are read. Rachel came to me asking for advice on her creative work in writing and photography during the upcoming season. We met at a local teahouse and cast the *feda* to see what potential directions her work might take and how she might more fruitfully explore her talents in those fields.

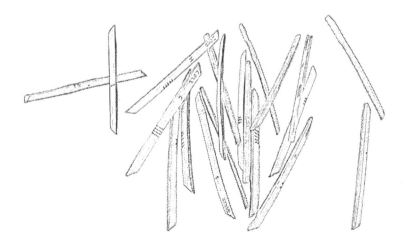

Random cast with full twenty-fid set

When the *feda* were cast, the first thing we noted was that Tinne, Coll and Beith were all lying atop other *feda*. These seemed to be the place to start, as everything was closely grouped and there didn't appear to be a central focus to the reading nor any significant outlying groups distinguishing themselves visually.

Tinne, the ingot, suggested not money, but mastery in this situation. Rachel was not so much interested in creating a business using her writing and photography as she was in expressing herself fully and creatively. Coll suggested using words with wisdom, while Beith as purifications and a new beginning offered the advice that it was a good time to be moving forward with new ventures.

Beith crossing Onn suggested that in her photography, she might be travelling to find subjects for her photos. She's already been doing this to some extent and hopes to expand on that aspect of her work.

Coll, crossing Ruis and nGétal, suggests that her writing in particular will be where she finds her passion, and together with nGétal, that writing will be a healing and strengthening path for her.

Tinne, crossing over Straif, Dair, and Sail, offers the thought that writing will be transformative for her, but that she needs strength and the patience of water wearing away at stone to bring the work to fruition. Straif touching Idad, at the top of the reading, brings in the idea that the writing may also be a way for her to connect with the past and with tradition and her ancestors in some way, perhaps through telling family stories and speaking the truth about her life in that way.

The other end of Straif touches Fern, the alder, which guards the heart. Lying directly alongside Fern are Ailm and Nin. Rachel's interest in writing has been growing a more feminist dimension lately, and these *feda* advise her to guard her emotions and grow a thick skin when it comes to how her writing may be received. Ailm is the cry of birth and death, and where this may be a new beginning and the birth of a new direction in her writing, it may also mean leaving old patterns of though and writing behind. Nin's connection with words and weaving brings an emphasis within the context of the reading to writing within a community of women, and expressing her opinion on women's issues.

Off to the right of the reading we find Lus covered by h-Úath, framed by Ceirt and Úr. This tells her that she needs to be careful not to let fear and frustration bury her writing or stop her from doing her creative work. Getting negative responses and fear of that potential should not rule her urges to use her creativity to advance her causes. Gort is near Úr, bringing a positive, earthy connection to the situation, showing that the soil of Úr does not have to be a death of her creativity should she find resistance, but the ground for cultivating her writing as a seed gestates within the earth before showing itself above the surface.

Last, we find Edad and Muin. Both of these *feda* have the potential for falsehood, trickery, illusion and deception. At the same time, Muin is about love and esteem, and about the strength of the ox. If Rachel holds to her principles, artistic and ethical, speaking her truth in her writing and photography, she can cut through illusion to the beauty she wishes to express.

Three Currents of Glas

The biggest innovation I've made in working with the ogam is to separate the interpretation of each *fid* into three currents of meaning and manifestation. These were touched on briefly in previous chapters and meanings were given for each of the currents under the entries for each *fid* in Chapter 2. It's important to understand how and why each of these currents was derived in order to know how to use them in divination and ritual. This understanding will also help you categorize any new connections and meanings that you derive for each *fid* as your work and study progresses.

Part of the inspiration for this division was the runic work of my friend Bjoern Hartsfvang,[125] who has been reading for many years now with three sets of runes made of different materials to represent the heights, the depths, and Midgard or the human world of manifestation. I was very impressed by this approach and asked if I could adapt it to work within the ogam system and he was kind enough to agree.

Another inspiration was a divinatory practice from volume four of the *Carmina Gadelica* that involved three stones used in a ritual manner to discern whether a problem was rooted in the mind, the heart, or the body for the restoration of a person's "displaced heart". The passage in question is worth quoting in full, as the context is fascinating and sheds much light on how

---

[125] More information about Bjoern and his work and techniques is available at his website, http://www.elvenstarstudios.com/ElvenStarStudios/bjoern.html -- Runes, ogam *feda* and other items are available there as well.

the soul was viewed. The account appears to be incomplete, as it does not describe what happened after the divination was done, but the circumstances and the way the person is viewed are part and parcel of how the three currents approach was imagined.

Tionndadh Cridhe: Displacement of the Heart

The following cure is to replace the heart after a fright: Go to a stream under a bridge over which the living and the dead pass. Take water from the stream in a wooden 'cuach,' cup. Lift three stones from the stream in the name of the Father, of the Son, of the Spirit. One stone must be round to represent the head; one must be triangular to represent the heart; one stone must be oblong to represent the body. Put these three stones in the cuach of water and carry them home. Put the stones one by one into the fire until they are red hot. Then take one stone out of the fire and place it in the water in the cuach, observing carefully for how long it fizzled in the water before it was cooled. Do the same to the second and third stones. The stone which makes the most prolonged and mournful sound indicates the seat of the trouble, whether it be the head, heart or body that is affected.[126]

The third piece that brought the idea of the three currents home for me was how the color *glas* is conceptualized, translated variously as green, blue, or grey. All of these colors are connected with the sea, the sky, eyes, and the Otherworld. In looking at the

---

[126] Carmichael 1978, 207

concepts of heights, depths, and center, and of the body, head, and heart, I saw that the three colors of *glas* could signify these ideas while still transcending boundaries through the metaphor of the mist.

For me, green is a manifestation of the physical realm, in all its verdant abundance. It is the body, and in Bjoern's model would be the realm of Midgard, where physical life happens. I designated the things related to this color as chthonic, for the embodied qualities of the land and the things hidden within the earth. It shares resonances with *Coire Goiriath*, the Cauldron of Warming that deals with physical health and energy. *Glas* as green is also associated with the Otherworldly realm of the ancestors and the direction where the spirits of the dead go when they are buried in the earth.

Following this thread of thought, the chthonic current of each *fid* expresses the qualities of what is physical, earthly, or solid. It deals with things that move slowly or take time to manifest, or things that are rooted and difficult to move. The animal and instinctual part of our nature is here, bound up in our body and biology. Seeds that lie in darkness are a part of this current, giving rise to the origins of things. It is generative and can be nurturing, but it can also be dissolving as a body breaks down in the grave. Some aspects of the chthonic current may be seen as "negative", for instance Úr's connection with physical death and the clay of the body. Others are regarded as much more positive, like Gort's peaceful garden or Tinne's material prosperity.

Remembering that no individual current is either positive or negative is important to the process of discerning if a meaning or concept belongs in a given current. Each current has manifestations that can have a beneficial, neutral, or harmful effect, depending on the *fid* being expressed through it. The meanings associated with a *fid* can't be divided into "bad" physical and earthly manifestations and "good" spiritual and heavenly categories -- life is never that simple and the realities of *Filidecht* reflect this complexity.

The grey of *glas* manifests as the mists. It is the mysterious depths of the heart and the emotions. This current is a part of the depths of the sea, and all things that are hidden or in motion. This is the current that carries the secrets of emotional reaction and passionate action, and is expressed in part through *Coire Érmae*, the Cauldron of Motion. It represents the heart, which is always in motion while we are alive. Emotions are a whirlpool at times, and like the whirlpool, this current may pull things in until they slip beyond your control. Mist is a transitional, liminal space in insular Celtic lore, where Otherworldly things happen that may bring joy or terror, and the physical manifestation of mist is itself always in motion, swirling and floating in the air around us, moving like a living thing. Ambiguity and uncertainty are a part of its identity.

This grey *glas* current is oceanic and deals with everything in transition. Emotion and passion are found here, as is a certain primal, creative chaos. The oceanic current deals with the obscured aspects of each *fid*, and with places where boundaries can be crossed for good or ill. When a concept is neither fish nor fowl, not one thing or another, it is most likely a property of the oceanic current of that *fid*. This is a twilight place, the dawn and dusk of passing boundaries and borders; emotions are neither a product solely of the body nor of the mind, but of some glimmering mix of both. Anything that is flexible, fluid, tidal, changeable, creative, or in motion is a part of this current; all that shapeshifts is found here. This is a current of energies and acts rather than static physical objects.

Glas blue is the stark depth of the heavens. The energies tend to manifest in orderly ways. They also express themselves as cyclic time, which can be understood as the stars in their eternal circle about the sky. Much of this current touches on things in the mental or spiritual realms. It partakes of the energies of *Coire Sofhis*, the Cauldron of Wisdom, but it should be remembered that wisdom and understanding can be twisted as easily as anything else. The celestial current, like the chthonic, is neither wholly good nor bad. Because all things are sacred within an animist worldview and because spirit and deity are immanent in all of nature, the celestial current is not considered any more sacred than the chthonic or the oceanic. While the sky realm is where the Tuatha Dé Danann originally came from, it is not the only place where the Gods dwell.

This current deals with the mind and the imagination. It's where the Gods may touch a situation, and when deity and order come together we find both the ideals and the abuses of law and regulation. The celestial current of a *fid* deals with mastery and intellectual connections, ideas and ideals, the electric spark of inspiration, and how spirit interacts with the physical world. The head was seen as the physical seat of the soul and the source of a person's power; heads were taken in battle and there are tales of severed heads speaking and revealing secrets.[127] This current touches on that connection between soul and breath found in the resonance between *anam* and *anál*.[128] The celestial current derives order from the chaos found in the oceanic current, but it should be noted that under some circumstances, order might be stultifying rather than organizing.

While I use the colors green, blue, and grey to represent the three currents, shapes can also be used, like the stones in the *Tionnaidh Cridhe* ritual. Using a circle for the celestial current, a triangular shape for the oceanic and an oval for the chthonic would work just as well, and provide a tactile distinction for those with vision problems. Engraving each *fid* deeply into wood or stone on differently shaped bases would provide a way for a blind ogam student to work with the system, for instance.

Another idea that I incorporated into my three currents work was the Irish Christian idea of the three colors of "martyrdom." Some might wonder why I would bring Christian ideas into a work on Pagan-focused divination and spirituality, but the underlying concepts are interesting and potentially applicable within the historical and modern cultural context of CR. My interpretations of the material are obviously going to be different from those of the medieval Christians who first discussed the ideas, but we live in a different time and are approaching it from a different religious perspective.

The three colors in question are white, red, and *glas* -- the green/blue/grey spectrum discussed regarding the three currents above. Within the Christian context, white martyrdom was pilgrimage or deliberate separation from everything one knew and loved for the sake of God. Red martyrdom was suffering and physical death, "endurance of a cross or destruction for Christ's sake,"[129] as the *Cambrai Homily* says. *Glas* martyrdom, which I'll render as "green" for the sake of this discussion, is asceticism and fasting for spiritual purposes.

Pilgrimage is a practice found in every religion, and one that can be undertaken by nearly anyone. Sacred places are everywhere, and even if you can't make a pilgrimage to holy sites in Ireland or Scotland, there are still places near your own home where the spirits have a strong presence. Making actual pilgrimages to Ireland and Scotland is a good practice, even if

---

[127] Davidson, 1988, 11, 74-75
[128] Both words carry implications of being the non-corporeal vehicle of life and, when it leaves the body, life ceases.
[129] Siewers, 2005, 33

you can only go once in your lifetime, but to be in those landscapes, walking the earth where the tales took place and seeing the places spoken of in the creation-tales of the *Dindsenechas* gives new depth to understanding and practice.

This "white martyrdom" is movement in the physical world, but its intent is spiritual blessing, and so I placed white with the celestial current. This provides a contrast of white against the blue of sky and symbolizes the stars circling above.

Red martyrdom's shedding of blood falls into the paradigm of sacrifice and offering within a CR context. It isn't unreasonable for people growing their own food and raising animals for that purpose to offer a sacrificial ritual when the animals are slaughtered, though it's certainly not a common practice in CR by any means. Comparatively speaking, though, raising an animal at home and knowing exactly what it eats and how it has lived before it's killed quickly and humanely is a far better way to deal with eating meat than to support the current commercial slaughterhouse and factory farm system. Sacrifices are often cosmological in nature, seen as a renewal of the world or of the contracts between humanity and the spirit world.

Because this is the most physical manifestation of all the colors, red is wedded with green's chthonic current, expressing the life and death of the body or the destruction or offering of physical objects as sacrifices to the deities and spirits. We know that both animals and objects were sacrificed. Ritual objects and weapons were also frequently thrown into pits, lakes, or rivers after they had been broken so that no human would be able to use them.[130]

Fasting and asceticism are associated with green martyrdom. While it can't be said that the pre-Christian Celtic peoples were particularly ascetic as a whole -- they were known for their feasting, their drinking, and their fighting -- it stands to reason that some within that culture would pursue an ascetic path as a part of their pursuit of wisdom. The sensory deprivation practices associated with the Stone on the Belly exercise certainly qualify as ascetic, and we know that there were "mad" poets called *gealta* who were said to live on vegetarian diets, far from society. The *gealta* also had a firm link to wilderness and the writing of nature poetry, for which Suibhne was famed. [131]

---

[130] Cunliffe, 1986, 90-95

[131] Chadwick, 1942, 109, Regarding the famous *geilt* Suibhne, Chadwick says, "His poems are full of lamentation over the hardness of his lot in being restricted to a

Asceticism, the madness of the *gealta* and the emotional matrix in which it occurs suggests its connection with the oceanic current, and so I've placed the green upon the grey in my system -- both of them *glas*, both of them in a liminal state, bridging the body and the spirit. Asceticism speaks to the heart and focuses the way it reaches out to deity and spirit, and is practiced in many traditions. Fasting, sleep deprivation, and isolation, for example, are core practices associated with the *hanblecheyapi* vision quest or "crying for a vision" ceremony of the Lakota, and this kind of pattern is repeated in any number of cultures and countries.

In working with these currents in divination, it helps to see each *fid* within this context. These understandings will also help when negotiating new associations and meanings for a *fid* that arises organically out of the traditional meanings and language. These shades and subtleties of interpretation offer a wider range for divinatory and magical work and also help to focus and sharpen a reading's details.

In some ways, working with the currents is a much more complex issue than using a single set of *feda*, but it could be said to simplify the choices made when attempting to discern which of a *fid's* meanings is emerging within the matrix of *feda* on the table. While in part the choices of a *fid's* meanings can be determined by sensitive attention to the context of the reading as a whole, the ability to observe the currents in action makes the choice a little easier. As with the single set, learning to work with the triple set of *feda* is most easily approached by using patterned layouts and then moving on to random castings. It takes time to appreciate the way different currents feel in a reading and does add another layer of initial memorization to the process of learning the ogam. That said I feel the benefits of the way the currents refine the system outweigh any difficulties initially encountered in the learning process.

Using the three currents and keeping the concepts that gave rise to them in mind adds a richness beneath the bare bones of language and fragmentary lore that has until now defined the use of ogam outside the tree-based systems. There are now sixty

---

vegetable and berry diet." At 120, it is shown that Suibhne was not the only one observing these dietary restrictions: "It is still believed in many parts of Ireland that all the lunatics of Ireland would make their way, if unrestrained, to a valley in the county of Kerry, called *Gleann na nGealt*, and remain there feeding on the herbs and watercresses of the valley until they should recover their former sanity."

subtle varieties of experience and understanding to work with rather than a mere twenty, and that in itself cannot help but expand the reader's repertoire.

Sample Three Current Cauldron and Tree Reading

The reading below uses the basic Cauldron and Tree layout, but here we include the refinement of working with the three currents and a sixty-*feda* set from which to draw the oracle. To distinguish the currents drawn, I use CH for chthonic, OC for oceanic, and CE for celestial.

Lee is a harper who came to me to ask if he should follow his calling and go into music therapy. He hopes that this will be a fulfilling path for him and isn't as concerned with the monetary outcome.

Cauldron of Wisdom   Path to the Future

                                      ⊥⊥⊥⊥   Sail

⊥⊥   Lus   CH

CE

Cauldron   World Tree
of Motion

⧣   Úr   ⊨   Lus
CH   OC
Cauldron
of Warming

╈   Ailm
CH

When the *feda* were laid out, I could see right away that this was the proper thing for Lee to be doing. Ailm and Úr in the chthonic current are the manifestations of birth and death, the times and places where healing harp are often called for. The music eases these transitions, and within the Irish tradition the three harp strains of laughter, weeping, and sleep are associated with stilling the pain of the dying and women in childbirth.

Lus appears twice in this reading, showing a connection with inspiration in its celestial current, and the process of healing in its oceanic current. My feeling was that the hand of Brighid was strongly influencing this decision.

Sail, in the final position, is the willow tree from which the bodies of harps were traditionally made. It also relates to the voices of ancestors, and Lee used to play music for his grandmother until she died. When he started playing again, he decided to learn the harp, and his progress was very quick and easy. There is a potential implication of his grandmother's approval in this reading as well.

Whether or not Lee manages to make a living doing this work, it is very likely to be a spiritually fulfilling path for him, so long as he takes care and prepares himself to deal with the difficult emotional nature of work with the dying, and with the physical realities of the organic processes of death and birth and what they do to bodies and to the people who are there with the dying and with mothers giving birth.

Within a week of receiving this reading, Lee was offered a place in a healing harp program on scholarship that paid his entire tuition. Before the reading he had not even been aware there was a program available in his area. He felt very strongly that this was a confirmation of Brighid's involvement and approval of his work.

Sample Three Current Random Casting With Nine Feda

Nolan is a magician who wanted to know if his magical work was moving in the right direction, or if there was another place he should focus as he works his way along his magical path.

He chose nine *feda* without looking and cast them onto the reading cloth. Three *feda* fell face down. Those falling face up were Ailm's celestial current, Ruis in the chthonic current, Fern's oceanic current, Nin's celestial current, Onn in the celestial current and nGétal in its oceanic current.

The *feda* fell in a very scattered pattern, so there was no grouping to move out from. This indicated that Nolan's energies were very scattered as well, and that he was feeling like he had no direction at the moment and wasn't sure where to go with his work. Lacking a particular focus to start from, I began at the top of the casting cloth.

☐ = Cthonic
▨ = Celestial
☐ = Oceanic

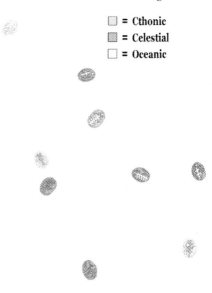

Nine Feda Three Current Casting

Ailm at the top, particularly in the celestial current, suggested beginnings and inspiration, with the potential for a stroke of enlightenment, but it was blocked from the rest of the reading by the chthonic current of Ruis, Redness, representing his anger, frustration and rage at the circumstances of his life. He was feeling helpless about situations regarding family and his physical surroundings. He felt a certain amount of guilt over a parent's failing health and was having a lot of difficulty dealing with the situation.

Oceanic Fern revealed that he had been tending to retreat to guard himself from emotional engagement over his anger, and that he had been having a very hard time expressing his needs and boundaries in the situation. Nin's celestial current falling nearby offered a potential way through the thicket if he was willing to engage in clear communication regarding his needs. Celestial Onn suggested spiritual journeywork and communication with the spirits he works with to help him find solid ground upon which to stand, and to find ways to resolve his rage and guilt.

At the bottom of the reading was nGétal's oceanic current, showing a need for healing and an imbalance in his life that must be dealt with before his magical work can proceed fruitfully.

Working in the Otherworld with his spirits and speaking in both the spiritual and the mundane realms to claim his own space and unclutter his life in a number of ways seems to be the best route to achieving his magical goals and finding his magical direction.

Nolan felt that the message was clear and relevant enough to his question and his situation that we didn't need to turn the face down *feda* and read them as well.

Sample Advanced Three Current Random Casting

Working beyond the use of a fixed number of *feda* can be useful. While nine is a good symbolic number for a variety of reasons, sometimes pulling a random handful of *feda* from the bag will reach deeper into a situation. It allows for more variables to be expressed and broadens the field of interpretation as well. More complex patterns can come into play, as they do with the single-set twenty *fid* casting method. I wouldn't usually recommend the use of more than about twenty *feda*, as that becomes unwieldy, but if you want to, feel free to use more. Using more than about thirty for a random cast, though, crowds the reading too much for my taste and seems to muddy the interpretation rather than sharpen and enhance it.

In readings like this the use of a pendulum tends to be more frequent as a tool for deciding which face down *feda* are relevant, or for tracing the energy flow in the patterns on the table. The more *feda* of different currents that are on the table, the more your intuition comes into the process as well. Weaving the reading together into one coherent whole is an art that takes time to master. Understanding which *feda* appear to be more emphasized than others, and where the focal points in a reading are also takes time and practice.

Remember too that not all questions or issues will need to be explored with advanced or in-depth readings. As you gain experience, you'll start to get a feel for how to approach each question or situation and decide whether to use a standardized layout, a random casting, or to design a more specific and intricate layout to address the issue at hand.

Skye came to me, never having had a reading of any kind before. She is a survivor of breast cancer and has had a double mastectomy. Over the course of her recovery, her partner has become more distant both physically and emotionally. Over the years, she has had a very androgynous identity, and the mastectomy has only served to emphasize this in her presentation socially. She has been reaching out but until very recently there has been no reciprocity and she has been feeling very alone physically and emotionally.

Part of what she wanted to know was if the relationship was salvageable. She was also concerned with her long-term health and survival regarding the aftermath of the cancer and its treatment regimen.

This reading had a somewhat spiral shape to it, with a few outliers. The first thing I noticed was that a couple of letters showed up twice, giving emphasis to their messages. We started looking at the reading from the center, where Muin's oceanic current was partially obscured by a hidden *fid*. Muin here often manifests as deception, hidden agendas, half-truths or fickleness. Insincerity and manipulation can be present in a situation like this. Next to it and touching it was the oceanic current of Onn. Here it seems to be indicating a change of heart and a journey taken for deep emotional reasons. In talking with Skye, it seemed that these two related to her own desire to leave the relationship she is in, and that the conversations they have been having may

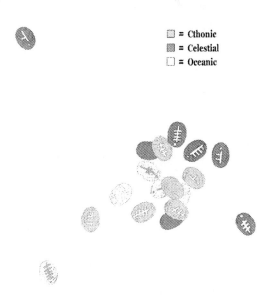

☐ = Cthonic
▨ = Celestial
☐ = Oceanic

Random toss reading for Skye.
17 feda appeared, with 5 face down.

285

be deflecting attention from her desire to leave and to emotionally prepare for that departure.

Next to Muin is the chthonic current of nGétal, which seems to refer to the surrounding health issues of the cancer and her recovery, giving context to the emotional drift and conflict at the heart of the reading.

Above nGétal, and to the right, is chthonic h-Úath, indicating fights and difficulties, as well as a feeling of being trapped and unable to escape. This accurately described her situation. That feeling of being trapped has been very destructive for her.

Around to the left and above, we found the chthonic current of Úr. This is the soil and the clay of the body, but strongly offers the opinion that there is a need to let go of what is passing and attempt to move on. Stagnation becomes a distinct possibility if the death indicated is not transcended.

Touching that *fid*, just slightly above and to the right, we had the celestial current of Edad, the Amanita. This offered advice to dream and envision a new life for herself, and suggested that deity was present, even if that presence was hidden. It advised a need to communicate with spirit, even if it seemed futile at first. Skye had been feeling lost spiritually, wavering between belief and unbelief, uncertain of her direction, and this advice seemed to affect her a great deal.

Next to Edad was the celestial current of Sail, the willow. This *fid* says that there's a proper time for everything, as the tides ebb and flow when they should. When Edad's dreams and visions are considered, they can be brought forth at the proper time. Lus was next to it in its celestial current, representing the fires of inspiration that supported Edad's advice to envision a new life, and suggesting taking up a regular spiritual practice of some sort to regain an emotional and spiritual steadiness that will give a good place from which to proceed.

Circling around and down toward the outside right of the reading we find Úr again, this time in the celestial current. This suggests that the changes are inevitable, and that there is a need for what almost might be termed an emotional exorcism of that which has festered within her life. This offers strong advice to move on from a stagnating relationship.

Moving around to the left again, we come back to Coll in its chthonic current, isolated from the body of the reading by a face down *fid*. Its advice is to listen to the evidence of her senses, a thing she has been hiding from for some time.

Below that is Idad's oceanic current. This represents the bond between generations and speaks of her concern for her children in the situation, but the distance between this *fid* and the rest of the reading suggests that dealing with her own health and sanity is the primary concern, and that what helps her will ultimately help them.

At the far left top of the reading is the celestial current of h-Úath. This represents her fears of abandonment and how she worries about loneliness and isolation, being without help or friends or love. The celestial current of this *fid* also advises facing one's fear. Because it is so far from the body of the reading, it exists only in potential and is not a true motivating factor. The fear of abandonment is more real than the loneliness itself.

Overall, the advice of the reading seems to be to prepare herself to leave the situation, paying attention to her needs and then attending to those of her children.

To see what the hidden heart of the reading was, we turned up the single *fid* in the center that was covering Muin. This was the chthonic current of Nin, symbolizing weaving and connection, communication, and potential legal issues. It urges the use of Skye's creative power and her contacts with others to give her strength and find ways to resolve her dilemma. Nin calls for making connections, creating community, and attending with proper attention to any legal issues that might surround custody of her children in the event of her leaving her relationship. Developing face to face connections with others who can support her emotionally is the hidden challenge of the reading, and what needs to happen to resolve the situation successfully.

In our discussion afterward, she asked if it was necessary to leave the relationship. In truth, if the communication suggested by Nin is established within the relationship and things change enough, leaving the old patterns of relating behind and creating wholly new ones could be enough to qualify as exorcising what has died and leaving the past behind. She left the reading feeling that whichever path she chose there was a positive option at the outcome.

It helps to remember that there are many ways in which a reading can be interpreted. Be sensitive to various ways to read each *fid* within the context of the situation and consider alternatives to the most obvious answers. A good reading should explore the situation and leave room for thought and meditation about the potential outcomes.

The best readings present options and open up minds to new possibilities.

AFTERWORD

Following the path of ogam, like the study of any divinatory system, can be the work of a lifetime. And just as with other systems of divination, the ogam can be fruitfully used in magic and ritual. The size of this book prohibited a more in-depth discussion of ogam in ritual, and there is a great deal yet to be said about the use of ogam in magic and healing. The material and methods presented here are enough to give you a good start toward understanding and working with this fascinating and unusual system. Reading and working with the material in the bibliography will give you a good grounding in the traditions surrounding the creation and development of the ogam, as well as the lore that gives it life.

It's my hope that this work has sparked your interest as well in the Gaelic languages and cultures from which ogam arose, for what is an alphabet without the language it was born to express? The poetry and music of the Gaelic-speaking peoples is deep and rich and well worth the time to explore thoroughly, whether in translation or in the original languages.

As Robert Frost once said, poetry is what gets lost in translation.[132] I urge you to listen to Gaelic poetry in the original language, to hear the rhythms of the tongue and the shapes of sounds, even if you don't learn the language thoroughly and use it fluently in your everyday or ritual life. It is the shape of Gaelic that gave birth to ogam, and it is the poetry of that language that fostered the practice of *Filidecht*. Letter and language together define the path.

May your way be blessed and may wisdom find you when you least expect it. *Slán leat!*

---

[132] Hirshfield, 1997, 62

Erynn Rowan Laurie

GLOSSARY AND
PRONUNCIATION GUIDE

In the pronunciations below, most sounds can approximate to something in English relatively easy, despite how different the phonetics may look in print. The one exception is the Old Irish *ch* sound, which is a guttural, and pronounced like the Scottish/Irish "loch" or the German "Bach." To distinguish it from the typical English "ch" sound, in the pronunciation guide below it is given as *kh*.

Aes Dána (ace DAW-nuh): "People of Art." The class of professionals, poets, and artists in Irish society.

Aicme, aicmí (AHK-meh, AHK-mee): "group(s)." A collection or group of five ogam letters sharing the same structure. They are named for the first letter in each group, for instance "B *aicme*" or "A *aicme*".

Aidhircleóg (AH-her-cloag): Lapwing.

Ailm (AHL-um): No established meaning. Used as "Cry" of ah! for the letter A.

Ainm (AH-num): Name.

Airmid (AHR-mid): Irish Goddess associated with herbal healing.

Aisling, aislinge (ASH-ling, ASH-ling-uh): "dream(s), vision(s)." A dream or the class of Gaelic stories about dreams.

Aislingthe (ASH-ling-theh): A class of vision-seeking rituals involving dreams or journeys into the realm of the sky.

Aiteal (A-chel): Juniper.

Aiteann (A-chen): Furze, whin, gorse.

Alad (AH-luhd): Piebald, speckled.

Anál (AH-nawl): Breath.

Anam (AH-nuhm): Soul.

Bán (bawn): White.

Basogam (BAHS-awe-gum): Palm of the Hand Ogam.

Bean sídhe (ban shee): "Fairy woman." A female spirit often attached to a particular family whose cry portends a death in that family.

Beith (bayth): Birch.

Besan (BESS-uhn): Probably a pheasant.

Bile (BILL-eh): Sacred tree.

Brecht: (brekht): Speckled.
Brí (bree): Strength, vigor, force or significance. Energy.
Briatharogam (BRI-ath-ur-AWE-gum): "Word ogam". Kennings and poetic phrases associated with each ogam letter that shed light on its meanings.
Brigid, Brighid (brih-gihd): Irish Goddess of poetry, smithcraft and healing. She was absorbed into the Christian religion as a saint.
Caorann (KOH-run): Rowan.
Ceirt (kyert): Rag. Shrub. The letter Q.
Clíath (KLEE-uth): The top of a ridgepole.
Coire Érmai (KOHR-uh UR-muh): Cauldron of Motion, associated with the heart.
Coire Goiriath (KOHR-uh GORE-ee-uth): Cauldron of Warming or Incubation, associated with the body.
Coire Sofhis (KOHR-uh HOH-ish): Cauldron of Wisdom, associated with the head.
Coll (kull): Hazel.
Conasg (KUN-asg): Furze, whin, gorse.
Córr (kohr): Crane or heron.
Corrguinecht (KOHR-gwin-ekht): "Crane magic." Battle sorcery performed standing on one leg with one hand behind the back and one eye closed.
Crann (krahn): Tree.
Crann bethadh (krahn BETH-uh): "Tree of Life." The sacred tree of a tribe.
Crann creathach, chraobh chrithinn (krahn KRE-thakh, khrav KHRI-thin): Aspen.
Crann soirb (krahn sorv): Service Tree.
Crann fír (krahn feer): "Test tree," "truth tree."
Crón (krohn): Brown.
Cú Chulainn (KOO KHOL-in): The "Hound of Culann," a great Ulster hero and warrior.
Cuileann (KWIL-in): Holly.
Dair (dar): Oak.
Dán (dawn): "Gift, applied skill, art, poem," but also has implications of fate. The gift may be material, but it can also be a spiritual gift.
Dathogam (DAHTH-awe-gum): Color ogam.
Dearg (jerg): Red.
Dian Cécht (JEE-un kekht): Chief healing deity of the Irish.
Dindsenachas (DINN-hen-uh-khus): Land-naming tales.

Dlí (dlee): Law or binding principle. Can be used to express the concept of the way the universe works in its natural state.

Draighean (DROY-yun): Blackthorn, sloe.

Draoí (dree): Druid. A ritualist, magician, philosopher, and priest of pre-Christian Celtic religions. Sacrificial rituals were unable to proceed without their presence. They were the class of learned nobility among the early Celtic peoples.

Draíocht (DREE-uhkht): The craft of the Druid. Also magic or spellcraft.

Droen (drain): Wren.

Dubh (duv): Black.

Eala (YAW-lah): Swan.

Ebad (AY-vud): Salmon? One of the *forfeda*.

Echtrae (EKH-trah): "Adventures." A class of tales about adventures into the Otherworld through the *Sídhe* mounds or into the forest, or rituals involving Otherworld journeys around or beneath the land.

Edad (AY-dad): Nonsense word associated with the letter E. Used in this book to symbolize the *Amanita muscaria* or Fly Agaric mushroom.

Edeand (AY-dun): Ivy.

Emancholl (EM-un-khull): Twin Hazel, one of the *forfeda*.

Erc (erk): Red-speckled.

Faelinn (FWAY-lin): Gull.

Féige Find (FWEE-guh FIN): Fionn's Window or Fionn's Ridgepole. A glyph consisting of five concentric rings with the ogam *feda* laid out upon it.

Fennid (FAY-nid): A warrior usually living outside the tribe but acting in its defense.

Fern (fairn): Alder.

Fid, Feda (fid, FED-uh): "wood(s)." Usually translated as "letter(s)" of the ogam alphabet.

Fidlanna (FID-lawn-uh): "Divination by wood."

Fili, Filid (FILL-ih, FILL-id): "Poet(s)." Practitioners of traditional Gaelic poetcraft. This could include poetry, law, genealogy, history, grammar, magic, mysticism, vision-seeking, oracular work and divination, inauguration of kings, and other duties within early Irish and Scottish society.

Filidecht (FIL-lih-dekht): "Poetcraft." The practice of traditional Gaelic poetcraft. In the modern world, this includes poetry, divination, and practices of nature-based mysticism as well as the study and teaching of lore and magical arts.

Finemain (FIN-eh-vwin): Grape vine.

Fír Flatha (FEAR FLAW-thuh): "King's Truth." The concept that the king must engage in true and accurate judgment in harmony with the land and his sovereignty for his kingdom to prosper.

Flann (flahn): Blood red.

Fomoire (FOHV-or-uh): A chthonic race of people who lived in Ireland before the arrival of the Tuatha Dé Danann. They are linked with the power of the land and sometimes perceived as chaotic or destructive, yet fertile, figures.

Forfeda (FORE-fay-duh): "Extra letters." The fifth and final *aicme* of the ogam alphabet, added as individual figures over a long period of time to fit foreign sounds in the Gaelic alphabet.

Fraoch (FRAY-ukh): Heather.

Fuinseóg (FWIN-shug): Ash.

Gàidhealtachd (GYAL-takhd): The areas where Gaelic is spoken as a living language (in the Scots-Gaelic spelling of the word).

Geilt (gyelt): One who flees in terror. A sacred madman/madmen, often associated with spirit flight, nature poetry, and unusual spiritual powers.

Geas, geasa (GESS, GYA-suh): Ritual strictures or taboos. Things that must or must not be done on pain of Otherworldly retribution; in Old Irish it would be *geis, gessi* (GESH, GESH-EE)

Géis (gaysh): Swan.

Giolach (GYOH-lokh): Broom plant.

Giúis (GYOO-ish): Pine. Fir.

Glannad (GLAHN-ud): Cleansing or purification.

Glas (gloss): A color covering the range of blue/grey/green. Associated with the Otherworlds.

Goibhniu (GOYV-noo): Irish God of smithcraft and the host of the Feast of Age that fostered the deities in their immortality.

Gorm (GORE-um): Blue.

Gort (gort): Garden, field.

Grianainech (GREE-un-ehkh): "Sun-face." An epithet of Ogma.

h-Úath (oo-uth): Fear, terror.

Hadaig (HOD-ug): Night raven.

Ibar (IH-vuhr): Yew.

Idad (IH-dahd): Nonsense word used to represent the letter I. Interpreted in this book as "Age."

Illat (ILL-ut): Eagle.

Imbas (IM-boss): Ecstatic poetic inspiration. It is seen as a particular type of enlightenment attained through poetic practice and the processing of deep and powerful emotions within the *Fili*'s internal cauldrons.

Imbas forosnai (IM-boss FOR-oss-nuh): A vision-seeking ritual involving sacrifices, sensory deprivation and deep trance work.

Imbolc (IM-bulk): Brighid's feast day, February 1st.

Immram, immrama (IHM-ruv, IHM-ruhv-uh): A class of tales involving sea voyages, or rituals involving journeys over or into the realm of the sea.

Iphin, Pín (IF-in, PEEN): One of the *forfeda*.

Irfind (IR-vind): "Very white."

Iúr (YOOR): Yew.

Lá Féil Bríd (LAW FAIL BREED): The feast of Brigid, also Imbolc.

Lachu (LAW-khoo): Duck.

Leamhán (LEH-vuhn): Elm.

Leannan sídhe (LEN-on shee): "Fairy lover." A spirit lover or spouse that may be of either gender.

Liath (LEE-uth): Grey.

Lorga fuach (LORE-guh FOO-ukh): "Stave of words" or "Staff of poetry." A ritual staff, rod, or wand of office used by *Filid* and *Draoí* to symbolize their status.

Lug (loog, with "oo" as in "book"): The God of many skills. His lineage was half from the Tuatha Dé Danann (by his father Cian) and half Fomoire (from his mother Ethliu).

Luis (loosh): Flame, Herb.

Manannán mac Lir (MON-on-ON mak leer): Irish and Manx God of the sea and the mists. Possibly a gatekeeper to the Otherworlds and psychopomp.

Mbracht (mrakht): Speckled, variegated.

Miach (MEE-ukh): Irish God associated with surgery, slain by his father Dian Cécht after outclassing him in his healing work.

Milbél (MILL-bayl): "Honey mouth." An epithet of Ogma.

Mintan (MIN-chin): Titmouse.

Mónóg (MOH-nohg): Bogberry, cranberry.

Muin (mwin): Love. Esteem. Trickery. Neck.

Naescu (NESS-koo): Snipe.

Necht (nekht): Clear, colorless.

Néldoracht (NAIL-dor-akht): "Divination by clouds." Its exact nature is uncertain, but some suggest that it should be translated as the practice of astrology.

Nentóg (NAIN-chog): Nettle.

Ngéigh (NYAY): Goose.

nGétal (NYET-all): Wound. Charm.

nGlas (*glas*) (gloss): Green.

Nin (nihn): Fork, Letter, Support.

Noinead (NOY-nyehd): A ritual period consisting of three or nine nights.

Núadha (NOO-uh-thuh): A king of the Tuatha Dé Danann.

Ochtach (OKH-tahkh): Pine. Fir.

Odhar (AW-thur): Dun colored.

Odoroscrach (AW-dur-oh-skrahkh): Scrat.

Ogam (AWE-gum): The 20 or 25 letter Irish alphabet.

Ogma (awe-gmuh): Irish God of eloquence and the creator of the Ogam alphabet.

Ogmios (awe-gmee-us): A Gaulish deity that the Greeks equated with Herakles. He may be cognate with Ogma.

Omen: a spontaneous, significant appearance of a sign or event with spiritual meaning that can be used for prophecy or divination.

Onn (own): Foundation. Wheel.

Ór (ore): Gold. One of the *forfeda*.

Oracle: a person who does divination or a tool for divination and the divinatory message received from that person or tool.

Pendulum: A tool consisting of an object at the end of a string or chain, held in the fingertips and allowed to swing freely, used for divination or dowsing.

Quair (kare): "Mouse-colored." Possibly grey-brown like a field mouse.

Querc (kirk): Hen.

Salach (SAHL-ukh): Dirty.

Sail (sahl): Willow.

Saildrong (SAHL-drawn): Willowbrake.

Scáthach (SKAH-thukh): Goddess or Demigoddess who trained the young warrior Cú Chulainn in the arts of war.

Sceach (shkaykh): Thorn.

sceach gheal (shkaykh yawl): Hawthorn, whitethorn.

Seg (shehg): Hawk.

Selkie: A seal spirit or a person in the shape of a seal.

Seun, sian (shun, shee-un): "Sain." A ritual or talisman used primarily for protection but also for purification and cleansing. The act of doing a sain is called saining.

SG: Shared Gnosis. Information and understanding not based in lore, but arrived at by several people within the community about a particular topic without prior influence on one another.

Shillelagh (SHILL-ay-leh): A club usually made of a blackthorn branch.

Sídhe (shee): A burial or other mound seen as an entrance into the Otherworld, or the people who dwell inside these mounds. Often used to describe Gods, "fairies," or other types of land spirits.

Smólach (SMOW-luhk): Thrush.

Sodath (SOH-duth): "Fine colored."

Sorcha (SORE-khuh): Bright.

Straif (strayf): Sulfur.

Temen (CHEH-vehn): Dark grey.

Tiarna nan Cheo (CHEER-nuh nun khyoh): "Lord of Mist." An epithet for Manannán mac Lir.

Tinne (CHIN-uh): Ingot, bar of metal.

Toradh (TOHR-uh): Produce, energy or substance. It is this that is taken from offerings by the spirits, and the remaining body of the offering is no longer considered healthy for human or animal consumption.

Trom (trahm): Elder tree.

Truith (trooth): Starling.

Tuatha Dé Danann (TOO-uh-thuh DAY DAH-nun): The Tribe of the Gods of Danu. Dé should always be capitalized because it means "Gods." It is not the article "of."

Raith (rawth): Fern.

Rócnat (ROWK-nut): Rook.

Ruadh (ROO-uh): Red-(haired).

Ruis (rish): Redness.

Uillend (OO-len): Elbow. One of the *forfeda*.

Uinnsiu (WIN-shoo): Ash.

Uiseóg (WISH-ohg): Lark.

Úll (ool): Apple.

UPG: Unsubstantiated Personal Gnosis. Information and understanding derived from research-informed dream and vision work, meditation, and other non-lore-based sources.

Úr (oor): Soil.

Usghda (OOS-yuh): "Resinous color."

Erynn Rowan Laurie

SELECTED BIBLIOGRAPHY

Breatnach, Liam, "The Cauldron of Poesy," *Ériu* 32 (1981), pp. 45-93

Breatnach, Liam, *Uraicecht na Ríar: The Poetic Grades in Early Irish Law*, Dublin: Dublin Institute for Advanced Studies, 1987

Breathnach, Breandán, *Folk Music and Dances of Ireland*, Cork: Mercier, 1986

Calder, George, ed., *Auraicept na n-Éces: The Scholar's Primer*, Dublin: Four Courts Press, 1995

Campbell, John Gregorson, *The Gaelic Otherworld*, ed. Ronald Black, Edinburgh: Birlinn, 2005

Carmichael, Alexander, *Carmina Gadelica: Hymns and Incantations*, vol 3, Edinburgh: Scottish Academic Press, 1976

Carmichael, Alexander, *Carmina Gadelica: Hymns and Incantations*, vol 4, Edinburgh: Scottish Academic Press, 1978

Chadwick, Nora K., "Geilt," *Scottish Gaelic Studies* 5.2 (1942), pp. 106-153

Chadwick, Nora K. *Poetry and Prophecy*, Cambridge: Cambridge University Press, 1952

Cross, Tom Peete and Clark Harris Slover, *Ancient Irish Tales*, Totowa: Barnes & Noble, 1988

Cunliffe, Barry, *The Celtic World: An Illustrated History of the Celtic Race, Their Culture, Customs and Legends*, New York: Greenwich House, 1986

Darwin, Tess, *The Scots Herbal: The Plant Lore of Scotland*, Edinburgh: Mercat Press, 1996

Davidson, H. R. Ellis, *Myths and Symbols in Pagan Europe: Early Scandinavian and Celtic Religions*, Syracuse: Syracuse University Press, 1988

Dinneen, Patrick S., *Foclóir Gaedhilge agus Béarla: An Irish-English Dictionary*, Dublin: Irish Texts Society, 1927

Dwelly, Edward, *Dwelly's Illustrated Gaelic to English Dictionary*, Glasgow: Gairm Publications, 1994

Eliade, Mircea, *Shamanism: Archaic Techniques of Ecstasy*, Princeton: Bollingen, 1974

Ellis, Peter Berresford, "The Fabrication of 'Celtic' Astrology," *The Astrological Journal* 39.4 (1997) http://cura.free.fr/xv/13ellis2.html

Evans, E. Estyn, *Irish Folk Ways*, London: Routledge, 1988

Fairfield, Gail, *Choice Centered Tarot*, Seattle: Choices, 1984

Gantz, Jeffrey, *Early Irish Myths and Sagas*, London: Penguin, 1988

Gray, Elizabeth A., *Cath Maige Tuired: The Second Battle of Mag Tuired*, Dublin: Irish Texts Society, 1982

Henry, P. L., "The Cauldron of Poesy," *Studia Celtica* 14/15 (1979/1980), pp. 114-128

Hirshfield, Jane, *Nine Gates: Entering the Mind of Poetry*, New York: HarperCollins, 1997

Kinsella, Thomas, *The Tain*, Philadelphia: University of Pennsylvania Press, 1985

Koch, John T., and John Carey, eds., *The Celtic Heroic Age : Literary Sources for Ancient Celtic Europe & Early Ireland & Wales*, Fourth ed., Aberystwyth: Celtic Studies Publications, 2003

Laurie, Erynn Rowan and Timothy White, "Speckled Snake, Brother of Birch: *Amanita Muscaria* Motifs in Celtic Legends," *Shaman's Drum* 44, (1997), pp. 53-65

Lazar-Meyn, H. A., *The Spectrum of Old Irish*, unpublished Masters thesis, University of Pennsylvania, 1979

Lescure, Brigitte, "The Hillfort and Sanctuary at Roquepertuse," in *The Celts*, ed. Sabatino Moscati et al, New York: Rizzoli, 1991, pp. 362-363

MacAlister, R. A. S., *Corpus Inscriptionum Insularum Celticarum*, Dublin: Irish Manuscripts Commission, 1945

MacCana, Proinsias, *Celtic Mythology*, New York: Hamlyn, 1970

Mac Coitir, Niall, *Irish Trees: Myths, Legends & Folklore*, Cork: Collins Press, 2003

MacKillop, James, *Dictionary of Celtic Mythology*, New York: Oxford University Press, 1998

McManus, Damian, *A Guide to Ogam*, Maynooth: An Sagart, 1997

Mac Mathúna, Liam, "Irish Perceptions of the Cosmos", *Celtica* 23 (1999), pp. 174-187

McNeill, F. Marian, *The Silver Bough*, Edinburgh: Canongate, 1989

Martin, Martin, *A Description of the Western Isles of Scotland*, 1695, http://www.appins.org/martin.htm

Meroney, Howard, "Early Irish Letter-Names," *Speculum*, 24.1 (1949), pp. 19-43

Megaw, Ruth and Vincent, *Celtic Art From its Beginnings to the Book of Kells*, New York: Thames and Hudson, 1989

Milliken, William, and Sam Bridgewater, *Flora Celtia: Plants and People in Scotland*, Edinburgh: Birlinn, 2004

Nagy, Joseph Falaky, *The Wisdom of the Outlaw: The Boyhood Deeds of Finn in Gaelic Narrative Tradition*, Berkeley: University of California Press, 1985

NicDhàna, Kathryn Price, and Raven nic Rhóisín, "Tree Huggers: A Methodology for Crann Ogam Work (a.k.a. Raven and Kathryn Get Lost in the Woods)", 2006, http://paganachd.com/articles/treehuggers.html

O'Boyle, Seán, *Ogam: The Poet's Secret*, Dublin: Gilbert Dalton, 1980

Obrist, Barbara, "Wind Diagrams and Medieval Cosmology," *Speculum* 72 (1997), pp. 33-84

O'Daly, Máirín, *Cath Maige Mucrama*, Irish Texts Society, Dublin: 1975

Ó Dónaill, Niall, *Foclór Gaeilge-Béarla*, Dublin: Oifig an tSoláthair, 1977

O hÓgain, Daithi, *Myth, Legend & Romance: An Encyclopaedia of the Irish Folk Tradition*, New York: Prentice Hall, 1991

O'Keefe, J. G., *Buile Shuibhne: The Adventures of Suibhne Geilt*, Dublin: Irish Texts Society, 1913

Onians, Richard B., *The Origins of European Thought*, Cambridge: Cambridge University Press, 1994

Oppenheimer, Monroe and Willard Wirtz, "A Linguistic Analysis of Some West Virginia Petroglyphs", *The West Virginia Archaeologist* 41.1 (1989), http://cwva.org/ogam_rebutal/wirtz.html

Phillips, Roger, *Trees of North American and Europe*, New York: Random House, 1978

Quin, E. G., ed., *Dictionary of the Irish Language*, Dublin: Royal Irish Academy, 1990

Rees, Alwyn and Brinley, *Celtic Heritage: Ancient Tradition in Ireland and Wales*, New York: Thames and Hudson, 1990

Siewers, Alfred K., "The Bluest Greyest Greenest Eye: Colours of Martyrdom and Colours of the Winds as Iconographic Landscape," *Cambrian Medieval Celtic Studies* 50 (2005), pp, 31-66

Erynn Rowan Laurie

Sims-Williams, Patrick, "The Additional Letters of the Ogam Alphabet," *Cambridge Medieval Celtic Studies* 23 (1992), pp. 29-75

Thurneysen, Rudolf, *A Grammar of Old Irish*, Dublin: Dublin Institute for Advanced Studies, 1980

Wright-Popescul, Jean, *The Twelve Winds of the Ancient Gaelic World*, Halifax: Canso-Chesapeake Heritage Publishing, 1997

INDEX

Erynn Rowan Laurie

DID YOU LIKE WHAT YOU READ?

CPSIA information can be obtained at www.ICGtesting.com
Printed in the USA
BVOW02s0320160715

408899BV00001B/73/P

9 781905 713028

The source of the Teachings on Sakya Pandita's *Clarifying the Sage's Intent* is Khenchen Appey Rinpoche, the founder of the International Buddhist Academy in Kathmandu, Nepal. The IBA offers in-depth study of the essential classical Indian Buddhist texts which are taught directly in English to students from all over the world by distinguished Khenpos. The IBA's Language School offers introductory courses, Tibetan Language Intensives and a program for training translators. One of IBA's main purposes is publishing. This includes digitizing and publishing rare Tibetan manuscripts and producing translations of key Mahayana texts in various languages. Please explore our website to find other texts available and to participate in our endeavours.

www.sakyaiba.edu.np
info@sakyaiba.edu.np